Translating New York

Contemporary Hispanic and Lusophone Cultures

This series aims to provide a forum for new research on modern and contemporary hispanic and lusophone cultures and writing. The volumes published in Contemporary Hispanic and Lusophone Cultures reflect a wide variety of critical practices and theoretical approaches, in harmony with the intellectual, cultural and social developments that have taken place over the past few decades. All manifestations of contemporary hispanic and lusophone culture and expression are considered, including literature, cinema, popular culture, theory. The volumes in the series will participate in the wider debate on key aspects of contemporary culture.

Translating New York

The City's Languages in Iberian Literatures

REGINA GALASSO

LIVERPOOL UNIVERSITY PRESS

First published 2018 by
Liverpool University Press
4 Cambridge Street
Liverpool
L69 7ZU

This paperback edition first published 2021

British Library Cataloguing-in-Publication data
A British Library CIP record is available

ISBN 978-1-78694-112-1 cased
ISBN 978-1-80085-580-9 paperback

Typeset in Borges by
Carnegie Book Production, Lancaster

Contents

List of Illustrations

Acknowledgments

I am indebted to a great number of individuals who have contributed to the development of this book, and to my growth as a scholar. This project began as a doctoral dissertation at Johns Hopkins University, where I had the good fortune to work with the late José B. Monleón, Eduardo González, and William Egginton. From there, this project took on new directions during my years as a faculty member at the Borough of Manhattan Community College of the City University of New York and the University of Massachusetts Amherst.

In preparing this book, I received assistance from institutions, professional organizations, publishers, colleagues, students, friends, and family. I would like to thank the Faculty Publication Program at CUNY, under the guidance of Shelly Eversley, for the insightful comments on parts of this text. Financial resources from the College of Humanities and Fine Arts of the University of Massachusetts Amherst and the Massachusetts Society of Professors allowed me to attend conferences and to spend a semester away from teaching to research and write. William Moebius has been a supportive and encouraging department chair. I would also like to thank the program directors I have worked with for their support: Peter Consenstein, Carol Wasserman, David Lenson, Jim Hicks, Amanda Seaman, and Luiz Amaral. I am grateful for the valuable professional advice and continued guidance from Barbara Zecchi, Alicia Borinsky, and William Egginton. I am particularly grateful to the Northeast Modern Language Association, who granted me not only a Summer Fellowship which supported my research at the Fundació Josep Pla, but also awarded me the 2017 NeMLA Book Award for the manuscript of *Translating New York*. Marta Vergés at the Fundació Josep Pla patiently assisted me with material during my visits to Palafrugell. This book has benefited from exchanges I had with Edwin Gentzler, Carmen Boullosa, Helen Freear-Papio, Evelyn Scaramella, Sara Kippur, Charles Hatfield, Ilan Stavans, Claudio Remeseira, Esther Allen, Christopher Schafenacker, and my students. I thank Heather Dubnick for her assistance with preparing the manuscript of this book for submission. I am grateful to Chloe Johnson, the dedicated and detailed editorial team, and the anonymous reader at Liverpool University Press for their careful review of my manuscript. I would like to thank the librarians at the University of Massachusetts Amherst for helping me access material, and Laura Quilter for helping me to sort out copyright issues. I have tried to identify all copyright holders. I apologize for any errors or omissions. I would like to thank Anna Cabrera Hens and the Càtedra Gaudí for helping me with the cover image of this book. Friends and family on both sides of the Atlantic have provided much-needed affection and warmth. I am especially grateful to my mother, Paulette, for her constant support and love.

I owe much to my immediate family. I cannot translate into any language how lucky I am to share my life with Albert Lloret. This book is dedicated to him, and to our children Julia and Natalia, whose deep beauty and joyous energy make every day a celebration.

Introduction
New York as an Iberian City

N ew York, a city with a deep and dynamic history as a long-time receiver of individuals looking for a temporary or permanent home, has appeared in the work of writers from the Iberian Peninsula for more than a century. The city has not only been a place to write about but, as this book explores, it has been a way for Iberian authors to write in English, Spanish, and Catalan. *Translating New York* examines writers who have indulged in the fascination of New York for varying reasons and explores how the city shaped their careers, language, and literature. This book was born of the desire to diversify ongoing discussions about Iberian writers and the city, and it is thus a hybrid project that explores literature in three different languages, uses translation as an analytical tool, and reaches a site beyond the geographical borders of the Iberian Peninsula, while at the same time exploring how a city can be represented in literature beyond descriptive passages.

New York Moments

To set the stage for the discussion on New York in which this book engages, it is essential to first map out New York's position within the Iberian and Latin American worlds. There is no doubt that New York is a Spanish-speaking city: almost every variation of the language along with its particular New York offspring can be heard somewhere on its streets. It is, however, not as widely recognized that this language has been spoken in the city since the mid-seventeenth century. Since then, Spanish has become a language of commerce, religion, politics, art, literature, and community, boosting New York's position as a financial and cultural capital. Like the presence of Spanish itself in New York, the history of literary production in the Spanish language in or about the city—by visitors, immigrants, or other temporary, permanent, or imaginary residents—is long and diverse.

In an effort to make this history more apparent to a wider audience, in 2010 the New York Historical Society, in collaboration with El Museo del Barrio and a solid and expansive cohort of scholars, organized an exhibition titled *Nueva York, 1613–1945* and edited a volume of the same name to illustrate that although a large wave of Spanish speakers reached New York in the latter half of the twentieth century, the city's relationship with and participation in Iberian and Latin American spheres is in no way a recent phenomenon. This agenda was further supported by the publication of *Hispanic New York: A Sourcebook* (2010), edited by Claudio Iván Remeseira, which brings together reprints of milestone publications and fresh scholarly perspectives. Not too long after, scholarly and creative circuits curated further expressions of recognition, most notably the 2013 exhibit *Back Tomorrow: Federico García Lorca/Poet in New York* curated by Christopher Maurer at the New York Public Library, which brought together manuscripts, drawings, letters, and other material that surrounded Lorca while he wrote the poems of the unforgettable *Poeta en Nueva York* (1940), a book first published under the title *The Poet in New York and Other Poems* in a bilingual Spanish-English edition with translations by Rolfe Humphries. *Back Tomorrow* was accompanied by the grand-scale festival *Lorca in New York: A Celebration*, held throughout the city for more than two months. These efforts, to name just a few, attest to New York's outstanding presence in national literatures beyond the United States and provide an historical and cultural foundation uncovering fruitful ground for acknowledging an alternative, non-anglophone New York.[1] At the same time, the success of such initiatives creates a visibility that expands a literary corpus built upon a specific city and adds depth to our understanding of specific authors and texts.

The triumph of these far-reaching projects, aside from their inclusivity and accessibility to the general public, lies in the fact that they present the opportunity to revisit canonical works and (re)introduce overlooked texts, creating new readings and exposing cultural routes. Traditionally, scholarship on Iberian and Latin American literatures related to New York has had a tendency to focus on a single national group or a single author.[2]

---

1 In early 2007, five writers—Carmen Boullosa, Eduardo Lago, José Manuel Prieto, Eduardo Mitre, Sylvia Molloy, and Naief Yehya—all of whom live in New York and produce literary works in Spanish, wrote and shared their *Manifiesto Neoyorkino*, in which they state that their lineage has been submerged in the cultural memory of New York partly due to the "Anglo-centricity that has been simultaneously provincial and imperial" (Boullosa).

2 For a study that includes multiple authors and nations, see Dionisio Cañas's *El poeta y la ciudad: Nueva York y los escritores hispanos* (1994) as well as "New York City: Center and Transit Point for Hispanic Cultural Nomadism" by Cañas with several contributors in *Literary Cultures of Latin America: A Comparative History* (2004). Both are largely bibliographic in nature.

Academic and more casual literary conversations about Spanish-language literature and New York have elicited Lorca's poetry of the city or have called upon exile as an area of principal interest due to the Spanish Civil War and the resulting dictatorship that endured for over 40 years. While the war certainly forced many to relocate, the arrival of individuals from the Iberian Peninsula in New York occurred over a stretch of time rather than at a single moment. For instance, the foundation of the community which came to be known as "Little Spain," historically Manhattan's neighborhood on 14th Street between Seventh and Eighth Avenues, was made up of newcomers who came as merchant marines, both before the Spanish Civil War and during it (Balder). And this is not to mention those from the peninsula who arrived in the nineteenth century and founded periodicals such as *La Llumanera de Nova York* (1874–81) and later *La Prensa* at the start of the twentieth century.[3] Variety is contributed not only to the making of the Iberian community in New York, but also to the literary history accompanying the movement of writers on and off the peninsula. Lorca is not the only Iberian writer whose creativity and career were guided by the U.S. city at some point, but Iberian writers beyond Lorca are still peripheral to the panorama of these pieces of New York literature.

Expanding Iberian Literatures

One the primary goals of this book is to broaden the range of authors who enter the critical discussion of Iberian literatures in New York.[4] At the same time, *Translating New York* is neither an exhaustive nor a comprehensive

3 *La Llumanera de Nova York* was an illustrated periodical published monthly in Catalan in New York. Seventy-three issues appeared between 1874 and 1881. For more on this publication, see "The Catalan Migration to New York: A View from *La Llumanera de Nova York (1874–1881)*" by Lluís Costa. *La Prensa* was a Spanish-language New York newspaper founded by José Campubrí (the brother-in-law of Juan Ramón Jiménez) and circulated for a continuous span of about 50 years from 1913–63. It merged with its main competitor, *El Diario de Nueva York*, in 1962. For more on the Spanish-language press in the United States, see James F. Shearer's article "Periódicos españoles en los Estados Unidos."

4 While this book does not address Lorca in a major way, I would like to point out that scholars such as Christopher Maurer, Evelyn Scaramella, and Leslie Harkema continue to make significant contributions to the study of the role of translation in the literary production and culture surrounding Lorca. More specifically, I am referring to Maurer's forthcoming chapter "Lorca, from Country to City: Three Versions of *Poet in New York*" and Scaramella's book manuscript titled "Translating Republican Resistance: Anglophone and Hispanophone Writers during the Spanish Civil War."

study of the actual or imaginative place of New York in Iberian literatures;[5] instead I have carefully selected writers whose New York City texts have marked their careers and, in several cases, the history of their national literatures. I arrange a constellation of writers spanning about 50 years during the earlier part of the twentieth century: Julio Camba (1882–1962), José Moreno Villa (1887–1955), Josep Pla (1897–1981), and Felipe Alfau (1902–99). Two of these authors wrote in Spanish, one in Catalan, and one in English, but all wrote in relation to a city that transformed their writing and made telling textual connections. While the focus on four main writers might seem to offer a reduced scope, the expansion of Iberian literatures which this book aims to provide also calls for new critical connections with translation studies, the urban turn in Iberian cultural studies,[6] and comparative concerns in Iberian studies mostly seen as considerations of Spain that are beyond Spain in terms of geography and linguistic variety. It also enhances the emerging translation turn in Iberian studies which includes, but is not limited to, the work of Christopher Maurer, Jonathan Mayhew, Helena Buffery, Gayle Rogers, Ignacio Infante, Evelyn Scaramella, and Leslie Harkema. Thus, to maintain the hybrid nature of this book, I have opted for depth rather than breadth in the hope of creating examples of how studies of urban-centric texts might move toward language as a point of critical inquiry.

Since the authors discussed in this study are all male, I would like to point out that women writers have not been overlooked. During and after the period I study here, women writers from Spain did travel to New York and published as a result. For example, Concha Espina (1869–1955) traveled to America in the early 1930s and published the three-part book *Singladuras. Viaje Americano (Cuba, Nueva York, Nueva Inglaterra)* (1932). As the recipient of a Guggenheim in 1959, Rosa Chacel (1898–1994) lived in the city for two years, during which she worked on a book of erotic philosophical essays,

5 For a study that includes a wide range of poets, see Julio Neira's *Historia poética de Nueva York en la España contemporánea* (2012). For a comprehensive anthology, see Neira's *Geometría y angustia: Poetas españoles en Nueva York* (2012).

6 In the early 2000s, when reviewing three publications related to the urban context in Spanish culture, Malcolm Alan Compitello and Susan Larson note that the "urban turn in cultural studies and in Spanish cultural studies in particular has brought out hitherto neglected areas of inquiry and promises to push at some of the institutional and disciplinary boundaries that can sometimes limit our attempts to put forward new and important readings of the cultural production of Spain" (231). Larson's book series on Hispanic urban studies, which she edits with Benjamin Fraser, has also given more importance to the urban within the story of Iberian literatures. Fraser himself has made a number of book contributions, including *Henri Lefebvre and the Spanish Urban Experience: Reading the Mobile City* (2011).

later published as *Saturnal* in 1972. Carmen Laforet (1921–2004) traveled to New York and other areas of the United States in the mid-1960s and then published the travel narrative *Paralelo 35* (1967). None of these texts marks a pivotal moment in their authors' careers, however. New York only appears in a section of each, and they all lack the urban-centric writing which this book celebrates. That said, when appropriate, I highlight the contribution of women writers to the international perspective of Iberian literatures which this book presents.

Another clarification needs to be made regarding terminology. In acknowledgment of the multicultural and multilingual traits of Spain and contemporary disciplinary trends that seek a more inclusive understanding of what Spain is and has been, in *Translating New York* I most often opt for the term *Iberian* over *Spanish*, but I recognize that *Spanish*, when used as an adjective to describe nationality, does not limit an individual's native or creative language to Spanish. At the same time, *Spain* is used to refer to the country regardless of language and cultural preferences. The many languages of the writers presented in this book also expand the linguistic diversity of literary production that might be encompassed in projects, such as the aforementioned exhibit *Nueva York*, which attempt to unearth a Hispanic New York literary tradition concurrent with its dominant anglophone counterpart. In this book, I focus on the repertoire of verbal and non-verbal languages of the texts studied in an effort to read their New York beyond an examination of the city's physical (re)presentation.

References to language or multilingual writing in relation to Hispanic literature at large, and to New York in particular, usually funnel through the same channels. Spanglish and other linguistic combinations that show an obvious textual movement between Spanish and English hold a central position, especially in more recent literature.[7] Likewise, contemporary writers who have predictable ways of moving between English and Spanish because they frequently travel between New York and their homelands, who do not share the same birthplace with previous generations, or who conduct their social life in one language and their academic or professional life in another receive most attention in considerations of language choice and literary production. In other words, language, a writer's main tool, is often limited to a bilingual marriage that has its difficulties, intimate connections,

---

7 Nuyorican literature, for example, has made use of multiple languages in a single text since the 1960s. A more recent example is the self-described Puerto Rican poet, performer, professor, and polemicist Urayoán Noel's work *Buzzing Hemisphere/ Rumor Hemisférico* (2015), which has been described by critics as neither Spanglish nor a translation. Literature from the Iberian Peninsula seldom enters the realm of multilingual literature in the U.S. context.

and fiery disconnections. This book expands the language dynamics and their penetration of the textual surface, which reaches beyond reflections on choosing between Spanish and English to look at how Spanish might carry traces of English, or how English might sound in Spanish, or how any of the other spoken, visual, or musical languages of New York touched a sample of Iberian literatures. *Translating New York* considers these aspects and shows that it is no coincidence that some of the most important literary texts or writers of twentieth-century Iberian literatures were inspired by a trip to New York.

Despite the deep presence of the Spanish language and the long tradition of writers from the Iberian Peninsula moving in, out of, and within New York, scholarly work in this area is either heavily bibliographic, collecting texts pertaining to this group, or tends to be robustly biographic as it strives to recuperate the itineraries of specific authors. Additionally, criticism devotes many pages to a discussion of whether writers have a favorable or unfavorable opinion of New York City, which is not surprising given some of the striking comments which writers and literature have shared about the city. For example, before Lorca's trip to New York, he told Carlos Morla Lynch (1885[?]–1969):[8] "Nueva York me parece horrible pero por eso mismo me voy allí" [New York looks horrible to me but that's why I'm going there] (qtd. in Stainton 195). Lorca's comment aligns with the representation of the city in European art and literature before 1929, such as in the film *Metropolis* (1927), said to have resulted from Fritz Lang's first trip to New York in 1924.[9] Another influential source of dislike for New York is the poem "La gran cosmópolis (Meditaciones de la madrugada)" (1915) by Rubén Darío (1867–1916),[10] as demonstrated in Julio Camba's recollection of it. In his

8 For more on the relationship between Morla Lynch and Lorca, see Morla Lynch's *En España con Federico García Lorca* (2008).

9 Stainton says that "*Metropolis* constituyó un punto decisivo—y un cambio radical—en la historia de la representación estética de Nueva York" [*Metropolis* was a decisive point—and a radical change—in the history of the aesthetic representation of New York] (194). In the same article, Stainton says that in the decade after the First World War, "Nueva York atrajo a la imaginación europea como ninguna otra ciudad del mundo, y pocos comprendieron esto mejor que García Lorca, cuyo viaje a América, según el mismo confesó, cambió el curso de su obra" [New York attracted the European imagination like no other city in the world, and few understood this better than García Lorca, whose trip to America, according to what he himself said, changed the course of his work] (191). *Metropolis* was shown in 1928 in Madrid and Granada. Juan Cano Ballesta writes about how it spoke to Lorca's generation in *Literatura y tecnología. Las letras españolas ante la revolución industrial (1900–1933)*.

10 Darío visited New York in 1893, 1907, and for several months at the end of 1914 and the beginning of 1915.

own New York writing, Camba incorrectly cites lines from the first stanza of Darío's poem:

> Poco antes de su muerte, Rubén Darío estuvo en Nueva York. La gran ciudad no le entusiasmó gran cosa. Estas casas de cincuenta pisos se le venían encima. Bajo la inmensa prosperidad material, Rubén Darío sentía palpitar aquí el dolor humano más agudo que en ninguna otra parte:
>
> > *Casas de cincuenta pisos,*
> > *millones de circuncisos*
> > *y dolor, dolor, dolor ...* (qtd. in Llera)

[Shortly before he died, Rubén Darío was in New York. He was not very enthusiastic about the great city. These 50-story houses were too overwhelming for him. Beneath the immense material prosperity, Rubén Darío felt the most acute human pain beat here more than anywhere else:

> *Houses fifty stories high,*
> *millions of circumcised men*
> *and pain, pain, pain ...*][11]

Yet, while the actual city might be portrayed negatively in literature, criticism's focus on such readings of the city nourishes the creation and persistence of stereotypes of New York and remains attached to the very place, or physicality, of the city, closed off to what lies beyond the visual. Because the zenith of these singularly successful Iberian writers' lives results from a visit to or the image of New York, their texts must contain the city in ways other than the extremes of affection or disdain for the place. Besides the poems he wrote from New York, Lorca also composed a collection of letters to his family and friends back in Andalusia. In these letters, he provides a wider understanding of his experience in New York, one that goes beyond the pain, disgust, and coldness expressed in his poetry. Having been in the city for about six months, in December of 1930, he reports to his loved ones: "estoy hecho *un niño de moda* después de mi utilísimo y provechoso viaje americano" [I have become a *stylish boy* after my extremely useful and beneficial American trip] (Stainton 191).[12] New York, then, beyond

---

11 All translations are mine unless otherwise noted.

12 Stainton thanks Christopher Maurer for granting her access to this letter, which is found in the Archivo de la Fundación FGL, Madrid.

being a place to like or dislike, more importantly awakened creative options for the literary writing of Lorca, and others. *Translating New York* attempts to get at how "New York, as an idea, [has] hijacked [the] imagination" (3) of Iberian writers, to borrow the expression used by Christopher Lindner in the opening pages to his recent book *Imagining New York City: Literature, Urbanism, and the Visual Arts, 1890–1940* (2015).[13]

Traveling, Translating

All the writers in this book are travelers, although some to a greater degree than others, and all have different itineraries. Therefore, the link between travel and translation is a fundamental point of departure. Travel and translation have endured an imbalanced relationship within translation and literary studies. Travel is a frequently used metaphor for translation. From the ancient Roman idea of *translatio studii et imperii*, translation has served to denote the travel of knowledge and power across cultural boundaries. And since the cultural turn in translation studies of the 1990s, the notion of translation as a form of travel has been a guide for understanding the ways in which texts traverse national and linguistic boundaries. However, the degrees of translation involved in travel have not shared the same trajectory, as contemporary critical discussions of travel and urban-centric writing overlook the idea of travelers as translators. For example, Enric Bou, who dedicated a chapter of *Invention of Space: City, Travel and Literature* (2012) to travel writing, noted that "travelers have to deal with space (geography) and people (sociology, anthropology)" (171). Language, however, is not directly mentioned as something the traveler must deal with, even though much of the discussion on travel writing echoes what is also said about translation. For instance, Bou proposes that "travelogues explore freedom from the limitations imposed by the culture of whomever is traveling/writing/reading. The separation from home provokes a significant contradiction between this state of maximum freedom, attained when traveling, and the laws and restrictions of normal life" (171). Bou's assessment of travel writing as a way to reach beyond the established norms strongly recalls Eliot Weinberger's view of translation as a way to liberate the translation language by allowing for new aspects to come into language (18). Translation is also an opportunity to abandon, if only momentarily, the restraints of the culture and language surrounding the translation language. Thus, travel, much like translation, allows the

---

13 Lindner's book draws from a wide range of examples to examine how certain city spaces came to stand for the modern condition.

writer an opportunity to do things he has never before done with his language, to introduce new arrangements of words, new phrases, and literally a new language to the home language.

Beyond travel's ability to shake up, invigorate, and agitate the home language, it also creates a tension between how much of home is to be left behind and how much is taken on the journey. Bou acknowledges this when he says: "When traveling we are normally carrying our visions and pre-concepts, we close our eyes and we are devoted to comparing the new things that we see with things we already know, with what is familiar and quotidian, which unconsciously we refuse to leave behind us" (178). Once again, Bou's assessment of traveling connects with the way that translators carry within them the text they are translating and the text they are writing in the translation language. The blend of the new with the familiar is what translators, like travel writers, place in dialogue in their writing. In doing so, the travel writer, like the translator, chooses from a variety of textual strategies that might embrace foreignization or domestication, or opts for a range of strategies that perhaps change over the course of a text and over time.

In *Across the Lines: Travel, Language, Translation* (2000), Michael Cronin notes an indifference to the question of language in many of the key texts on writing and travel, thus leading to a serious misrepresentation of both the experience of travel and the construction of narrative accounts of these experiences (2). Travelers, when they are writers, artists, or other producers of culture, make several kinds of translational efforts during their creative acts. When a writer travels to lands of new languages and decides to continue writing for the home audience about a new place, for whatever reason, he does a great deal of translation. Cronin's work has brought new perspectives to travel accounts, encouraging readers and critics to look beyond considerations that judge the accuracy of the descriptions of the places they depict. The complexities of travel writing have exploded because of Cronin's work, as it opens new avenues for reading the work of travel writers departing from the premise that "critical writing on travel ... has largely neglected ... the relationship of the traveller to language" (2). Turning to Roman Jakobson's description of three different kinds of translation—intralingual, interlingual, and intersemiotic—Cronin explores the work of writers in situations in which they speak the same language, speak it to some degree, or not at all.[14] Attuned to several moments of different kinds of translation, *Translating New York* has benefited greatly from Cronin's scholarship on thinking about just how much translation a

14 See Jakobson's "On Linguistic Aspects of Translation."

traveler, and accordingly a writer, must do. Reading literature inspired by travel and written with translation in mind creates a new appreciation for how writers experienced the city, especially in cases of lesser-known authors and texts, desiring a more robust understanding that otherwise might not fulfill established literary conventions.

In New York, the fact that visitors from the Iberian Peninsula encountered Spanish, including international and local variations,[15] and other Iberian languages created a unique translational situation further colored by the sounds of English as a backdrop. This book proposes that this climate granted Iberian writers an additional edge within the urban experience, influencing their literary language and approach to writing New York. In this sense, New York offered the writers discussed here an urban experience which differs from that found in major Iberian cities such as Madrid and Barcelona. While Madrid and Barcelona were also international and multilingual cities, they were not as multilingual as New York. Another and perhaps more important major distinction among the authors I study here is that they could speak Spanish, the dominant language of Madrid and Barcelona. They could not, however, speak English, the dominant language of New York, with the same fluidity, thus leading to a distinctive linguistic situation. Finally, they all did not produce work about Madrid or Barcelona which matched their New York corpus in significance.

In New York, writers were transitioning back and forth between interlingual and intralingual translation. For many Iberian writers experiencing New York City, translation is more of a process than a state, to paraphrase Michael Cronin and Sherry Simon in their essay "Introduction: The City as Translation Zone" (124).[16] Although much of this theory relies on

15 To illustrate the flavor of the Spanish language in New York City, Nicolás Kanellos and Helvetia Martell have noted that the city's Spanish-language periodicals were "as cosmopolitan [or] as pan-Hispanic as the magazines and newspapers of New York," mostly because no other U.S. community was "as tied to the rest of Spanish America and Spain through trade and commerce as was the port city of New York" (72). Another example is Antonio Muñoz Molina's essay "Spanish in New York: A Moving Landscape," discussed in Part I.

16 In the same essay, Cronin and Simon outline key terms for their discussion of the city as a translation zone. First, they differentiate between the multilingual city and the translational city. For them, "multilingualism calls to mind a space of plurality and diversity, with no particular idea of hierarchy or organization," while "translation proposes an active, directional and interactional model of language relations" (119). For Simon, a scholar of translation studies and francophone literature, New York is not a divided city linguistically speaking but rather a multilingual city and one in which "English is the dominant language, the single gateway to social promotion" (*Cities* 2), though the distinct place of Spanish in the

contemporary technologies that create "a new kind of translational reality for the migrant" in the context of the multilingual city, Cronin and Simon explain the difference between the two conditions. Translation as process results from "repeated contact with fellow native speakers of a language in the country of origin" (124). The situation of continuous daily movement in and out of and around their home language or languages, however, is also applicable to what Iberian writers face in New York due to the presence of Spanish and their association with Iberian colleagues and friends already established in the city, facilitating a "much more vivid sense of translation as *process*" (124).

Aside from Cronin, an essential reference point in developing the theoretical framework of this book has been Simon's work on cities and translation. With *Translating Montreal: Episodes in the Life of a Divided City* (2006) and *Cities in Translation: Intersections of Language and Memory* (2011), Simon moved discussions of urban-centric writing away from an exclusive focus on spatial relations and turned toward a "new angle of perception" (*Translating* 18) that centralizes language and translation, arguing that "the audible surface of languages, each city's signature blend of dialects and accents, is an equally crucial urban element" (*Cities in Translation* 1). In her scholarly work as a whole, Simon has demonstrated that the ability to hear the city "introduces the observer into layers of social, economic and cultural complexity" ("Across Troubled Divides"). This complexity, partially fueled by the unique linguistic circumstances of New York, impacted Iberian literatures just as much as the physical uniqueness of the cityscape. Translation as a tool of literary analysis helps to unpack thinking about the representation of a city beyond its visual aspects. Simon's broad definition of translation in the city context as "writing at the intersection of languages, writing under the influence of, in the company of, with or often against other languages" ("Across Troubled Divides") has been an

---

city turns on the behavior of translational cities. Cronin and Simon then discuss how the term "translation zone" "was developed through analogy with Mary Louise Pratt's (1992) influential 'contact zone,' which she defines as 'social spaces where disparate cultures meet, clash, and grapple with each other, often in highly asymmetrical relations of domination and subordination-like colonialism, slavery, or their aftermaths as they are lived out across the globe today' (ibid. 4)" (121). Next, they turn to Emily Apter's (2006) *The Translation Zone*, in which "she uses a zone to imagine a broad intellectual topography, a zone of critical engagement." As a result, "translation zone" came to be the term used to "refer to the cultural and geographical spaces that give rise to intense language traffic" (121). While New York could be a translation zone for Iberian writers, the traffic surrounding the movements in and out of languages and through them is one that, although inspired by an actual location, happens in the abstract place of literary creation.

influential undercurrent in the writing of this book, allowing literary and cultural histories to emerge. Simon is part of a group of women translators and scholars, including Esther Allen, Edith Grossman, and Susan Bassnett, who have been a guiding force in the conceptual framework of this book. Over the past ten years, they have shaped the way translation is considered both within academic circles and by the general public.

One of the core questions which *Translating New York* explores is why the city has repeatedly appeared in the work of so many Iberian writers, yet scholarship has made few attempts to study these authors collectively or to look beyond the fascination with New York as a motivator of literary production. Following Cronin and Simon's "Introduction: The City as Translation Zone," the trope of translation as a way of understanding the construction and representation of New York City in Iberian literatures offers a more dynamic approach to the texts in question. Translation provides a framework that allows the complexities involved with travel to and the experience of a multilingual city to emerge. Moreover, translation, as a lens for literary analysis, makes way for new critical discussions that surpass the physical aspects of a city as a centerpiece. In doing so, *Translating New York* does not aim to assess the accuracy of the representations of New York in the texts it examines. In other words, it does not strive to determine whether the literary New Yorks live up to the actual place that inspired them. Instead, departing from Cronin's scholarship on travel and translation, and Simon's engagement in translation and the city, this book opts for an approach that treats translation as an interpretive act full of a myriad choices.

In her defense of why translation matters, Edith Grossman follows up on issues which Walter Benjamin set out in "The Task of the Translator" (1923), noting that literary translation infuses a language "with influences, alterations and combinations that would not have been possible without the presence of translated foreign literary styles and perceptions, the material significance and heft of literature that lies outside the territory of the purely monolingual" (16). *Translating New York* proposes that this is precisely what the city did for the work of the authors identified above. A visit to, or the idea of, New York offered new creative possibilities, thus "revivifying" and having an "expansive effect" on Iberian literatures as the resulting New York texts each hold a distinguished place in the *œuvre* of their author and attracted the critical eye of fellow writers (Grossman 16).

In writing about Gaudí (1852–1926), Josep Pla includes segments from a conversation he had with the architect, art historian and critic, essayist, and poet Josep Pijoan (1881–1963) in Lausanne. Pijoan concludes:

You know I am convinced that emigration is good for Catalans, mostly if they are intelligent. This is true for the whole peninsula. Once abroad, they feel nostalgia, certainly, but living amid a more authentic society, one more open to positive merits, they can produce great things. In general, the Catalans' output at home is quite weak, excepting some rare cases, mostly those of erudites; work at home is by and large disconnected from the tenor of the times. ("Antoni Gaudí" 163)

In speaking of the Catalan context while in the French-speaking part of Switzerland, Pijoan hints at the benefit of travel abroad for Iberian artists and writers in general in order to prevent their work from stagnating. Ironically, he and Pla are talking about an architectural genius who never traveled (Lahuerta 191). This is not to say, however, that imagining his work outside Catalonia did not alter the path of his projects at home.

During the first decade of the twentieth century, in the spring of 1908, two U.S. financiers traveled to Barcelona for a two- to three-week stay in the city and met with Gaudí. They discussed plans for him to design a luxury hotel "decorative in the traditional spirit, but much more monumental, much more exotic than strictly functional," which would be "joined by rapid transport to the centre of the city, and visible for miles" (Collins, "Postmodern" 93). The hotel's projected location was the southern tip of Manhattan, and its name was to be Hotel Attraction since the structure would serve as an "all-purpose tourist attraction," a destination in its own right, like many hotels of the time (Davidson 125). The hotel was to exceed the world's tallest building, the Eiffel Tower, measuring 1,181 feet. Glenn Collins further describes the project:

Gaudí had planned something typically gaudy: like some of his works in Barcelona, the hotel was to have been rainbow-hued in tile and marble. The hotel would have been a group of clustered towers, of reinforced concrete over steel, in Gaudí's sturdy trademark parabolic shapes that also animate the 330-foot-tall Sagrada Familia. The hotel's 360-foot-by-360-foot ground floor was to contain a titanic reception hall, surrounded by large saloons connected to a clutch of outbuildings and towers containing meeting rooms, apartments and hotel rooms. In the central tower there were to be five monumental dining rooms dedicated to five continents; each was to seat 400. Yet another dining room on the sixth floor was to be topped by an exhibition hall, and above that was planned a theater conference room. Atop that was to be a cathedral-like 375-foot-high space honoring all the American presidents, in a hall decorated with stained glass windows, mosaics and frescos. (Collins, "Postmodern")[17]

Gaudí is said to have worked on this project for three years, from 1908 to 1911, yet architectural plans are scarce. Moreover, the project was little known until the summer of 2002, when the Lower Manhattan Development Corporation announced a worldwide request for proposals for the 16-acre site of the former World Trade Center. A team in Barcelona and U.S. artist-architect Paul Laffoley independently submitted proposals calling for the building of Gaudí's structure.[18] What remains of Hotel Attraction are seven original drawings by Gaudí and his "right hand" Lorenzo Matamala, which were saved from the disastrous fires of the Spanish Civil War and kept by Lorenzo's son, Joan (Collins, "The American Hotel" 201). Joan Matamala, who worked in Gaudí's studio, created ten additional drawings based on his memories of the work done in 1908 (Collins, "Postmodern").

The reasons why the project was never started remain unknown,[19] and scholars doubt its authenticity. Regardless, the imaginative possibilities generated are of great import in the context of Iberian artistic production. On the one hand, the possibility of such a project makes way for fantasies

17 For more details and sketches of the design of this project, see George R. Collins's chapter "The American Hotel."

18 The year 2002 was also the Year of Gaudí. Events and exhibitions displayed "The American Hotel" Project. In the exhibition catalogue *Universo Gaudí*, a chapter dedicated to New York mentions another project intended for construction in New York titled "Office Building": "Ignasi Brugueras presentó en Reus, en 1952 también, y supuestamente realizado asimismo para Nueva York, el dibujo del 'Office Building' que el visitante puede ver aquí. La misma organización que en el proyecto de Matamala: torres fusiformes organizadas alrededor de una central, y unas plantas bajas que ahora interpretan, con dificultades, recogiendo formas de un *art nouveau* más internacional, más *standard*, las tribunas de la Casa Batlló. Según Ignasi Brugueras, este proyecto le fue encargado a él mismo en 1917, aunque, como en el case del 'Attraction Hotel,' hasta los actos de celebración del centenario de Gaudí nadie tuvo conocimiento de ello" [In 1952, Ignasi Brugueras also presented in Reus the drawing "Office Building," for the New York project, which visitors can see here. It was organized the same way as Matamala's Project: spindle towers arranged around a central tower, and the lower levels—now echoed in the galleries of the Casa Batlló, although it is a stretch—that recall a more international or more standard form of Art Nouveau. According to Ignasi Brugueras, Gaudí was charged with this project in 1917, although, similar to "Hotel Attraction," nobody knew about it until the celebration of Gaudí centenary] (191).

19 Laffoley speculates about the possible reasons why the project was never realized in "A Grand Hotel on the Hudson." According to him, Gaudí's paranoia played a large role in the failure to even begin this project.

about how New York could play out in the local culture; the idea of a New York version of Gaudí allows viewers to envision the familiar filtered through a new lens. In other words, New York injected Iberian cultural production with a new vitality. On the other hand, today's viewers, with access to the images or knowledge of the project, are able to expand their everyday cityscape, stepping out of the usual if only momentarily, imagining the international impact of Catalan *modernisme* during the rise of New York.[20] For example, returning to the dialogue between Pijoan and Pla, Pijoan elaborates: "About Gaudí, let me tell you he would have been the person—the only person in the world—capable of building a cathedral for New York had that city decided to build a cathedral in proportion to its volume and its spirit" (163). From what is cited of their exchange, it is unclear if Pijoan is aware of the Hotel Attraction project; however, this conversation with Pla illustrates that New York is a place where the scale of greatness of Iberian artistic production can be achieved.

From this example, and others throughout this book, New York becomes a site of experiment, a site on which to physically or imaginatively rehearse new directions for artistic projects. For centuries, writers have invoked literary translation to practice and innovate their own writing. New York has been able to attract a range of writers for more than a century because the city, given its key dialogue with Iberian and Latin American cultures, is a place that is familiar yet in perpetual transformation, enabling the production of rich textual diversity.

Outline of the Book

There is no shortage of books on New York. José Luis García Martín opens his introduction to Julio Camba's *La ciudad automática* pointing out that "[h]ay ciudades que constituyen por sí mismas un género literario: Venecia es una de ellas; Nueva York, otra" [there are cities that make up a literary genre of their own: Venice is one of them; New York is another] (9). However, this is not simply another book about New York. *Translating New York* is also about writing the city and analyzing texts that speak to travel and the multiple dimensions of experiencing the city. It does not intend to ignore monumental literary works. On the contrary, it further contextualizes them

20 Robert A. Davidson remarks that, if constructed, "[n]ot only would such a project have fulfilled the latent potential for exporting Catalan architectural *modernisme*, and thus fully capacitated the movement as an active contributor to an international dialogue [...], it would have created on different levels an intriguing resonance of modern Barcelona in New York" ("Periphery" 172).

by exposing the networks in which these authors and their texts circulated, as well as those that preceded and followed them. As such, this book carries an intentional bibliographical and biographical portrait of its authors and their texts.

Bibliographical and biographical information have two main functions in *Translating New York*. First, they seek to introduce an anglophone audience to authors who have been underappreciated within and beyond Iberian studies. Second, the foundational premise of this book is that New York City has an important role in Iberian literatures because a notable number of authors traveled to the city, wrote about it, and recorded its transformative power, marking a special place in their overall biographical and bibliographical profiles as writers. This discussion could not be possible without addressing the authors' relationship to language and travel. New York forced each of these writers to confront his own linguistic situation. The book is not organized according to an author's personal relationship with the city, however; rather, it is arranged according to translational situations. In the book's three parts, I provide a revisionary account of Iberian literatures provided by a source beyond the peninsula. While the parts loosely follow a chronological organization, the limitations are fluid and require transgression. The organizing principle was the motivations for traveling to New York—circumstantial, personal, professional—and the kinds of translations of New York undertaken by a single, but significant writer, or a remarkable pairing. Collectively, these three parts open new ways of thinking about Iberian writers' participation on an international, multilingual literary scene as well as reading urban-centric texts at large.

The focus of Part I, "Translational Language: Felipe Alfau's Iberian English and its Afterlife," is Alfau's English-language novel *Chromos*. Its publication in 1990, about 50 years after its writing, sparked significant critical acclaim, including a nomination for the National Book Award in the United States. Alfau's circumstances brought him to New York. As a Barcelona-born immigrant who lived more than 80 years in New York City, Alfau's decision to write in English—but not only that, a unique English bearing a deep imprint of Spanish influence—struck critics as an odd choice. The choice, however, is not all that shocking in light of Alfau's day job as a translator in a city bank, a detail discarded in criticism on his literature. In this first section of the book, I postulate that translation is indeed critical to Alfau's literary craft. His proximity to the practice of translation is responsible not only for the extraordinary language of *Chromos* but also for its main themes, as the novel repeatedly questions the relationship between original and translation in literature and other artistic works, particularly in situations of relocation. In the context of New York, the novel is not forced to choose between old and new, here and there, past and present, Spanish and English, but rather to make them coexist, overlap, and amend each other. I argue that *Chromos* suspends the process of translation, rather than defining itself as an original or translation. Then I move to a discussion of Eduardo Lago's first novel, *Llámame Brooklyn* (2006), which pays homage to Alfau by including him as a character as well as forming other structural and thematic threads with the late author's writing. This revival of Alfau exposes the deficiencies of existing literary criticism and histories in dealing with Iberian writings on New York. Both *Llámame Brooklyn* and *Chromos* propose a treatment of New York that questions the cultural boundaries of Spain and problematizes the coexistence of the Spanish and English languages.

Part II, "The Source of an Avant-garde Voice: Music and Photography in José Moreno Villa," studies the New York prose and poetry of José Moreno Villa, one of the most overlooked cultural figures of twentieth-century Iberian studies. He visited the city for personal reasons in 1927, two years before Federico García Lorca and about ten after Juan Ramón Jiménez, and produced two books that remain in the shadows of these two widely recognized writers. As a gateway to the context of Moreno Villa's New York, I begin this part with a prefatory discussion of Lorca and his epistolary writing, in which he regards travel to New York as one of the most useful experiences of his life while also repeatedly noting the continuous linguistic negotiations surrounding him in the city. Since Lorca wrote his most influential book of poetry at a time when he moved between Spanish, English, and French, the relationship between travel, translation, and creative writing presents innovative channels for addressing what New York meant for Lorca and the other writers of this book. I then introduce Moreno Villa and the fruits of his transatlantic travel, *Pruebas de Nueva York* (1927) and *Jacinta la pelirroja* (1929), and I contend that the marginal place of these texts within literary criticism is due to the absence of a stereotypical New York in favor of one that depends on representing the city through its sounds and non-literary discourses. I suggest that Moreno Villa's past experiences, coupled with his vulnerable linguistic position due of travel, tuned him into the languages of photography, jazz, and the careful use of Spanish, English, and other languages. In doing so, I propose that Moreno Villa's literary New York brought his readers more than a superficial experience, also introducing new discourses and considerations of language and its relationship to other media.

While introducing Julio Camba and Josep Pla to anglophone audiences and highlighting the backstories of their New York writing, Part III, "Travel in Translation: Julio Camba and Josep Pla Write for a Home Audience," leaves behind the avant-garde writing that preceded the Spanish Civil War and shifts focus to the travel texts of two writers from opposite sides of the Iberian Peninsula who wrote the city for professional reasons. Both are esteemed writers in the regions where they were born and currently receive wide recognition throughout the Iberian Peninsula and internationally, particularly Pla.[21] This section analyzes how New York also entered the imagination of an Iberian audience through the travel narratives of writers who, unlike the other authors studied thus far, were assigned to experience New York and bring the city to readers. At times these non-fiction pieces were released in book form, while at others they appeared periodically in newspapers reaching a wide audience. Among the many who wrote New York during the early to mid-twentieth century, the works of Camba and Pla present curious cases regarding translation and the city given that they both are from regions in which Spanish is not the sole language (Galicia and Catalonia, respectively), they both traveled extensively, and both dedicated at least an entire book to New York City. In drawing associations between the two writers, Part III identifies strategies employed by Camba's and Pla's texts in order to discover other avenues these writers explored beyond the physical to deliver New York to readers. In other words, I outline what they were they able to give their readers of New York beyond another description of the cityscape. As Camba's and Pla's New York experiences and the resulting texts strikingly marked the timeline of their work, this part argues for travel as an event that sharpens and broadens the creative imagination of writers, and for a more robust reading of travel narratives as complex texts that carry within them aspects of the city that exceed the visual.

Together, these three parts outline a tradition of writing New York in Iberian literatures that demonstrates the city's standing as much more than a touristic or curious destination for these writers. The quantity and quality of these texts raises New York's status as perhaps the city most often imagined by the greatest diversity of writers from the Iberian Peninsula. For these writers, New York is a complex image of creative options that permeates their respective writing in myriad ways, which are illuminated by shifting from the physical aspects of the city to its array of languages. This book follows how those languages were translated in order to expand the options of literature in English, Spanish, and Catalan, further advocating for "translation as the appropriate hermeneutic for a city" (Cronin and

---

21 Peter Bush recently published two translations of Pla's work: *The Gray Notebook* (2014) and *Life Embitters* (2015). In 2016, a new Spanish-language edition of Pla's *Week-end (d'estiu) a New-York*, titled *Fin de semana en Nueva York*, was released. New editions of Camba's New York work have been printed, in 2008, 2009, and 2014, but he remains inaccessible to the monolingual anglophone reader.

Simon 128) in understanding the city's contributions to the development of literature. The Coda identifies other translational phenomena related to writing New York that cover the latter part of the twentieth century to the present and reflects on the possibility of New York City as a classic in Iberian literatures open to multiple re-creations.

PART I

Translational Language: Felipe Alfau's Iberian English and Its Afterlife

Finding Felipe Alfau

In 1985, Steven Moore (1951–), an editor at Dalkey Archive Press, picked up a copy of *Locos: A Comedy of Gestures* at a used bookstore in Marlboro, Vermont, for ten dollars.[1] The book had been published 49 years earlier, in 1936, by Farrar and Rinehart in New York City.[2] Soon after reading it, Moore looked up its author, Felipe Alfau (1902–99), in the Manhattan phone book.[3] He successfully reached Alfau, who was living alone in Chelsea, and told him he wanted to bring *Locos* back into print. Alfau agreed. He refused an advance, instructing Dalkey to use whatever profits the book made to publish other forgotten work. While *Locos* was in production, Moore asked Alfau if he had written anything else, and Alfau sent him a photocopy of a yellowing manuscript that had been buried deep in a dresser drawer since 1948.[4]

1 Dalkey Archive Press was founded in 1984 by John O'Brien and modeled after other "small houses that published quality literature and experimental fiction," such as Grove Press and New Directions (McDowell, "Small-Press Celebrity"). When Dalkey published *Chromos*, the house had three full-time and two part-time employees, and published about 15 titles per year (McDowell, "Small-Press"). Moore joined Dalkey in 1988. Alfau's *Locos* and *Chromos* were among the first titles he brought to the press, making it one of the top literary presses in the United States. Moore resigned from Dalkey in 1996.

2 The book was included as one of the first titles in Farrar and Rinehart's Discoverers Series, distributed to subscribers by mail (Stavans, "Felipe Alfau: Curriculum Vitae" 143). Alfau received $250 for the edition of 1,500 copies (Martín Gaite, "Triunfo" 179).

3 There is a story that runs counter to this. Chandler Brossard suspects that he might have loaned Moore his own copy of *Locos* (196). Moore refutes this and tells of Brossard's involvement in Alfau's rediscovery in "Recalled to Life."

4 Doris Shapiro remembers the manuscript in "Hidalgo Remembered." Moore claims that Alfau had corrected it. Alfau gave Moore the original manuscript when Moore went to see him in May 1991.

It was *Chromos*.[5] Dalkey published the book, which was one of four finalists for the 1990 National Book Award for fiction in the United States.[6]

Although *Locos* and *Chromos*, Alfau's only two novels, drew the support of respectable publishers in the United States, he did not consider himself a writer. Between 1923 and 1987, Alfau wrote poetry. Ilan Stavans (1961–) collected, edited, and translated his verses from Spanish to English in the volume *Sentimental Songs (La poesía cursi)*, also published by Dalkey in 1992. But despite more than 50 years of composing verses, Alfau did not identify himself as a poet either. His contributions to cultural production did not stop there. Between the ages of 18 and 25, he occasionally wrote music criticism for the New York-based Spanish-language daily *La Prensa*,[7] but those articles remain unidentified.[8]

5 Alfau's friends Chandler Brossard, Charles Simmons, and Daniel Talbot circulated the manuscript among editors with no success (Stavans, "Felipe Alfau: Curriculum Vitae" 144). However, Gayle Rogers claims in *Incomparable Empires: Modernism and the Translation of Spanish and American Literature* (2016) that the manuscript was "in galleys in the late 1940s when [Alfau] abruptly pulled the text from production" (220).

6 In the *New York Times* announcement about the nominations for the National Book Award, Edwin McDowell writes that *Chromos* is "About Spaniards who move to New York in the 1930s. Mr. Alfau, who is 88 years old, completed the novel in 1948 but did not find a publisher for it until this year." The other nominees for fiction that year included *Paradise* by Elena Castedo, *Dogeaters* by Jessica Hagedorn, *Middle Passage* by Charles Johnson, and *Because it Is Bitter, Because it Is My Heart* by Joyce Carol Oates. That same year, Oscar Hijuelos (1951–2013) won the Pulitzer Prize for fiction for *The Mambo Kings Play Songs of Love* and Octavio Paz (1914–98) won the Nobel Prize for Literature.

7 *La Prensa* was founded by José Campubrí, the brother-in-law of Juan Ramón Jiménez. See Emilia Cortés Ibáñez's "José Campubrí y *La Prensa*, pilar del Hispanismo en Nueva York" (2013). For more information on *La Prensa* and other Hispanic periodicals published in New York, such as *El Diario*, see Nicolás Kanellos with Helvetia Martell, *Hispanic Periodicals in the United States, Origins to 1960: A Brief History and Comprehensive Bibliography* (2000).

8 Regarding Alfau's relationship to music, he said that he had "always wanted to be an orchestra conductor" (Stavans, "Anonymity" 149). Anna Shapiro proposes that the "shape of *Locos* is musical—a set of themes and variations" (204). Philippe Villenueve studied the musical allusions in *Locos* and *Chromos*. In Chapter 4 of his dissertation, he proposes that "since *Chromos* is about Spanish exiles living in New York, and since it continually recalls and discusses the cultural heritage of Spain, its food and wines, music, dances, and bullfights, one could read the novel as a rewriting of the zarzuela *La Gran Vía* for an émigré audience, Spaniards who were forced into modernity and distanced from traditional Spain by spatial, not temporal, displacement" (125). Alfau's own writing on music, however, has yet to be identified. Stavans published a piece in *El Diario/La Prensa* in 2007 in which he expressed his desire to find these articles in order to complete his biography of Alfau.

During the rediscovery of Alfau in the United States in the early 1990s, further attempts to recover and introduce his work to a wider audience, particularly a Spanish-speaking one, were made by the prominent writer Carmen Martín Gaite (1925–2000), who produced a Spanish translation of Alfau's first book *Old Tales from Spain*, a collection of children's stories, published as *Cuentos españoles de antaño*.[9] In 1991, the Spanish publishing house Siruela printed the translation accompanied by "diecisiete primorosas ilustraciones de corte modernista de Rhea Wells" (Martín Gaite, "Introducción" xxii) ["seventeen beautiful modernist illustrations by Rhea Wells," Martín Gaite, "Triumph" 179], which first appeared in the 1929 edition initially released by Doubleday, Doran & Company (see Fig. 1.1).[10] Martín Gaite was surprised that the book had remained unknown—"Lo único que no me explico es que de este libro, para mi gusto el más original de los tres de Alfau, nadie hubiera dicho hasta hoy ni una palabra" (Martín Gaite, "Introducción" xxii) [I don't understand why it's unknown; I think it's the most original of Alfau's three books. Not a word has been said about it][11]—considering its careful presentation and inclusion in Doubleday's Junior Books series. Martín Gaite's praise and her translation, however, did not persuade Alfau of his status as a writer either.

What is more, regardless of having produced a wide range of literary texts and receiving recognition from notable publishers and writers, Alfau showed little appreciation for his own writing or for literature in general: "I don't see how anybody could like my books or even understand them. They are unreadable" (Stavans, "Anonymity" 147). He denied having read major authors (Stavans, "Anonymity" 152), and personal accounts about him, such as that of U.S. novelist Chandler Brossard (1922–93), note that he "wholeheartedly hated the New York literary world" (195).[12]

---

9 Martín Gaite includes her own "Introducción: El triunfo de la excepción" to her Spanish translation, in which she gives some biographical information on Alfau as well as providing a discussion of his short stories. Siruela published three editions of *Cuentos españoles de antaño*. Martín Gaite also translated into Spanish the work of Charlotte Brontë, Emily Brontë, Virginia Woolf, and Gustave Flaubert, among others.

10 Rhea Wells (1891–1962) was an author and illustrator of children's books, and worked most prolifically during the 1920s and 1930s. See the 1973 M.A. thesis by Carolyn Sue Usary for more on his life and work.

11 Stavans produced an English translation of Martín Gaite's introduction, "The Triumph of the Exception." All translations of this text are his unless noted otherwise. This translation is mine.

12 Alfau claimed never to have heard of Jorge Luis Borges, Luigi Pirandello, or Vladimir Nabokov (Stavans, "Anonymity" 152). Martín Gaite explains his detachment from literature: "Felipe Alfau ha declarado orgullosamente en muchas ocasiones que se dedicó a la literatura de forma autónoma, y que no había leído (y

Fig. 1.1 Rhea Wells. Title page,
Old Tales from Spain
by Felipe Alfau, 1929.

Never considering himself a professional writer, Alfau claimed that only by necessity did he receive payment for his work (Stavans, "Anonymity" 146), since his job as a translator in the basement of Morgan Bank in Manhattan offered him a steady income (Stavans, "Anonymity" 151).

Chromos features characters who are writers and who also hesitate to identify themselves as such and find it impossible to produce a text on their own.[13] For instance, Garcia, whom Gayle Rogers noted to be a "doubling

---

ha seguido sin hacerlo) a ningún novelista español posterior a Galdós. Frente a esta manifestación, insiste en cambio en reconocer su deuda con la literatura española del Siglo de Oro, y sobre todo con Cervantes" ("Introducción" xxvii) ["Alfau has proudly stated many times that he came to literature as an amateur, not as a professional; that he never read (and continues not to read) Spanish novelists after Galdós. Yet he insists he owes a debt to the Spanish Golden Age, and especially to Cervantes"] ("Triumph" 182).

13 Anna Shapiro also talks about *Locos*'s characters, who are also writers. See "Sixty-one Years of Solitude," originally printed in the *New Yorker*.

of Alfau himself" (222), often talks about his writing projects, but never finishes one, and shares how during the creative process he wishes to call upon a translator to assist him. In doing so, Garcia brings attention to creative writing, especially when working in a new city, New York, and in a new language, English. Thus, in Alfau's work, when frontiers are crossed and the everyday becomes destabilized by the interference of another language, the interest in creative efforts is heavily weighted toward exploring the dynamics of preparation, process, and collaborative efforts, and the intricacies of each stage.

Alfau's silence about himself as a writer has also been a feature of the literary criticism surrounding his work. Despite his National Book Award nomination and the brief critical enthusiasm of the early nineties, critical texts on Alfau are relatively scarce. In 1993, Stavans and David Bellos edited a special issue of the *Review of Contemporary Fiction* dedicated to Alfau and Georges Perec (1936–82). The volume collected the majority of the extant texts on Alfau, including reviews, critical essays, personal commentary, and a bibliography, along with an interview that Stavans conducted with him. Critical essays on Alfau's *Chromos*, mostly published after his rediscovery, have addressed topics such as the defiance of the naturalization of nationality (DeGuzmán), the detective fiction aspects of his work (Sweeney), identity (Castillo, Ramos, Scott, Villeneuve), memory (Villeneuve), and, more recently, multilingualism and narration (Rogers).[14]

Some of the most revealing readings of Alfau and of *Chromos* are by literary translators and creative writers.[15] For example, *Chromos* captured

---

14 Villeneuve's doctoral dissertation, "Confabulation, Collaboration, and Chromolithography: Memory as a Construct in the Works of Felipe Alfau," is the second study to focus solely on the work of Alfau. Joseph Scott's master's thesis, "Thundering Out of the Shadow: Modernism and Identity in the Novels of Felipe Alfau" (2005), was the first master's thesis dedicated to Alfau, in which he studies "identity, both personal and collective, as a constructed, not a natural, category" (1) in *Locos* and *Chromos*. In doing so, he argues for Alfau's place among modernist rather than postmodernist writers.

15 I am mainly interested in Rabassa's and Eduardo Lago's readings of Alfau, but it is also noteworthy that U.S. editor and novelist Charles Simmons (1924–) included Alfau as a character in his novel *Powered Eggs* (1964). In a brief introduction to a selection from *Powered Eggs*, he writes: "One could not know Felipe Alfau, be a novelist, and not write about him. [...] In his early middle age, when I knew him, he had everything needed for a fictional character and, in the colloquial sense, a character—luminous intelligence, outrageous perversity of opinion, and a straight-faced delivery of genius. I put him in my first novel, *Powered Eggs* (E.P. Dutton, 1964), as Jose (no accent) Llano, and ascribed him the book's Very Tales, which were my inventions but were inspired by Felipe's style of thought and

the attention of Gregory Rabassa (1922–2016), a translator of Spanish and Portuguese texts who also wrote literary reviews and critiques, and established meaningful personal connections with some of the authors he translated.[16] In "The Power of *Chromos*" (1990), Rabassa commented that the novel "is a remarkable book, not only for what it says, but also for what it is struggling to say, often with strangely successful insights" (224). In *Gregory Rabassa's Latin American Literature: A Translator's Visible Legacy* (2011), María Constanza Guzmán describes Rabassa as fundamental in shaping how anglophone audiences receive and read Latin American and—to a lesser, but no less significant extent—Spanish- and Portuguese-language literature. Rabassa's visibility is unique for a literary translator, a role that receives limited recognition in the United States, to the degree that he "is accorded nearly co-creative status with the original author" (Thomas Hoaksema qtd. in Guzmán 14). As such, his commentary on *Chromos* carries significant weight, as it captures the exploratory, experimental vibe of the novel. At the same time, Rabassa's words make evident his sensitivities to the use of language as a literary translator, bilingual reader, and long-time resident of New York City: attributes that are not necessary but that could arguably favor the detection of complexities of the text not immediately available on its surface.

More recently, Eduardo Lago (1954–), the Madrid-born, New York-based writer, literary translator,[17] critic, and university professor, resuscitated Alfau as a character in his first and award-winning novel *Llámame Brooklyn* (2006), and established other structural and thematic connections with Alfau's writing.[18] Lago has also paid homage to several other aspects of Alfau's profile and literary production in public interviews. His placement of Alfau in a fictionalized New York literary scene not only satisfies readers'

talk. When the book was done I showed it to him, wondering whether he would be offended. He wasn't. He understood. I think, Jose Llano was an *hommage*" (186). In addition, Barcelona-born writer Enrique Vila-Matas (1948–) includes Alfau in his novel *Bartleby y Compañía* (2002) as an example of a writer who decides to cut off his career by ceasing to write.

16 For more on Rabassa's career, see his memoir *If This Be Treason: Translation and its Dyscontents* (2005).

17 Lago has translated Henry James, William Dean Howells, John Barth, Sylvia Plath, and Junot Díaz, among others.

18 *Llámame Brooklyn* won the Premio Nadal, Spain's oldest literary prize, the Premio Ciudad de Barcelona, and the Premio de la Crítica de narrativa castellana. In 2013, *Llámame Brooklyn* was translated into English as *Call Me Brooklyn* by Ernesto Mestre-Reed and published by Dalkey Archive. Since *Llámame Brooklyn*, Lago has written two more novels: *Ladrón de mapas* and *Siempre supe que volvería a verte, Aurora Lee*.

longing to imagine Alfau still occupying an active place in the cultural landscape of the city, but can also be seen as an interpretation of Alfau's role and work in literary history, opening new avenues of inquiry regarding the literary interactions between the Iberian Peninsula and New York.

Besides being said to have an "engaging meta-literary style, clearly too advanced for his epoch" (Stavans, "Felipe Alfau: Curriculum Vitae" 143), one of the reasons Alfau has been neglected by critics is because he did exactly what Lago did not do: he wrote *Locos* and *Chromos* in English. One of the obvious consequences of this decision is that Alfau struggled to be fully embraced by either Spanish or U.S. audiences and critics. But those readers who do find his work are often tripped up by Alfau's decision to opt out of Spanish as his novelistic language, and early critical commentary superficially highlights the distinct English that this choice produces.[19] However, pushing the conversation about Alfau's language beyond the binary choice of Spanish and English presents fresh readings of his work.

From the scarce biographical information on Alfau, a wealth of insight can be gleaned from the fact the he worked as a translator at a Wall Street bank for many years, before retiring in 1954 (McDowell, "Small-Press Celebrity"). This substantial part of his life has been dismissed as bearing no relation to his creative writing. Although there are great differences between translation for technical purposes and translation for creative purposes, Alfau was nonetheless immersed in personal and professional spheres that moved between Spanish and English. I open this book with an exploration of translation in *Chromos* and in relation to Alfau's literary profile as a way of expanding translation's role in literary analysis, especially in contexts in which multiple languages intimately circulate. From the novel's very language and one character's dependency on translation to complete his own creative projects, to the conversations that reveal the language choices and complications of being an Iberian writer in a context dominated by the English language, among other examples, *Chromos* engages in the centrality of translation in situations of relocation. After all, *Chromos*'s opening sentence is the most frequently quoted—"The moment one learns English, complications set in"—as it sets the tone and overarching theme of the novel (7).

In the first part of this book, I postulate that Alfau's work is keenly aware of the dynamics of language that occur in travel, relocation, and city life where signs of an individual's past and present cohabit with all that is new. Translation is critical to Alfau's literary craft, and the decision

19 Villeneuve argues that the lack of criticism on Alfau is due to that fact that critics have had a difficult time moving beyond the metafiction angle of his work.

to write his novels in English instead of Spanish is not solely a strategy to avoid translation, or being translated—although Alfau might have preferred that—but rather centralizes translation as a way to encounter the complexities of representing a new place, whether literary or actual, as a result of travel or relocation. However, as I argue in this section, Alfau's English presents a new feeling that seeks to combine the strange and the familiar due to the acute awareness of translation as a shaper of everyday life. Translation is not only responsible for the extraordinary language of *Chromos* but also for its main themes. Thus, Alfau's literature has much to say about how New York is experienced, especially for those, like Iberian writers, whose first language is Spanish. By destabilizing expectations of Spanish and English,[20] Alfau calls attention to the process of translation, or the state of translation, rather than to the finality of the movement from one language to another that characterizes the starting point and products of the process.

Finally, I conclude Part I with a discussion of how Eduardo Lago's revival of Alfau in *Llámame Brooklyn* exposes the deficiencies of existing criticism and histories in dealing with Iberian literary production on and in New York. Although their publication is separated by 16 years and their creation by more than 60, both *Llámame Brooklyn* and *Chromos* propose a treatment of New York that questions the cultural boundaries of the Iberian Peninsula and problematizes the contact of the Spanish and English languages. Although their trajectories have differed, Alfau and Lago both established New York as their adopted home and wrote from the city. Looking at what New York allows their literature to do, ultimately the first part of this book introduces a critical framework with which to study the city's influence on Iberian literatures by shifting the focus from the visual impact of a city on literature to language's role in molding literary creativity.

---

20 DeGuzmán also notes the way in which *Chromos* plays with readers' expectations between a "work of art and its supposed real referent" (247). She pairs *Chromos* with Kathy Acker's *Don Quixote* and examines how these texts play with readers' expectations of word and image: "A common complaint about these two works is that they produce an uncomfortable epistemological vertigo and confusion. I contend that this effect is created by their substitution of a constantly shifting performance for the type of verbal description that offers iconic stasis or familiar grounds according to readers' expectations" (247).

Alfau's Language

Felipe Alfau was born in Barcelona on August 24, 1902 into a family of journalists, politicians, diplomats, and artists, and spent his childhood in several cities around the peninsula, including the Basque Country, and in the Philippines and the Caribbean.[21] During the First World War, at the tender age of 14, he moved to New York with his family and was a resident of the city until his lonely death in a retirement home in Rego Park, Queens, on February 18, 1999.[22] His 38-word obituary in the *New York Times* simply identifies him as "author of 'Locos' and 'Chromos'" ("Felipe Alfau"). Most of Alfau's known literary production took place during the early years of his time in the city. Within a little over ten years of being in New York, he had already authored two books in English. In 1928, at the age of 26,

21 Little has been published about the life of Alfau. The Perec/Alfau special issue of *The Review of Contemporary Fiction* (1993) includes a brief biographical piece on Alfau by Stavans, who is working on a biography of Alfau. See Stavans's "Anonymity: An Interview with Felipe Alfau" and "Felipe Alfau: Curriculum Vitae." Stavans met Alfau in May 1991 at his retirement home in Queens, New York, after trying to visit him several times with no luck at his previous address, 436 West 27th Street, Apartment 9H in Manhattan ("Felipe Alfau: Curriculum Vitae" 144). Prior to that, Alfau had lived on the Upper West Side on West 78th Street (Talbot 183). He married and divorced twice. Chandler Brossard's essay "Two or Three Things I Know about Him" shares some details about Alfau's family life. He had a daughter, Chiquita Villet, with his first wife, Esther Goodman, born in New York City on February 24, 1928. Villet died on May 25, 2014 in California. Stavans says that Alfau was close friends with Luis Muñoz Marín (1898–1980), Puerto Rico's first elected governor from 1948 until early 1965 ("Felipe Alfau: Curriculum Vitae" 144). More information on Alfau's family can also be found in the entry for his older sister Jesusa Alfau de Solalinde (1890–1943) by Daisy Cocco De Filippis in *Latinas in the United States: A Historical Encyclopedia* (2006). Alfau's parents were Antonio Abad Alfau Baralt and Eugenia Galván Velázquez, and his grandfather was the "illustrious" Dominican Manuel de Jesús Galván (Cocco De Filippis 37). His father was editor of the weekly newspaper *Las Novedades: España y los pueblos hispano-americanos*, published in English and Spanish between 1916 and 1918. Alfau de Solalinde married the distinguished Hispanic studies professor Antonio G. Solalinde. At the age of 18, she wrote the novel *Los débiles*, which was published in Spain four years later. Although there have been claims that an English translation of this novel exists, Cocco De Filippis notes that it has not been located. Two editions of this novel were published in the United States. The J. Horace Nunemaker edition published by Prentice-Hall includes a prologue, the only section written in English. The other edition, by Cocco De Filippis, includes eight articles previously published in *Las Novedades*.

22 According to Toby Talbot, Alfau returned to Spain once for a week in 1958, when Talbot and her family were living there. See Talbot's essay "The Return of the Native" for details of his visit.

Fig. 1.2 Felipe Alfau.

Alfau had completed *Locos*, the first of the two novels he would write, and found a publisher for it in 1936. The first work he published, in 1929, was a collection of children's stories, *Old Tales from Spain*. Soon after, he began to write *Chromos*, which would remain stored away in a draw, hidden until Alfau was well into his late eighties.

When published, long after they were written, in 1989 and 1990 respectively, *Locos* and *Chromos* were reviewed in publications such as the *New Yorker*, the *Atlantic*, the *New York Times Book Review*, *World Literature Today*, and the *New Republic*, to name but a few.[23] *Locos* was praised for its avant-garde techniques, including the creation of a "proto-postmodernist universe" (Stavans, "Felipe Alfau: Curriculum Vitae" 143) and a preoccupation with "the nature of fiction" (Shapiro, "Sixty-one" 203). Susan Elizabeth Sweeney pairs Alfau with Jorge Luis Borges (1899–1986) and Vladimir Nabokov (1899–1977), who "explored the frightening and exhilarating space between naming and identity, between narration and story, between language and what it would describe" (207). Doris Shapiro's review of *Locos* in the *New*

---

23 Most of the reviews of *Chromos* were overwhelmingly positive, but a few did criticize the book for being lengthy (Begnal), for obfuscating its main concerns (Brenkman), and for being nothing more than a literary curiosity (Iannone).

Yorker says that he had "predicted the discoveries of the great magic realists" (201). Stavans applies the description "Alfauesque narrative exercises" to Georges Perec's *Life, A User's Manual* (1978), Julio Cortázar's *Hopscotch* (1963), and other "classic novels written in Europe and Latin America in the sixties and after" ("Felipe Alfau: Curriculum Vitae" 143).[24] In July 1991, Chandler Brossard said that *Chromos* was slowly winning Alfau recognition as one of the most significant twentieth-century writers (197), although Alfau still has not achieved the same recognition or critical regard as Nabokov, Brodsky, or Conrad, other "writers who have mastered a second language and used it to write their oeuvre" (Stavans, "Anonymity" 149).[25]

As these remarkable writers and many more have proven, opting to write in a language other than one's first is not rare.[26] Nor is an Iberian author writing in English during the same years in New York.[27] Although born on

24 For example, in the prologue to *Locos*, the author invites the reader to read the stories in any order, a detail that is reminiscent of *Hopscotch*. Rabassa makes a connection between *Chromos*'s Garcia and *Hopscotch*'s Morelli: "García is the Morelli of this remarkable story, anticipating, as does Alfau's earlier book [...], that great outpouring of good fiction that has come to be known as the Latin American 'boom' and which, in light of this book, might well have resulted from some condition that is inherently Hispanic and which goes back to *Don Quixote*" ("Power" 224). Anna Shapiro further speaks to the reader's interaction with Alfau's work: "it's a pleasure to read *Locos* with a pencil in hand, riffling backward to pounce on a clue as suggestive as a detail remembered from a dream" (203). Along the same lines, Mary McCarthy refers to *Locos* as a detective story, "but one in which the mystery is identity and the detective is the reader" (Shapiro 203).

25 While critics have repeatedly praised Alfau for being a writer well ahead of his time, some have traced obvious influences on his work, such as Miguel de Unamuno's *Niebla* (1914) (Martín Gaite) and de Unamuno's work in general (DeGuzmán 247), Ramón María del Valle-Inclán (DeGuzmán 247), *The Late Mattia Pascal* (1904) by Luigi Pirandello (Zangrilli), and Max Beerbohm's *Seven Men* (1919) (Villeneuve).

26 For examples of Spanish-American writers who write in languages other than Spanish, see *Unhomely Rooms: Foreign Tongues and Spanish-American Literature* (2002) by Roberto Ignacio Díaz, in which he "reconfigure[s] Spanish-American literature as an entity with no fixed linguistic midpoint" (26). Among the writers he studies are Comtesse Merline, W.H. Hudson, and Carlos Fuentes.

27 While in New York at the end of the nineteenth century, José Martí (1853–1895) wrote an article titled "Impressions of America (By a Very Fresh Spaniard)" for the city's publication *The Hour*. Martí wrote the article in English, and it was published with "errors of spelling and grammar usage" (Allen 5). As Martí is chiefly known for his contributions to Cuban independence and identity, Esther Allen points out that "in order to address New York [...] he had to adopt the persona of a Spaniard— not only in the title and by-line of the article, but in its pages as well, where Martí consistently includes himself in a European 'we'" (5). This episode marks an early

opposite sides of the Atlantic, discussions in literary criticism tend to place Felipe Alfau and the New Yorker Prudencio de Pereda in the category of "first- and second-generation Spanish-Americans," along with Mercedes de Acosta (1893–1968) and José Yglesias (1919–15) (Varela-Lago 12).[28] Four years before Alfau arrived in New York, de Pereda (1912–) was born in the Spanish colony in Brooklyn to parents from Spain. De Pereda authored short stories and three novels in English: *All the Girls We Loved* (1948), *Fiesta: A Novel of Modern Spain* (1953), and *Windmills in Brooklyn* (1960). He collaborated with Ernest Hemingway on the Spanish Civil War films *Spain in Flames* and *The Spanish Earth*, both released in 1937. Other widely recognized individuals, such as Joris Ivens, John Dos Passos, Archibald MacLeish, Orson Welles, and Lillian Hellman, also participated in the making of these films. In addition, de Pereda translated the Argentine Alberto Gerchunoff's *Jewish Gauchos of the Pampas* (1910) into English in 1953. Coupled with Alfau because of the link to the "Spanish diaspora in the United States" (Varela-Lago 13), this brief sketch of de Pereda's career reveals aspects absent from that of Alfau: productive collaboration with other writers, embrace of the U.S. market, commitment to literary and creative production in English, and willingness to maintain expectations of a "Spanish" or "Spanish-American" writer, as de Pereda's three novels are either set in Spain or explicitly depict Brooklyn's Spanish colony in a conventional narrative style that was immediately accessible. For example, de Pereda's success as a writer for an expansive audience can be shown by the fact that *All the Girls We Loved* had two paperback editions and sold over 500,000 copies (Ordaz).

While Alfau did not collaborate with major writers from the anglophone world, testimonies, such as that by Brossard, who met Alfau through a woman from the Canary Islands, Eulalia Cabrera, whose father had been a professor,

---

instance of the de-foreignization of "Spanish." While Martí's English might contain errors, a "Spaniard" writing in English brings "Spanish" closer to the anglophone community.

28 Mercedes de Acosta was born and died in New York City. A child of wealthy immigrants from the Iberian Peninsula, she was an author, poet, and playwright. She was known for her love of women and romantic conquests, which included Greta Garbo and Isadora Duncan, among others. See *"That Furious Lesbian": The Story of Mercedes de Acosta* (2003) by Robert A. Schanke. Of Spanish and Cuban descent, José Yglesias was born in Tampa, Florida, and died in New York City. He authored 15 books and articles for prominent periodicals such as the *New Yorker* and the *New York Times Magazine*. In the introduction to her dissertation "Conquerors, Immigrants, Exiles: The Spanish Diaspora in the United States (1848–1948)," Ana María Varela-Lago briefly situates Alfau's work in "Latino" and "Hispanic" categories. See her dissertation for an exploration of "how the legacy of Spanish colonialism in America contributed to shaping the Spanish diaspora in the United States" (15).

indicate that he had at least some contact with other Spanish speakers living in New York City: Eulalia and Alfau "were good friends because the two belonged to the same social strata, had the same points of reference" (Brossard 194).[29] Additionally, Brossard describes: "The New York of that epoch" as "a fabulous city. Felipe would know the best restaurants. For instance, there was a place called El Mundo in Spanish Harlem in which he was well known. He was a real gourmet" (195). Thus, Alfau did enjoy New York, especially during the city's participation in the "Spanish craze," which began in the late 1890s and lasted until the early 1930s, just before he began *Chromos*, "when seemingly everything Spanish—art, music, language, literature, architecture, and more—was in vogue" (Kagan 25). Kagan clarifies that "this craze was not exclusively Spanish in the peninsular sense of the term" (25). Alfau was not always as dark and isolated as he is portrayed in his later years.[30]

In addition, Alfau took a class on Iberian letters with one of the pillars of U.S. Hispanism, Professor Federico de Onís (1888–1966),[31] joining the

29 I have questioned whether this Eulalia Cabrera is the same Eulalia Cabrera Duval, known as Nina, who married the Mexican-born poet José Juan Tablada (1871–1945), who also spent time in New York. According to Brossard, Eulalia's father was a professor, and she was from the Canary Islands. Nina's father was a landowner and the family was from Cuba. The dates align, as do the potential social circles. At times, however, Brossard's information is not accurate. I consulted with the literary critic and historian Rodolfo Mata, who believes that they are not the same person. Nina met Tablada when her parents hired him to teach her French. The two married in 1918 and lived in New York City and Mexico. See Mata's article "José Juan Tablada: Translator" (2011) for more on New York in the work of Tablada and Nina's book *José Juan Tablada en la intimidad: con cartas y poemas inéditos* (1954) for more on the couple's relationship.

30 The Alfaus were friends of the family of Joaquín Torres-García (1874–1949), who traveled to New York City from Barcelona in the early twenties. Torres-García writes about the Alfau family in his life narrative *Historia de mi vida* (1939). His description gives insight into the familial surroundings: "En medio de aquel ambiente de negocios, aquella gente consagrada al arte, a la filosofía, a la literatura y a la música, hacían un notable contraste en aquella ciudad" [In the middle of that business-driven environment, those people, devoted to art, philosophy, literature, and music, were a notable contrast in that city] (168). Torres-García also writes that it was Alfau's mother who was devoted to music (169). He mentions Alfau's two sisters Jesusa and Monna by name, but says nothing more about Felipe other than the fact that he was one of three siblings (169).

31 Onís founded the Spanish Department at Columbia University in 1916. It was outstanding "in terms of the number of students it produced, and the most dazzling with regard to its list of visiting professors" (Young 268). In 1930, he founded the Casa Hispánica, and four years later the journal *Revista Hispánica Moderna* (Young 268). See Howard Young's brief essay for an outline of Onís's contributions to Hispanism at Columbia and in the United States more widely.

list of Iberian and Latin American writers—including José Moreno Villa, Federico García Lorca, and Carmen Martín Gaite—for whom Columbia University provided an intellectual environment of growth and exchange (Stavans, "Felipe Alfau: Curriculum Vitae" 143).[32] Contact with de Onís and an inconspicuous enjoyment of New York's version of "Spanish" kept Alfau on the margins of literary history, not only due to his choice of language, but also to the characteristics of his literary language and the content of his writing. In his blurb for the National Book Award, Paul West described *Chromos* as:

> Finished in 1948, [it] sets an imaginary Alfau dreaming in front of old calendar pictures by the light of a match. Before the flame gutters, a real novel has come to him: a tart and eloquent, sly and feisty kaleidoscope of New York Spaniards, wrought in fire amid the *cante hondo* of the heart by a hunger artist almost lost, unpublished, to oblivion. (243)

West's description presents an obscure yet intriguing novel. *Chromos* displays the "kaleidoscope" of New Yorkers in a collage-like structure, including interspersed stories of another set of characters across the Atlantic in Madrid, and other parts of the peninsula in an English that requires more than just knowledge of the language to appreciate its unique characteristics as it holds onto Spanish in an unobtrusive manner. Anna Shapiro gives a sense of what it is like to encounter Alfau's language in a review of *Locos* in the *New Yorker* titled "Sixty-one Years of Solitude": "there are phrases in *Locos* that read like translations or like the overcorrect diction of a non-native speaker ('a rogue after whom the police had been after for some time')" (205). Shortly after, Gregory Rabassa's review of *Chromos* comments that "the very language of [Alfau's] narration is perfectly good English, and yet it is not English. Nor is it Spanish either in a free or in a literal translation" (224). Rabassa, a keen bilingual English-Spanish reader and literary translator, pinpoints that the origin of the uniqueness of Alfau's language as a fusion of Spanish and English. In Alfau's own words: "My English is Iberian—an acquisition. It's half English and half my own creation, the result of an immigrant experience" (Stavans, "Anonymity" 151). With his "Iberian English," he maintained Spanish, the visibility of the translation process undergone by many of the novel's contexts, and English, or the inescapable language of his new city. In this way, Alfau's language is distinct because it refuses to surrender to choosing between Spanish or English, but rather

---

32 In his interview with Stavans, Alfau says that he took philosophy courses at Columbia and does not mention Onís.

holds on to Spanish while being visibly English. The language of *Chromos* has captured translation.

The use of Iberian English subverts ideas about language choice and supports the novel's ideas about nationality. At the beginning of the novel, a discussion about Spaniards' resistance of the idea that an individual in New York could really be from Spain, even less so Madrid, "as if it were an empty city or a place which no one can ever leave" (10), presents the complexities of this situation. In an attempt to avoid being doubted so often, the first-person narrator says that he is "a Latin American and save[s] [himself] a good deal of trouble" (10). In fact, the majority of Iberian emigrants to New York came from the northwestern region of Galicia.[33] At the same time, this statement also speaks to the normalcy of movement from Latin America to New York during this period. More interesting, however, is the culmination of this discussion when the narrator directly addresses the reader:

> I take this opportunity to advise all my countrymen who read this to carry their passports with them at all times and thus squelch any doubts as to their nationality and if they come from Madrid, to run to the nearest consulate and there have the fact stated in bold type. (11)

Continuing with the humorous tone, the narrator confirms his origins and thus calls further attention to the language of *Chromos*. Language turns out to be a faulty indicator of origin, a topic that María DeGuzmán explores in her book *Spain's Long Shadow: The Black Legend, Off-Whiteness, and Anglo-American Empire* (2005). Instead of focusing her study on Alfau's language *per se*, in the book's fifth chapter DeGuzmán discusses how *Chromos* denaturalizes nationality with the technique of imposture (274).

If the narrator confirms that he is from Spain and that other individuals from his country are reading this book, then the absence of Spanish in the novel's pages leads to questions about language and, more specifically, about translation. Given that the text is aware of a potential bilingual reader, why doesn't the language resort to more instances of code-switching, or the alternation of Spanish and English, the chosen avenue for numerous contemporary writers in Alfau's same situation?[34] Perhaps, in order to

---

33 See the documentary *Little Spain* (2011) by Artur Balder for more on the history of Iberian immigration to New York City and more specifically the area surrounding Manhattan's 14th Street. See also James D. Fernández and Luis Argeo's *Invisible Immigrants: Spaniards in the U.S. (1868–1945)* (2015).

34 In literary studies, code-switching it is often associated with Latino writing in the United States. See Lourdes Torres's article "In the Contact Zone: Code-switching

avoid an overtly bilingual text, the role of the narrator as a translator surfaces in that he relates in English situations which happened in Spanish. Alternatively, readers may believe that the text before them is a translation of an unseen text.

Translation, however, is absent from criticism on Alfau. Doris Shapiro, who was a friend of Alfau, laments that in addition to living in a basement apartment, he spent many years "travailing at a desk in the basement of a bank, reached by subway, where he translated commercial papers of no interest to him" (199). Philippe Villeneuve blames Alfau's job for his failure to keep writing: "Alfau turns his back on novel writing in mid-life for a practical, bread-winning job in a bank, the locus *par excellence* of meaningless action" (160). It was at this bank desk that *Chromos* came to life. Edwin McDowell of the *New York Times* reports that Alfau told his publisher that "Chromos ... was written at the office between translations, to pass the time" ("Nominees"). On another occasion, Alfau says: "I was a translator at Morgan Bank in Manhattan for many, many years. In the office, between one document and another, I would write a paragraph or two" (Stavans, "Anonymity" 151). Shapiro's comment understands there to be a disconnection between this type of translation and creative writing: Alfau used the writing as an escape from the mundane bank-related translations. While translation for business purposes lacks the inherent creativity necessary for literary translation, Alfau's occupation adds to the multiple quotidian ways of moving among languages, be they technical, creative, or as a matter of survival. Attention to language and translation constantly surrounded Alfau, an emigrant to New York, while he inhabited the city. In fact, attention to the intricacies of language was the foundation of some of his social relationships. The literary translator, theater founder and owner, and educator Toby Talbot, who befriended Alfau in 1953 while he was living on Manhattan's Upper West Side, says that "he shared my fascination for words, sherry, and garlic" (183).[35] Additionally, Brossard aligns Alfau's work as a translator in a bank with his own start as a writer: "He was already working as a translator at the Morgan Bank. When we first

Strategies by Latino/a Writers" (2007) for some examples of authors who incorporate code-switching into their writing. *Chromos* was published at the dawn of the decade in which Latino literature was "finally recognized by mainstream publishers as a legitimate, indeed integral, part of American letters," as explained by Margo Gutiérrez (1998).

35 Talbot opened the New Yorker Theater on the Upper West Side with her husband. She also translated many Spanish literary texts, including works by Rocco Negri, José Ortega y Gasset, Benito Pérez Galdós, Jacobo Timerman, and Luisa Valenzuela.

became friends, I was just beginning to write" (195). Translation, then, is not a parallel activity to Alfau's writing. On the contrary, translation, as the link to some of his social relationships, is also the force that sustains his literary language and the central theme of his second novel about displacement, relocation, acculturation, alienation, and creative production. Just as Esther Allen reminds us that a literary translation "embodies a theory of the text it represents" ("Perils"), *Chromos* beholds a theory of writing in situations of movement, travel, and adaptation to a city's life that seeks to centralize the constraints of a language, their creative opportunities, and the shifts made to language that respond to the host environment.

Apart from the fact that Brossard held onto Alfau's employment as a translator, he also observed Alfau's actual use of language and offered insight on the choices he made:

> Poetry is intimate in a way fiction is not and Felipe's native tongue was always very important to him. I remember, for instance, how, a long time ago, when Toby Talbot first met him, she would speak to him in Spanish but he would answer in English simply because he didn't recognize her Spanish as his. People saw him as arrogant but he was a purist. He would only use Spanish with Eulalia. (197)[36]

While it may seem that Alfau was adverse to non-native accents, Alfau's decisions about language were far from simplistic, as Brossard further notes that Alfau "was very bright and always had a terrific ear for languages" (197).[37] Besides justifying Alfau's language choice for poetry, Brossard touches on how Alfau selected the language he would speak with people, which seems to make it all the more significant that his novelistic language purposefully hovers between Spanish and English as it emphasizes the detachment experienced when one undergoes a transition that involves linguistic movement and exchange.[38] In other words, his novelistic language

36 Alfau himself commented on his use of Spanish for writing poetry: "The poems I wrote in my mother tongue because poetry is too close to the heart, whereas fiction is a mental activity, an invention, something foreign, distant" (Stavans, "Anonymity" 149).

37 Alfau tells that "it took a while" to switch from Spanish to English in his writing. He explained how he learned English: "I never studied English in school. My parents, after a life of wandering in the Philippines, the Caribbean, and several cities on the Iberian peninsula, emigrated to the United States. I arrived when I was fourteen, in 1916. A child picks up new linguistic patterns rather easily. An adolescent has a harder time, and an adult may never accomplish the task of mastering a second language" (Stavans, "Anonymity" 149).

38 In the introduction to *Bilingual Games: Some Literary Investigations*, Doris Sommer

goes beyond a standard English or Spanish, attempting a state of fusion of the two. Rabassa has suggested that in Alfau's language, "we might be witnessing linguistic transformation here, what happened when the Franks and Goths began to speak Latin or the Normans Anglo-Saxon" (224), a remark that offers high praise for Alfau attempt to literally put into language rather than a mere description the experience of an Iberian individual in New York.

In "Introduction: The City as Translation Zone," Michael Cronin and Sherry Simon thoroughly discuss the implications of bringing the words "translation" and "city" together. They explore what translation means in the digital city of today:

> In a world of Skype, Viber, Facebook, text messaging, the near instantaneity of contact with elsewhere makes staying in touch both economically and technically feasible. This, in turn creates a new kind of translational reality for the migrant in the multilingual city space. Repeated contact with fellow native speakers of a language in the country of origin or technically mediated communication with fellow nationals in the host city leads to a much keener perception of *translation as process* as opposed to *translation as state*. (124)

With the term "state," Cronin and Simon refer to the result of language distance in the predigital setting, where the "translated subject with the language of origin [i]s an increasingly marginal presence in the language life of the migrant" (124). Although Alfau wrote from a predigital New York, his professional life and social circles frequently wove together Spanish and English in the city. The "repeated contact" with Spanish in a city dominated by English mimics, to an extent, the way in which Cronin and Simon describe the translational reality of migrants.

Albert Mobilio's review of *Chromos* for the *Village Voice* describes the novel as "an extended mediation on exile, especially the linguistic limbo that divides the new language from the old" (18). Additionally, Rabassa

---

discusses Wittgenstein (1889–1951) in England, his use of German and English, and his ultimate decision to avoid bilingual games and "stay inside one language at a time" (5). Alfau did cross over the language lines in his literature and put "universalism [on edge] in the field of bilingual games because they don't play evenhandedly" (Sommer 6). Sommer's work helps to further understand the rewards and consequences of a text's bilingualism: "The players take advantages [sic] of the uneven playing field where a powerful language expects to win every match, but where other languages jostle and rub power [sic] to win some points. Using more than one language causes problems for universal, across-the-board games of politics, philosophy and aesthetics" (6).

comments that *Chromos* "is a remarkable book, not only for what it says, but also for what it is struggling to say, often with strangely successful insights" (224). Both statements hint at the treatment of language ingrained in the novel but do not elaborate on how Alfau's literature uses language itself not only as a means but also as a message. Alfau's understanding of and commitment to translation as part of the experience of travel and relocation are responsible for his Iberian English: a language that relies on knowledge of both Spanish, the old, and English, the new, without making the former entirely visible. There is something more to the language of *Chromos* that reaches beyond the influence of Spanish on English. Translation is not only a purely linguistic question, but also a conceptual one, as questions of translation permeate several levels of *Chromos*'s narrative.

Translation Happens

Alfau's explanation of how he wrote *Chromos*, interspersing writing with his translation work at the bank, emphasizes the book's patchwork spread or collage of stories, also echoed by the title itself. "Chromos" refers to chromolithograph calendars, the "gaudy commercial prints of the period, calendar art" (Rabassa 224), which, adapted to a book form, are similar to vignettes. In his discussion of *Chromos*, Gayle Rogers has also proposed that the title "looks like it is suspended between two tongues," noting that it "might appear to an anglophone audience to be a Spanish word" (*Incomparable* 220). This suspension between languages is a characteristic of the novel. *Chromos*'s cast includes four primary characters, all of whom are from the Iberian Peninsula: the narrator, Garcia the writer, Dr. José de los Rios, and Don Pedro Guzman O'Moore Algoracid, an occasional bandleader known to his U.S. audience as Pete Guz and to friends as the Moor.[39] Together they walk the streets of New York City, spend time in parks, gather in apartments, and meet at the Lower East Side bar El Telescopio, named for the image of an individual throwing back a bottle of wine. Beyond that, nothing significant happens in terms of an overarching plot; it is the novel's aesthetic, philosophical, and linguistic ruminations that are of interest. Garcia's writing projects in progress are interspersed with the characters' meanderings and conversations, and are often interrupted by the narrator's comments.

The characters of *Chromos* face some of the same dilemmas, particularly those regarding language choice, associated with Alfau's literary profile.

---

39 See DeGuzmán's chapter on Alfau for a reading of the significance of the characters' names.

Early in *Chromos*, Garcia reads the narrator a portion of the novel he is writing about a family in Spain and asks for his opinion:

> "Well?"
>
> "Oh, it is fine, fine—the only thing: to come all the way to New York to write a novel about a family in Spain ..."
>
> "I did not come here to write it, you ought to know that. I am here and I happened to think of writing it. That's all."
>
> "But who is going to read it? Unless it is for your own satisfaction or records ..."
>
> "I am not thinking of publishing it in Spanish here. I have in mind one or two publishing houses in Latin America, or perhaps even Spain, although I would rather—but what I was really thinking is that you might help me with the English translation. I will show you some other parts I have already written out, even if they still need a little polishing."
>
> "Well, I don't know about that. My English is not so good." (34)

On the one hand, their conversation concerns the extra-textual situations surrounding the proposed text: audience, publisher, and language.[40] If Garcia chooses to write in Spanish, he expresses a desire to look beyond New York in order to publish his work, despite the fact that there might already be options for Spanish-language publishing for him in the city; and if he chooses to publish it locally, he must translate it into English. Whether it is published outside New York or translated to keep it in the city, the novel undergoes a detachment from its initial conditions of creation. This could also be understood as a detachment from its source, its original language or birthplace, further illuminating the dynamics that arise when multiple languages intersect and literary activity is involved.

Throughout *Chromos*, Garcia and the narrator take the opportunity to discuss his novel's plot and questions of language, especially aspects that will be of concern for its English translation. They begin a conversation about language choice but do not arrive at any definitive conclusion about which option would be best given the extra-textual circumstances.

---

40 As literary studies advance in the twenty-first century, the limitations of a single-language/single-national literary history paradigm do not accommodate certain texts, or aspects of certain texts. In their discussions of literary history, Mario Valdés and Linda Hutcheon acknowledge that "literature does not exist in isolation from the culture in which it is 'experienced'—that is, the culture in which it is both produced and received" (12). The narrator and Garcia's conversations exhibit these same concerns.

Instead, Garcia is convinced that the process of translation will accompany the creation of his version of the text.

Garcia's preoccupations not only concern how a specific word will translate, but also how an English-speaking audience will receive the plot.[41] Included in Garcia's novel is a passage about the 16-year-old Julieta Sandoval and her special maid, who discusses "forbidden subjects with her mistress" (61). At this point, the narrator discovers "a pornographic turn" in Garcia's text, which he finds "uncalled-for" and "irrelevant," and he warns him that "if I had anything to do with the translation, I would not tolerate any more of such passages which could only offend the ears of the English reader" (62). However, the section of the novel that the narrator finds inappropriate is not included in *Chromos*: the text has already been censored. The narrator's plans for the English translation are already carried out in what is deemed to be Garcia's version. The narrator's reaction takes into account cultural aspects, or what is appropriate for a given audience. The novel has already done what the translator suggests.

What is remarkable about *Chromos* is not the emphasis on cultural differences, but rather the acknowledgment and visibility granted to the role of translation and its presentation as an opportunity for revision. Garcia solicits the translator's input, permitting him to become the co-author of the text. The translator, instead of holding a peripheral position regarding the source text, has an essential relationship to it, detracting from the independence and absolute authority of Garcia. Garcia relies on the translator in order to complete his novel, thereby inverting the relationship between translator and author. In *Chromos*, the author does not have a text without the translator.

In her preface to the third edition of *Translation Studies* (2002), Susan Bassnett outlines the history of the discipline. She indicates that "in the new millennium translation scholarship will continue to emphasize the unequal power relationships that have characterized the translation process" (5). Questions of power and authority became the focus of debates on translation during the nineties, when the relationship between "what is termed 'translation' and what is termed 'original'" became a major concern ("When" 25). The origins of the focus on this topic go back to Jacques Derrida's reading of Walter Benjamin, in which the translation of a text is its "after-life," how a text survives. Thus, the translation becomes the original (Derrida). *Chromos*, written during the 1940s, deconstructs inequalities

---

41 For example, the narrator comments: "The word 'cursi' is difficult to translate, its meaning almost impossible to convey with any other word, and the closest I can find to it in English is the word 'corny'" (58).

associated with the translation process by presenting neither the original as superior nor the translation as inferior. In *Chromos*, each depends on the other for the creation of the text.

Garcia's role as an author not only becomes secondary when working on this novel, but also in the creation of another story that he is writing about a character named Julio Ramos, a man from the Iberian Peninsula who never returns to his home after he leaves in search of a new life in New York. This story, similar to the one about Julieta's family, exists as a text imbedded in *Chromos*, but proposes a bolder measure that involves moving from text to screen. As Garcia tells the narrator about his ideas, he also insists that the best way to convey this story is a "moving picture because of the more flexible technique" (51), which "could show the shifts and changes of scenery and the action much better" (81). Once again, Garcia explains that he is relying on "a lot of translating and perhaps a little collaborating" on the part of the narrator in order to complete his new project (51). As the story leaves the Iberian Peninsula, it is not only language that becomes a concern for artistic production, but also medium. Garcia sees that movement to a new location opens creative possibilities that expand to the incorporation or transfer to other media. This new direction is a possibility that other writers from the Iberian Peninsula experiment with through their work either via their texts or via the actual passing to a form of non-written expression. Although Garcia is an active author, working simultaneously on two projects, both remain in the developmental stages. Language and medium, as barriers to his realization of these projects with his current resources, speak to the necessity and integral role of translation cast on Garcia as a writer from this new location.

The collaboration between the narrator and Garcia involves an English translation of Garcia's texts; however, as the texts are already in English, even though the two characters speak about the Spanish-language versions, expectations of translation are put into play. In other conversations between them, a similar situation occurs. Upon leaving the Spanish theater and commenting on a production of the classic *Don Juan Tenorio*, the narrator says to Garcia: "If we were speaking English, I could say that the drama was not ghostly but ghastly, get it?" (48). The narrator-translator shows his knowledge and confidence in English as he tags the comment with the colloquial "get it." At the same time the text, although presented in English, makes clear that the conversation is not conducted in English. In this sense, *Chromos* refers to an existence in Spanish for its own characters beyond the text itself, leaving traces of a translation and destabilizing the relationship between the source and translated texts.

To further attest to the awareness of a Spanish version of the text beyond the boundaries of the page, certain words are in Spanish because the narrator confesses that he cannot provide an English equivalent. When describing another character, he says: "The man who had spoken the castigating line was middle-aged, very happy and antipático—I can't find another word" (129). The use of "antipático," followed by an explanation for its inclusion, speaks to the sensitivity to language in the text and makes apparent the narrator's efforts and process as a translator. The narrator not only communicates to the reader information that does not appear in the characters' conversations, thus establishing intimacy with the reader, but also implies the special effort made to search for the right word and to then cushion the text upon failing to do so. The narrator suggests that he would like this text to be in English and therefore needs to justify the retreat to Spanish. At the same time, by not italicizing "antipático," a foreign word in English, the narrator creates a smooth textual surface naturalizing the term in English and even questioning the need for translation in this situation. What is more, readers of both Spanish and English might find humor in the contradiction of the two adjectives, happy and *antipático*.

Because of these aspects, *Chromos* could be described as a "pseudotranslation," a concept developed by Gideon Toury in his 1984 essay "Translation, Literary Translation, and Pseudotranslation." Pseudotranslations are "texts which have been presented as translations with no corresponding source texts in other languages ever having existed" (*Descriptive* 40). In other words, the pseudotranslation is a text "that claims falsely to be a translation" (Bassnett, "When" 27). Toury's ideas about pseudotranslation are text-based in that the text itself, disguised as a translation, introduces to the target audience literary innovations that might not otherwise be accepted if the text were presented as an original. Although literary texts that claim to be fictitious translations are a long-established convention, Toury's essay marked a pivotal moment in translation studies.[42] *Chromos*, however, does not comply with definitions of pseudotranslation. The text is not presented to the reader as a translation *per se*. Instead, the language and content of the novel vacillates between its state in English and references to a

---

42 Brigitte Rath's chart on the usage of "pseudotranslation" is helpful as she indicates that it is an "idea of the (past decade)," roughly two-thirds of the sources that use the term having been published in the decade up to 2014. She also presents "fictitious translation," "assumed translation," "supposed translation," and "original translation" as alternative terms for pseudotranslation and suggests that critics are attempting to bring these terms together. See also Carol O'Sullivan's pseudotranslation entry in *The Handbook of Translation Studies* (2011).

Spanish-language context, and questions the relationship between the two languages. Moreover, while *Chromos*'s status as an English-language text might have increased its chances of being published in the United States, Alfau's lack of effort to actually publish the manuscript shows no indication that he was actively interested in using a pseudotranslation to innovate U.S. literature.

The aforementioned examples demonstrate awareness of language usage and choices that keep *Chromos*'s readers wondering what is being translated and by whom. Bilingual readers of Alfau are also implicitly asked to participate in the translation process. Because the novel features the process of translation, readers are asked to wonder what statement the text makes about the conditions of writing when linguistic and cultural borders are crossed. In this regard, the visibility that Alfau lends to the role of the translator and translation is a critical concern that is also ahead of his time. While translation's existence is just as long as literature's, it was not until the 1980s that "translation became a more prolific, more visible, and more respectable activity than perhaps ever before" (Trivedi 277). It is also during this decade that translation studies gained momentum in academia, led by the publication of Susan Bassnett's introductory book *Translation Studies* (1980). While *Chromos*'s macro structure might lack a strong plot, what the novel suggests about language is in and of itself moving. *Chromos* presents a puzzle involving language that reveals itself to be infinitely similar to the way that English forever complicates the life of the narrator and his fellow characters.

Español Is Not Spanish

The complications of learning English not only affect Garcia and the narrator, but also extend to the wider network of characters in New York. The opening and most frequently quoted lines of *Chromos*—"The moment one learns English complications set in" (7)—seem general at first, but it soon becomes clear that *Chromos* is heedful of the results of the coexistence and conflict of the two codes: "Try as one may, one cannot elude this conclusion, one must inevitably come back to it. This applies to all persons, including those born to the language and, at times, even more so to Latins, including Spaniards" (7). The subject of the characters' Spanishness becomes the main focus of their discussions as they learn that in the New York context *español* does not equate to Spanish, uncovering not only the complexities of translation, but also setting the text in the Manhattan of the time when "Spanish" already extended to Spanish-speaking regions beyond the Iberian Peninsula (Kagan 25). Spanish takes on other meanings in the city and provides a spark for constant conversation and invasion into the life of an individual.

The novel's unluckiest character, Don Hilarión, exemplifies the extent of these complications. The narrator explains:

> Don Hilarión was a notario, not a notary, mind you; that does not quite convey the meaning, but a notario. A notario in Spain, at least in Don Hilarión's day, was a title given to a man having achieved the summit of his career in the field of law. It was the coronation of every law student. (173)[43]

By describing how *notario* in Spain does not coincide with being a notary in New York, the novel addresses, with some exaggeration, the consequences of cultural translation, a term that gained recognition in the 1990s, the decade when *Chromos* was published, when Homi Bhabha used it to describe, as Bassnett summarizes, "encounters between cultures in a new kind of space where interlingual encounter is part of daily life" (Bassnett, *Translation* 55). Bassnett further explains that cultural translation became a "kind of rhetorical catch-all for processes of interpretation of the multiple sign systems across and between cultural borders in which numerous differentiating factors [are] at work" (*Translation* 55). Unable to practice his profession in New York, Don Hilarión encloses himself in his tiny office in his family's apartment. One day an insurance salesman visits him at home, and upon hearing that he is a *notario*, says: "Anybody can be one. All you have to do is pay a few dollars and you are a notary" (181). Shortly after hearing these words, Don Hilarión expires.[44] Humor is used here to address the severe consequences of rupturing the strong bond between a man and his profession, and to call attention to the irreversible damage that a mechanical, or strictly linguistic word-for-word translation can do. The monolingual salesman is unaware of the extra-linguistic measures involved in translation.

It was also during the 1990s that the cultural turn in translation studies occurred. This shift marked a new awareness of translation beyond a "transaction not between two languages, [...], but rather a more complex negotiation between two cultures" (Trivedi). This was a stride away from previous ideas about translation. Harish Trivedi points out that "before these new developments took place [...] translation was seen as a segment or sub-field of linguistics, on the basic premise that translation was a

---

43 Like *antipático*, "notario" is not italicized in *Chromos*.

44 Rabassa says that the Don Hilarión episode is reminiscent of García Márquez's *The Autumn of the Patriarch* ("Power" 224), which Rabassa himself translated.

transaction between two languages." He explains that in *A Linguistic Theory of Translation: An Essay in Applied Linguistics* (1965), J.C. Catford "defined translation as compromising a substitution of TL [i.e. target language] meanings for SL [i.e. source language] meanings" (Trivedi). Written about 50 years before the cultural turn in translation studies, *Chromos* set out the dangers of translation as a simple matter of replacing a word, since a matter of translation, or the failure to acknowledge the complexities of translation, causes Don Hilarión's hilarious demise. Don Hilarión's name echoes the Spanish word *hilarante*, a translation of the English *hilarious*. Since this pun speaks to readers with knowledge of both Spanish and English, the ability to "read" *Chromos* in both languages adds another layer to an understanding and enjoyment of the novel.

Chromos incorporates extraordinary situations and exaggerated conclusions to express the dangers and dilemmas of translation as a mere act of substitution, as well as wavering concepts of nationality when language takes on new meanings in new locations. María DeGuzmán discusses Alfau's work with regard to the denaturalization of nationality, or the idea that "nationality as an essence or as a fixed, unitary, or 'pure' identity, like essence itself, is a construction, a fiction, a collective hallucination" (276). *Chromos* shows that being "Spanish" in New York ceases to relate solely to a specific country and extends to anyone who is Spanish-speaking or seemingly Spanish-speaking. As a result, one of the narrator's interlocutors, Don Pedro is obsessed "with the position of the Spaniard in the world, with more assurance in Spain and with more complications in foreign lands—all right, in this country" (12). *Chromos* argues that in New York, being a Spaniard is particularly complicated due to the fact that "Spanish" ceases to mean the same thing as it does in Spain and, conversely, being outside of Spain forces one to ponder what it means to be Spanish.[45] On the final page of the novel, the narrator explains: "In Spanish one sees and things remain unquestioned and clear. In English, one studies and uncovers meanings that one does not understand. It is then that, as I said in the beginning, complications set in" (348).

These complications captured the attention of another cultural medium

---

45　Debra Castillo highlights another instance of the associations between Spain and other Spanish-speaking countries in the U.S. context. She quotes from Concha Alborg's novel *Beyond Jet-Lag: Other Stories* (2000):
> The minute we opened our mouths, we were foreigners [...] Like to answer the mantra question of "Where are you from?"
> —Espain, we'd answer in chorus.
> —Really? Oh! I love Mexico! (qtd. in Castillo 49)

El baile "español" en España y en los Estados Unidos

El furor "artístico" de moda—según los críticos—lo constituyen los bailes "españoles". Apenas hay en torno a Broadway cabaret que se estime, que no tenga en su programa algún número resonantemente "spanish". Y en efecto, al compás de música hispana más o menos atormentada por orquestas que desconocen totalmente el ritmo y el espíritu de las cadencias españolas, bailarines y bailarinas de fantasía "ejecutan" bailes españoles con tanta aproximación como—muy felizmente—representa la genial caricatura que publicamos. Nada más a propósito pudiera ponérsele, como título, que el de "De lo vivo... a lo estropeado".

Fig. 1.3 *La Prensa.* January 17, 1922.

in New York. *La Prensa*, New York's Spanish-language daily newspaper, printed the following caricature (see Fig. 1.3), on January 17, 1922.[46]

This "genial caricatura" [brilliant caricature], as the caption indicates, is a response to the numerous "bailes 'españoles'" ["Spanish" dances] that flood the Broadway cabarets announcing some supposedly "Spanish" number. The caption not only criticizes the orchestra's inability to play "el ritmo y el espíritu de las cadencias" [the rhythm and spirit of the cadences], but also the sorry attempts of the "bailarines y bailarinas" [male and female dancers] to "'ejecuta[r]' bailes españoles" ["perform" Spanish dances]. As the caricature juxtaposes Spanish dance in Spain and its U.S. version, in the drawing on the right, "el baile 'español'" [the "Spanish" dance] from Spain, the strong dancer wears typical dress and accessories as she confidently strikes a pose. In the drawing on the left, the skinny dancer dressed in any old skirt tries to appear "Spanish" and slouches in a sorry effort to perform. As a result, the caption suggests that the title of this caricature could be "De lo vivo ... a lo estropeado" [From the living ... to the ruined]. This New York interpretation of something Spanish is similar to that undergone by Don Hilarión. Representations of the city bring awareness to these remarkable transformations.

Because the specificity of *Chromos* plays intricately with the contact of Spanish and English, the novel provokes questions that lead to thinking about its own translation into other languages.[47] The peculiarities of *Chromos*'s language and the way in which the novel plays with translation on multiple levels speak to the challenges this text proposes for its translation into Spanish, for example. How would the Spanish translation deal with *Chromos*'s language? How would it translate the passage about *antipático*? In Don

---

46 The caption reads: "El furor 'artístico' de moda—según los críticos—lo constituyen los bailes 'españoles'. Apenas hay en torno a Broadway cabaret que se estima que no tenga en su programa algún número resonantemente 'spanish'. Y en efecto, al compás de música hispana más o menos atormentada por orquestas que desconocen totalmente el ritmo y el espíritu de las cadencias españolas, bailarines y bailarinas de fantasía 'ejecutan' bailes españoles con tanta aproximación como— muy felizmente—representa la genial caricatura que publicamos. Nada más a propósito pudiera ponérselo, como título, que el del 'De lo vivo ... a lo estropeado'" [According to critics, "Spanish" dances are part of today's "artistic" rage. There are hardly any cabarets on Broadway that don't have a number that sounds "Spanish" on their program. And, indeed, fantasy male and female dancers "perform" Spanish numbers very approximatively to the beat of Hispanic music more or less butchered by orchestras completely ignorant of the rhythm and spirit of Spanish cadences, as our brilliant caricature very happily captures. We could not give it a more appropriate title than "From the living ... to the ruined"].

47 Besides Spanish, Alfau's work has been translated into Italian, Dutch, and German.

Hilarión's story, would the Spanish translation incorporate an explanation of *notario*? Would the translation require instead an explanation of *notary*? With these examples, *Chromos* proves that translation is much more than substitution. A strategy based on equivalence would be severely reductive because what the novel has to say is deeply imbedded in its language.

In her aforementioned review of the novel, Anna Shapiro compares Alfau to Nabokov:

> Like Nabokov (again), Alfau is writing in the language of his adopted country, and one wonders what his history, or that of this book, would have been if he had written in Spanish and published in Spain or Latin America, where readers might not have been scared off by an air of "foreignness" (206)

But *Chromos* is only possible because of its existence in English as the book is based on the complications that arise when specific languages meet. If the novel were in Spanish, perhaps it would lack the "rhetorical vigor and lexical splendor" that West regarded as its outstanding qualities. Moreover, in a discussion of all the National Book Award nominees, he states: "Their estimable authors knew that prose is not a mere expository medium but an instrument to play, a voice to sing. No barbarous monotony here, but a straight line back to such illustrious forebears as Faulkner, Proust, Mann, Woolf, Nabokov, Beckett, and even Joyce" (West 241).[48] While Alfau claims to have been unaware of these forebears and detached from literature and the literary world, the Spanish translation of *Chromos* by María Teresa Fernández de Castro did pique his curiosity when it appeared in 1991 with the prominent Barcelona publisher Seix Barral. He was not fond of the Spanish translation:

> When I read the lousy Spanish translation, made in Barcelona, of *Chromos*, I thought my message had been deformed, my intentions inverted. The translator often misunderstands a sentence. Unfortunately, the mistakes are not rare. The art of translation is difficult, to say the least. One cannot substitute one word in a language with its equivalent in another. The task is to make two cultures find a common path, a bridge. I think translators must be anthropolinguists if they want to succeed in their profession. ("Anonymity" 150)

---

48 Beside Alfau's *Chromos*, the other nominees for the National Book Award included Mary Caponegro's *The Star Cafe*, and Elena Castedo's *Paradise*, to Joanna Scott's *Arrogance*, Steven Millhauser's *The Barnum Museum*, and Sandra Schor's *The Great Letter E.*

Alfau came from a family of translators. One of his sisters, Montserrat, translated her husband Felipe Teixador (Barcelona, 1895–Mexico City, 1980), with whom she collaborated on scholarly projects. Teixador translated from French and English. Felipe Alfau reports that his sister "did translations" and that she was going to translate *Locos*, although it never came to pass (Stavans, "Anonymity" 146). Stavans asked Alfau if he had ever attempted to translate his own work, and his response was "Never. Why would I?" ("Anonymity" 151). A writer of children's literature and novels, a poet, and a music critic, Alfau never authored a literary translation that we know of, perhaps because he understood all too well the frustrations involved. Alfau's comments on the Spanish translation prove his awareness of the arduousness of literary translation and reveal the necessity to go far beyond purely linguistic measures in order to cultivate a successful translation. The language of *Chromos*, along with the novel's interspersed stories that are interrupted by the narrator and his friends, does not opt for conventional standards of Spanish or English. The novel lingers in the area between the two languages, teasing the reader to consider the suspended state that dominates these characters' experience in New York.[49]

Similar states have been described by scholars who have written about the space between two cultures. For example, Gustavo Pérez Firmat opted for the term "life on the hyphen" in a 1994 book of the same name that speaks specifically about the Cuban-American context, while Ilan Stavans has talked about it as a condition in *The Hispanic Condition: Reflections on Culture & Identity in America* (1995). In *Chromos*, this state is given the name Americaniard by Don Pedro. "A word of his own composition" (13), Americaniard, described by María DeGuzmán as "Spaniards transplanted to the United States" (244), turns out to be much more than that. Americaniard, a word that is itself a combination of the English words *American* and *Spaniard*, explores the condition of being a Spaniard in New York with emphasis on the language politics at play in relocation and travel. The narrator relates that Don Pedro:

---

49 The basis for theorizing translation introduced by Friedrich Schleiermacher in the nineteenth century regarding foreignization and domestication, later developed by Lawrence Venuti in the twentieth century, has dominated translation studies. On the one hand, the language of *Chromos* adds a foreign flair to English, reminding the reader that the original came from a different world, but the novel is not offered as a translation, a text that was written in one language and then moved to another by the work of a translator. Thus, foreignization alone is not a convincing strategy to understand Alfau's writing. On the other hand, a domestication strategy does not apply to the language of *Chromos* as it is entirely its own.

had begun to originally employ [the term] when referring to Spaniards in the Americas and at one time might have included Latin Americans, but he had gradually varied the meaning until at present it applied to all Spaniards in New York and then by association even to other foreigners, especially of Latin origin, in the same circumstances. (13)

Americaniard could be considered a precursor of the label Latino as Stavans refers to Alfau as a Latino writer in *The Hispanic Condition* (175). Debra Castillo, however, disassociates the continuity between the two terms by placing them in opposition. She notes that Americaniard, on the one hand, "captures the ambiguity of identity" (49) but, on the other, lacks the "socio-political base" of "Latina" (57). Her suggestion, then, aims at shying away from terminology and "clutching to the 'idea of Latina'" (57) to transform disciplinary boundaries and restrictions relating to national literature and language. At the same time, literary studies should not shun the ideas behind Americaniard as the term is appealing to those authors and texts lacking the political implications of "Latino/a," but which nevertheless subscribe to a marginal literary tradition of New York.

In its early days, Americaniard had a broader definition as it incorporated "Spaniards in the Americas" but later evolved into a more pointed term focusing on New York and Spaniards, and consequentially any immigrant of Latin origin there.[50] *Chromos* demonstrates an awareness that "Spanish" is not limited to the classification of a particular national group and as a result is an inclusionary term. Don Pedro's definition comprehends that the condition of a Spaniard in New York is unique and therefore has nothing to do with that of a Spaniard in Florida, Texas, or California, for example, thus calling attention to the language politics of the city. The evolution of the definition of Americaniard exhibits the need to address a local phenomenon while at the same time being a flexible category that defies strict national classifications. Without being one or the other, it strives to create the bridge or, as Susan Elizabeth Sweeney has written, "seek such equilibrium" or balance that would successfully unite the two ("Aliens" 207). With the coining of Americaniard, *Chromos* presents an example of the work of an anthropolinguist, an individual skilled in

---

50 During the early twentieth century, there were other popular uses of the word "Latin" to refer to Iberians and Latin Americans. For example, in Al Jolson's rendition of the song "She's a Latin from Manhattan" in the 1935 musical film *Go into Your Dance* directed by Archie Mayo (1891–1968), the singer is mesmerized by a woman he spots in New York. He wonders "is she from Havana or Madrid" and then determines "by her mañana" that she is a Latin from Manhattan.

many languages who is attentive to the development of each, a key asset of a translator as proposed by Alfau.

Alfau's ideas about translation as expressed in his assessment of the Spanish edition of *Chromos* are similar to those of Homi Bhabha. Susan Bassnett explains that "Bhabha uses the term 'translation' not to describe a transaction between texts and languages but in the etymological sense of being carried across from one place to another" (*Translation Studies* 4th ed. 6). For Alfau, and as seen in *Chromos*, translation relies on the translator to provide the passage between cultures, but with no fixed or finite destination between the two. In providing a passage, *Chromos* invites the reader to also participate in negotiating the process of translation.

When Stavans asked Alfau if he still "felt Iberian, a citizen of Spain?" or "an American like everybody else around here [in the retirement home]?" Alfau responded, "neither one nor the other. I guess I am a frontier man that belongs to a world that is no more" ("Anonymity" 148). His refusal to choose one of the identities offered to him attests to his commitment to the translational area that marked the majority of his life and mirrors the lack of commitment in *Chromos* to fully surrender to English or to remain fixed in Spanish. Eduardo Lago, one of Alfau's successors, faced similar questions in early 2006, when won the Premio Nadal for *Llámame Brooklyn*. In interviews conducted in both English and Spanish, he was repeatedly asked for his affiliation: "Do you feel closer to American literature than to Spanish literature?" (Rodríguez Martorell, "Call Me Brooklyn" 20); "¿Se siente quizá un escritor más americano que español?" [Do you perhaps feel more like an American writer than a Spanish one?] (Azancot 7). These questions demonstrate the need to compartmentalize Lago, and the challenges of such a task when an author deviates from limited understandings of national literatures based on monolingual and geographically restricted guidelines.[51] *Llámame Brooklyn*, a novel written in Spanish that draws on U.S. and Iberian literary traditions, perplexes established categories, jeopardizing its inclusion in them, and, what is more, threatening its survival in literary studies. Debra Castillo expresses similar concerns about other authors from Spain who write in the United States in her article "Latina or Americaniard?" She begins her inquiry by stating that "Authors, texts, and ideas have always moved across international borders; yet to the degree that they confound monolingual and nationally based literary

---

51 Alfau's work was erroneously placed in a compilation titled *English Translations from the Spanish, 1484–1943: A Bibliography* (1944) by Remigio Ugo Pane. The collection includes one of Alfau's short stories, "Madrileños," from *Old Tales from Spain*. This text is not an English translation from the Spanish, despite its Spanish title.

projects, such as crossings and mediations have been insufficiently studied even by an academic audience that prides itself on its border-crossing analytic abilities" (47). When pressed to classify himself as either Spanish or American, Lago opted for Americaniard: "Soy también uno de los americanos con un guión; un español-americano, o como el escritor Felipe Alfau lo pondría como broma, un americaniard" [I'm also one of those Americans with a hyphen; a Spaniard-American, or as the writer Felipe Alfau would jokingly put it, an Americaniard] (Rodríguez Martorell, "Ode"). It is significant that Lago did not alter the term when speaking Spanish, as did Varela-Lago, who states that "the Spanish rendition of the term [Americaniards] would be 'Americañoles'" (13). Varela-Lago translated the term simply by turning English into Spanish, neither considering the context in which the term originated nor its development surrounded by the English language. Although her proposed Spanish translation strips the term of its complexity, at least it did not follow the solution of the Spanish translator of *Chromos* María Teresa Fernández de Castro, who turned Americaniard into *americanizado*, a choice that misses the interruption of the English language and the combination of two nouns that identify an individual's nationality. Lago, aware of the complexity of the term and its attachment to English, not only embraced Americaniard to skirt the question of identifying himself as one thing or the other, but also found a place for the term in his creative work, promoting a return to Alfau in stepping over the limitations of Iberian literatures with his own work.

Alfau in Literature

Given that Eduardo Lago and Felipe Alfau both came to New York, developed their literature in the city, and surprised the literary world as they received critical recognition at a relatively late stage in their lives, Lago should be considered a direct literary descendent of Alfau. In fact, Lago regards Alfau as his "literary 'patron saint'" (Rodríguez Martorell, "Hispanic" 5).[52] Alfau's influence on Lago's *Llámame Brooklyn* is apparent in numerous ways, ranging from setting to structure and theme. Both *Chromos* and *Llámame Brooklyn* include stories within stories that move between the Iberian Peninsula and New York, fueling their meta-narratives and nourishing a structure that relies on dependency. Fernando Valls describes Lago's novel as "una novela *collage*, un género de géneros, a la manera del tejido textual que muestra una

52 Alfau the character is not only part of *Llámame Brooklyn* but also of Lago's more recent work. His second novel, *Ladrón de mapas* (2008), includes a section entitled "La sombra de Alfau" [Alfau's Shadow].

historia, utilizando piezas de muy diverso calado y distinta procedencia" [a collage novel, a genre of genres, in the style of a textual weave that makes a story, using pieces of very diverse importance and different sources] (142). Valls does not explicitly state Lago's indebtedness to Alfau in his review of *Llámame Brooklyn* although his own description of Lago's novel echoes Alfau's description of how he wrote *Chromos*: "In the office between one document and another, I would write a paragraph or two. I then pasted together the whole book, as in a collage" (Stavans, "Anonymity" 151).

  Chromos and *Llámame Brooklyn* both expand literary New York by offering a version of the city that blends hispanophone and anglophone spheres while simultaneously recognizing Iberian literature beyond the peninsula. Lago's novel, however, has a stronger plot that links the city to the Iberian Peninsula via the adoption of an orphan by a Brooklyn couple who were members of the Abraham Lincoln Brigade. Born in Madrid in 1937 during the Spanish Civil War, Gal Ackerman grew up in Brooklyn to become a writer and translator. The novel opens with his death and his friend and fellow writer Néstor Oliver-Chapman's subsequent task to complete Gal's book *Brooklyn*. Gal did not intend for his manuscript to be published, but rather for it to be read by only one person: his beloved Nadia Orlov. Néstor, also known as Ness, not only consults journal entries, letters, transcripts of lectures, archives, and testimonies to complete the task he has inherited, he also relies on the help of another character, Frank Otero, a Galician-born New Yorker who runs a Brooklyn bar called the Oakland and who occasionally provides his own notes to make up for gaps in the manuscript. The process of producing this novel is just as visible as the final product. Similar to *Chromos*, authorship becomes a primary matter that requires collaboration. *Llámame Brooklyn* learns from *Chromos* that in situations in which complications arise from a life that is neither linear nor fixed to one location or language, authorial identity becomes destabilized, calling attention to a shift in the creative process.

  Gal presents a curious case of a life moving through Spanish and English and touching upon other variants of Spanish—or even other languages, as Nadia spoke Russian. Frank explains to Ness that the Spanish language was of utmost importance to Gal: "la cuestión del idioma cobró una importancia inusitada" (247) ["it was the key to his true identity" (217)]. Gal went to great efforts to retain the language, including becoming a translator and making frequent trips to Mexico.[53] Ness defines the circumstances in which Gal

---

53 The fact that Gal traveled to Mexico to maintain his Spanish, to hold on to his "true identity"—he was born in Spain—suggests a reversal of what James D. Fernández has labeled "Longfellow's Law," according to which, "U.S. interest in

would write in English or in Spanish, clarifying that the material intended for *Brooklyn* was 99 percent in Spanish. In Lago's novel, however, attention to language *per se* is not a dominant theme as it is in *Chromos*. While Ness might have done some translating to produce *Brooklyn*, authorial identity is not explored through the relationship between translator and author, but rather, as Ricardo Senabre has suggested, through that between philologist and text:

> Néstor es, en realidad, un compilador; su tarea se asemeja a la de un filólogo que trata de llevar a cabo la edición crítica de un texto del que se conservan testimonios dispares.

> [Néstor is actually a compiler; his work is similar to that of a philologist who attempts to produce a critical edition of a text of which there remain disparate testimonies.]

Without Gal, Ness must use his own resources to recover and construct the text. Moreover, Valls warns that:

> No hay que confundir, pues, la novela de Gal y Ness con la de Eduardo Lago, que la contiene. A este respecto, quizá no esté de más preguntarse sobre la autoría de esa curiosa obra cuyas peripecias compositivas también se narran en sus páginas. ¿A quién pertenece el resultado, a Gal, a Ness, o acaso a ambos?" (141)

> [One mustn't confuse Gal and Ness's novel with Eduardo Lago's, which contains it. In this respect, perhaps it wouldn't hurt to think about the authorship of this curious work whose compositional vicissitudes are also narrated on its pages. To whom does the result belong? To Gal? To Ness? Or perhaps to both of them?]

Since *Chromos* and *Llámame Brooklyn* are invested in the process of writing, both question the boundaries of authorship when circumstances reflect national and linguistic uprooting.

Via Ness, readers learn that Gal's grandfather David from Brooklyn belonged to a group of literary types of diverse backgrounds called los Incoherentes, or, as the English translation calls them, the Order of the

---

Spain is and always has been largely mediated by U.S. interest in Latin America" (124). Fernández uses the example of Henry Wadsworth Longfellow's son, who is motivated to go to Spain because of the importance of the relations between the United States and Spanish America. "Longfellow's Law" acknowledges Fernández's indebtedness to Richard L. Kagan's important essay "Prescott's Paradigm: American Historical Scholarship and the Decline of Spain" (1996).

Knights Incoherent, who would gather on the Lower East Side in the bar El Periscopio, recalling El Telescopio in *Chromos*. Three of the five founding members of los Incoherentes are Americaniards:[54] Felipe Alfau, Aquilino Guerra, and Henry Martínez.[55] The novel loosely identifies Americaniards as characters of Spanish descent, and in a transcript of his speech on the Chelsea Hotel, Alfau refers to other Americaniards as those living or working in the area around the hotel, a neighborhood of the city that was once known as Little Spain. These Americaniards are not isolated, however, since they mingle with other Spanish-speaking characters as well as with English speakers.

In Alfau's delivery of the annual lecture of los Incoherentes, open to the public, the audience is reminded of the non-committal status of the author. Just as *Chromos*'s Garcia relied on the narrator to participate as a translator in the production of his work, Alfau depends on the work of his research assistant, Murphy Burrell, for the content of his speech. Just as *Chromos*'s narrator freely comments on the development of Garcia's stories, Alfau continuously reminds the audience of Murphy's contributions to the lecture when he often refers to him during the speech and holds him responsible for any errors, again questioning the independence of the author. There would be no lecture without Murphy, not only because of his research but also because of the amount of attention he receives throughout its delivery.

During the lecture Alfau says "lo último que se puede hacer es aburrir al lector" (302) ["the last thing one can do is bore the reader" (272)], something that Alfau's own work tries to avoid. Overall, the reader of *Llámame Brooklyn* is not asked to be active in a way that questions language, but rather to participate in the same type of detective work which the construction of Gal's work and life demand of Ness. When Alfau says to his audience in his speech, "no tengo la menor intención de respetar ningún hilo narrativo y menos cronológico, y cuando así ocurriere, téngase por coincidencia" (299) ["I don't have the least intention to pay heed to any narrative or chronological thread; if it should appear that I'm doing so, I assure you that this will be a mere coincidence" (268)], he is consistent with the characteristics of the work of Alfau, the author. Not only does Lago remind the reader of Alfau's writing, but he also confesses that through the character Alfau, the reader is able to gain insight into his own interest in literature, forging his connection and

54 While *Chromos* does not italicize the word Americaniards, both *Llámame Brooklyn* and its English translation do, thereby giving the term extra prominence.

55 Besides Alfau, another character who has a real-life counterpart and who stands out for his role in literary history is Jesús Colón (1901–74), who wrote chronicles in English and Spanish for New York City newspapers. He is the author of *A Puerto Rican in New York and Other Sketches* (1961).

indebtedness to Alfau: "I took many liberties with Alfau's character. He was an interesting vanguard author, at times limited, but he was like a father to me in that tradition. In the novel, I use him to express my own ideas about literature" (Rodriguez Martorell, "Call Me Brooklyn").

Among the parallels between the literary and personal profiles of Lago and Alfau, each writer's relationship to the use of language marks a stark difference, which does not distance them but rather demonstrates the evolution of the dynamics of the Spanish language in New York. Although Lago had spent many years outside of Spain, dramatic alterations do not mark the Spanish of *Llámame Brooklyn*; at least, they have not been a topic of literary criticism.[56] On the contrary, Lago confesses that when he travels to Spain, his "accent seems distorted," and that he sometimes makes lexical choices associated with Mexican or Chilean Spanish (Rodríguez Martorell, "Ode"). When Lago entered the literary scene, New York was incomparably diverse in terms of the Spanish language. Antonio Muñoz Molina, who spends about half of his time in New York, describes the city as the "mejor atalaya para entender la lengua española [...] en Estados Unidos" [best observation point from which to understand the Spanish language [...] in the United States] (356) in his essay "Paisajes del idioma" (2007), later translated as "Spanish in New York: A Moving Landscape" (2010).[57] Muñoz Molina says that the city serves as a place "donde confluyen todos los ríos del idioma, todos los acentos" [a confluence for all rivers of the language, for every accent] (356). Besides listing the variations from Cuba, Mexico, the Dominican Republic, Puerto Rico, Guatemala, Colombia, the River Plate, Bolivia, and Chile, Muñoz Molina adds that one is able to hear "la más rara, la más antigua de las hablas españolas, el judeoespañol que algunos hijos y nietos—nietos sobre todo—de emigrantes llegados del antiguo imperio otomano quisieran nostálgicamente recobrar" [the rarest, the oldest of Spanish dialects, the Judeo-Spanish that some of the children and grandchildren—especially the grandchildren—of immigrants from the old Ottoman Empire now nostalgically wish to recover] (Muñoz Molina

56 Although New York has a long history as a Spanish-speaking city with a rich literary history in Spanish, in the past two decades there have been a notable number of literary productions, events, publications, and other initiatives to promote the Spanish-language literature of New York. In fact, along with Carmen Boullosa, José Manuel Prieto, Naief Yehya, Sylvia Molloy, and Eduardo Mitre, Lago composed the "Manifiesto Neoyorkino" calling for greater attention to the long tradition of writers from Latin America and Spain who have lived in the New York City.

57 Dan Newland's English translation of this essay was published in *Hispanic New York: A Sourcebook* (2010), edited by Claudio Iván Remeseira. I have quoted his translations.

356). His use of the image of rivers as a way to speak about the Spanish language in all its New York variants reverberates in Sherry Simon's 2013 lecture "Across Troubled Divides: Translation, Gender, Memory" at the Nida School of Translation Studies. She opens her presentation on cities and translation with the phrase: "All around the world, cities are rediscovering their underground rivers." Simon calls attention to the symbolic significance of city dwellers being reconnected with their city's natural history and the literal reminder of the city as a space of circulation:

> Cities are given life by what flows through them ... Circulation is a powerful figure for studying the cultural life of cities. Circulation, I think, is also a useful way to speak about the passage of language through cities. The way languages are always in movement and in contact with one another.

Languages in cities, circulating as rivers, provide an understanding of how they come into contact, coexist, transform, blend, rise, and fall, and moreover the image speaks to their inherent unpredictability and ever-changing nature in the city space.

In the 1940s, *Chromos* already detected the experience of the Spanish language in New York as a home for people from Latin American countries and the fluidity with which one could leave one's nationality and subscribe to another. These variations, however, did not impede linguistic comprehension among the Spanish-speaking community. Muñoz Molina describes the contemporary language scene as one in which

> Todas las variantes son inmediatamente inteligibles para cualquiera que hable la lengua: en vez de limitarla, la enriquecen, porque nos enseñan formas de nombrar las cosas que son distintas de las nuestras y sin embargo nunca nos niegan su significado, con sólo prestar un poco de atención. (356)

> [Each and every variation is immediately intelligible for anyone who speaks the language: instead of limiting it, they enrich it, because they teach us ways of calling things that are different from our own and yet never deny us their meaning—as long as we are paying attention.][58]

---

58 Muñoz Molina's essay is not only a celebration of the Spanish language in New York City but also argues against the balkanization of the language, especially as it is viewed in Spain. He argues for the universality of the Spanish language: "El español es un país que le permite circular a uno por una variedad ilimitada de paisajes sin que lo detengan en ninguna frontera, una identidad fluida y flexible que nos permite ser de muchos lugares y de uno solo" [Spanish is a country that permits one to travel

Spanish in New York, then, not only means moments of interlingual translation, the focus of Alfau's writing, when one language faces another, but also includes bountiful moments of intralingual translation, as detected in Lago's own lexicon. Intralingual translation, "the interpretation of verbal signs by means of other signs belonging to the same language" (Cronin 3), "is often disguised by writers and critics to create the illusion of linguistic transparency" according to Michael Cronin in *Across the Lines* (3). In Lago's novel, movement beyond the central question of languages in contact, paired with the way in which characters of multiple linguistic and cultural origins gather, suggests the long-standing presence of Iberian figures in New York and their points of interaction, while at the same time naturalizing the process of translation.

Llámame Brooklyn, written about 60 years after *Chromos*, at a time when the city's culture surrounding the Spanish language had transformed, introduces readers to the intriguing character of Alfau and extends the imagination about his life in New York, introducing circles of writers who worked in a multilingual and multinational setting. On the other hand, Lago's personal use of the term Americaniard opens a space for a literary history that does not conform to what has already been established. Lago's use of Americaniard, both in his personal interviews and in his own writing, speaks not only to the successful "anthropolinguistic" effort of Don Pedro for its implications reach beyond *Chromos*, but also to the transforming, extra-linguistic effects that translation can introduce to literary categories. Further, what Lago's artistic connection to Alfau's work demonstrates is that being an Americaniard does not emphasize finality regarding language, or a choice between Spanish and English. Rather, being an Americaniard leaves one in a productive limbo in which languages and their literary histories are constantly informing each other.

Conclusions

In the inclusive, multicultural environment of New York, *Llámame Brooklyn* presents the character Felipe Alfau as a "catalán de Barcelona" (272) ["Catalan from Barcelona" (240)] who "se consideraba vasco" (272) ["considered himself Basque" (240)]. Martín Gaite called Alfau the author an "emigrante catalán" ("Introducción" xxii) ["Catalan emigrant" ("Triumph" 179)]. He has also been labeled a "Spanish-American" (Villeneuve), a precursor of Latino

through an unlimited variety of landscapes, without being hindered at any border, a fluent and flexible identity that permits us to be from many places at the same time and from one alone] (358).

literature (Stavans, *Hispanic Condition* 175), "un escritor español" [a Spanish writer] (Ramos), a "Spanish author" (Scott), a "Spanish novelist" (Scott), and a "catalán" (Vila-Matas 22), and he is widely referred to online as a "Catalan-American." As a self-labeled "frontier man," Alfau likely would not have favored any one of these terms for himself or the character based on him. Moreover, he said that it is "by mere chance we are born in a specific geography and time" and that he had "always wished to travel through time, to champion a life beyond [his] individual boundaries" (Stavans, "Anonymity" 150). Alfau was never known to be politically engaged, much less an activist, although what has circulated about his political and social orientations has been anything but favorable. In fact, it has been said on several occasions that he supported Francisco Franco's dictatorship, favored tyranny over anarchy, was an anti-Semite, and complained that "many immigrants [invaded New York's] streets and neighborhoods, making it a violent jungle" (Stavans, "Anonymity" 152).[59] Such a profile could have also contributed to readers' difficulty with his works. The views on language, however, presented in *Chromos* are both innovative and provocative. Writing at the start of the twenty-first century, Doris Sommer says that "In today's readjustments to global dynamics, mono is a malady of adolescent societies. The world has outgrown a one-to-one identity between a language and a people" ("Introduction" xv). Alfau's writing and his own comments demonstrate a recognition of fading monolingualism, at least in artistic production, about 70 years earlier, when he reached New York and began to write the works that would later be published. His use of both Spanish and English in his *œuvre* and the unique language of *Chromos*, which looks English but hangs onto Spanish, promotes the rewards of knowledge of both languages. Bilingual readers of Alfau's work engage with the text in ways different from their monolingual counterparts. Bilingual readers are caught in a state of translation and asked to actively use their languages to grasp the humor and other textual complexities.

Attention to translation is a fruitful way to expose the complications, changes, and exchanges that travel, relocation, and mobility impose on literary production. *Chromos* shows that departures ignite a release from language and lead to translation, inviting an author to contemplate how his or her language can adequately write the host location. How much of the new language should the text incorporate? How much of the old language should it retain, and in what way? *Chromos* even broadens the discussion, although

---

59 For more on Alfau's political views, see his interview with Stavans, the texts by Chandler Brossard and Charles Simmons, as well as the interview with Miguel Ángel Del Arco.

secondarily, by including the capabilities of other media as a means to tell stories that involve multiple locations. Translation in this sense gives writers the choice to represent a city based not only on the mix of verbal languages they encounter but also on the techniques employed by cinema, music, visual arts, and any other sounds, sights, and sensations of the city.

Recognized for anticipating the work of some of the most influential writers of the twentieth century, Alfau also shows an interest in ideas about translation and the role of the translator that would later emerge in translation studies. Overall, *Chromos* is a story of Americaniards living in Manhattan, a story that would not be possible without the narrator's work to translate his interactions with other characters along with his fellow characters' creative writing. Movement, travel, temporary or permanent relocation—all involve new avenues for language. Although the portrait we have of Alfau is of a recluse, *Chromos* exposes a sharp awareness of how language is lived in New York and how it thrives on the creative energy and irreversible effects of the hurdles of mobility. Alfau's work is a fine example of the importance of context in language and writing, and the way in which the specificities of a city enter urban-centric writing. The characters of *Chromos* experience a city in which Spanish undergoes a transformation, with psychological or physical repercussions. Likewise, through his literature, Alfau sets up the edge that one encounters when language is challenged and then leads to literary works of wonder.

PART II

The Source of an Avant-Garde Voice: Music and Photography in José Moreno Villa

Travel to New York City was often a personal choice for Iberian writers, a choice not largely driven by the need to produce a text, but rather by the need to retreat. This has been the case for two writers from Andalusia: the well-known Federico García Lorca and the lesser-known José Moreno Villa, who each spent less than a year in the city due to personal circumstances. Their visits, however, would lead to the creation of literature written in situations that challenged their linguistic abilities, thus making them more receptive to other languages, sounds, and modes of expression in their surroundings. While highlighting the work of Moreno Villa, this second part considers the ways in which the city is brought into a text through an array of languages and discourses related to non-literary forms of artistic creativity.

Useful New York

Federico García Lorca's visit to New York City is arguably the most significant event in the history of literary relations between the Iberian Peninsula and New York.[1] From June 1929 to March 1930, the 30-year-old Lorca wrote most of the poems that would become part of the influential collection known to anglophone audiences as *Poet in New York*. Six years after his return from the United States, Lorca left the manuscript on the desk of his Madrid publisher, José Bergamín, with a note that said "Back Tomorrow," a message that the

---

1 James D. Fernández opens his essay "Poets, Peasants, Painters, Professors and Performers in New York" with the following sentence: "Federico García Lorca's *Poeta en Nueva York* is probably the best-known book written by a Spaniard in and about New York" (47). For further details about the atmosphere that surrounded Lorca while in New York, see the same essay.

main branch of the New York Public Library highlighted in a 2013 exhibit of the manuscript that had been lost for decades.[2] Lorca never returned to Bergamín's office, and scholars have questioned the whole provenance of the book ever since, not only because of the mystery surrounding the disappearance of the manuscript, but also the variations between published editions.[3] Nevertheless, *Poet in New York* has profoundly impacted multiple literary traditions, generations of writers, and other artistic media.[4]

Roughly a decade separates the composition of the poems and their initial publication. In 1939, a translation by Stephen Spender and J.L. Gili was published in Britain, and in 1940 the W.W. Norton Company published another translation in New York. For contemporary readers unaccustomed to seeing the name of a translator listed prominently on the cover of a book, and for literary translators who continuously strive to be recognized for their work, it is inspiring to see that the Norton edition of *Poet in New York* advertises Rolfe Humphries's English translations accompanying Lorca's poems. The book's cover includes the translator's full name in capital letters along with its English title *The Poet in New York and Other Poems*, noting the book's original Spanish version on the title page: "The Spanish text with an English translation by ROLFE HUMPHRIES" (see Fig. 2.1.). Besides the fact that the curious but under-informed reader might hold a first edition of this book and wonder about the nature of the relationship between the Spanish and English versions, it is significant that most anglophone readers have enjoyed some English version of *Poet in New York* for as long as they have known about the Spanish one. Since Humphries's 1940 version, *Poet in New York* has been translated into English three times: by Ben Belitt (1955), Greg Simon and Steven F. White (1988), and Pablo Medina and Mark Statman (2007); the complexity of the poetics Lorca developed in New York

---

2 Christopher Maurer and Andrés Soria Olmedo curated the exhibition "Back Tomorrow: Federico García Lorca/Poet in New York" presented by the New York Public Library and the Federico García Lorca Foundation. During the run of the exhibition, April 5, 2013 through July 20, a host of complementary events took place in New York City, including academic talks, theatrical productions, walking tours, and other performances.

3 Numerous scholars have noted the complexity of the manuscript. Notable is the work of Andrew A. Anderson. See his introduction and notes in the Galaxia Gutenberg edition of *Poeta en Nueva York*. See also Daniel Eisenberg's *Poeta en Nueva York: Historia y problemas de un texto* (1976).

4 The list of texts, performances, and films inspired by *Poet in New York* is extensive and includes Jonathan Mayhew's *Apocryphal Lorca: Translation, Parody, Kitsch* (2009), Jaime Manrique's *My Night with Federico García Lorca* (1995) and *Eminent Maricones: Arenas, Lorca, Puig, and Me* (1999), Jerome Rothenberg's *The Lorca Variations: I–XXXIII* (1993), and Nathalie Handal's *Poet in Andalucia* (2012).

Fig. 2.1 Cover of the first edition of *The Poet in New York and Other Poems*, 1940.

continues to fascinate translators and readers alike. Simon and White have revised their translation twice since 1988, and the volume's most recent English translators, Medina and Statman, are contemplating the reissue of a revised edition of their 2007 version.[5] In addition, at least three new Spanish editions of *Poeta en Nueva York* have been published since 2010.[6] Lorca's poetic achievement in the collection's individual verses and the uncertainties of the definitive version contribute to the text's place within literary history as a magnet for translations and other rewritings.[7]

From the release of the book to the impetus to create new versions of the work, translation is at the heart of the textual history of *Poet in New York* and is partially responsible for the book's continued success. Yet careful attention to the personal circumstances surrounding the writing of *Poet in New York*, including the initial purpose of Lorca's trip to New York and his own awareness of language use and conscientious discussions of the kinds of poems he considered these to be, further bring into question the acts of translation that shaped his New York experience. Travel to a diverse, dense, and dynamic city pushed Lorca's Spanish to write new things, contributing to the development of a poetry that ultimately internationalized literary traditions.

Lorca regularly wrote letters from New York to his family in Granada. In a letter dated August 8, 1929, he writes that his poems are "típicamente norteamericanos" [typically American] (*Prosa* 1069).[8] What Lorca meant by "norteamericanos" is unclear. Perhaps he was aware that they might be published first in English (*Prosa* 1069). Lorca could have also referred to them as "American poems" since they derived from an experience that was unique to the U.S. city itself: "Prefiero hacer la vida de los americanos" [I prefer to live the life of an American] (*Prosa* 1065). On the other hand, the "Americanness" of these poems could be indebted to the apparent freshness and innovation of his language, inspired by travels to and within the city. In

5 See my interview with Mark Statman in *Translation Review* (2014).

6 The following is a list of publishers that have recently published editions of *Poet in New York*. The quality of the editions varies greatly, but nonetheless they give an idea of the continued and widespread interest in *Poet in New York*: Galaxia Gutenberg; Farrar, Straus and Giroux; Red Ediciones; Diputación de Granada, Patronato Cultural Federico García Lorca and Román y Bueno; Lunwerg.

7 André Lefevere developed the concept of translation as rewriting. Rewriting includes any text produced based on another with the intention of adapting it to a certain ideology or poetics.

8 Christopher Maurer translated Lorca's U.S. letters in his edition of *Poet in New York*. All English translations from Lorca's letters are by Maurer. In Part II, however, all translations are mine unless otherwise indicated.

the same letter, he says: "Me interesa mucho Nueva York y creo que podré dar una nota nueva no sólo en la poesía española, sino en la que gira alrededor de estos motivos" [I am deeply interested in New York, and think I can strike a new note not only in Spanish but in all that has been written about these things] (*Prosa* 1069).

At the same time, the chronological distance we now have from Lorca's New York stay echoes in yet another way the influence of translation on the history of this text. His parents sent him abroad primarily to learn English, and this motivation informed his interactions with the city. Although he spent time with speakers of Spanish from his home country, Latin America, and the United States, in his letters he often notes the progress he is making in his English classes and the other venues where he could speak the language. In addition, he was given the opportunity to use his French when he met and formed a friendship with the novelist Nella Larsen.[9] She introduced him to other Harlem Renaissance luminaries as well as to Dorothy Peterson, who translated for him at social gatherings, as Evelyn Scaramella reveals in ("Literary Liaisons" 64). Peterson worked closely with Langston Hughes to translate Lorca and other Spanish-language poets into English (Scaramella 62).

Lorca also walked with Ángel Flores across the Brooklyn Bridge from Manhattan to the Brooklyn apartment of the North American poet Hart Crane (1899–1932) (Thompson and Walsh). What exactly happened once the two arrived is a mystery, but Lorca's limited English was very likely more advanced than Crane's Spanish. Did they speak French to each other?[10] Lorca's actual experience in the city, often negotiating between Spanish, English, and other languages, as well as enjoying the opportunities they provided, taught him something beyond Spanish, something "norteamericano," that would come across in his poetry as expressed in his personal correspondence.

In 1932 Lorca gave a lecture in Madrid that he would later repeat in cities around Spain as well as in Argentina and Uruguay. The lecture included a reading of poems from *Poet in New York* along with an explanation of how

9 For details of his time with Larsen, see Lorca's letter to his parents dated July 19, 1929. For more on Larsen see George Hutchinson's *In Search of Nella Larsen: A Biography of the Color Line* (2006). See Vera M. Kutzinski's *The Worlds of Langston Hughes: Modernism and Translation in the Americas* (2012) for more on the translation work of Hughes. For a focused discussion of Hughes and his translation work associated with the Spanish Civil War, see Scaramella, "Translating the Spanish Civil War: Langston Hughes's Transnational Poetics" (2014).

10 See B. Bussell Thompson and J.K. Walsh, "Un encuentro de Lorca y Hart Crane en Nueva York" (1986). For a poem inspired by this meeting, see Philip Levine's "On the Meeting of García Lorca and Hart Crane" (1992).

they came to be. Toward the end of his Madrid lecture, Lorca referred to his New York experience as the most useful of his life ("Lecture" 200). In a letter dated 1930 and addressed to Salvador Dalí, whom he had met before going to New York at the Residencia de Estudiantes in Madrid, Lorca invites the artist to return to New York with him: "You know how charming I am as a person and I believe that would be useful to you and that your marvelous spirit would see unheard-of things in that city, which is totally new and opposite in form and in dream to the renovated but rotten romanticism of Paris" (Maurer 106). The word "useful" seems uncharacteristic for a poet who, as he explained in his 1933 lecture "Theory and Play of the Duende" delivered in Argentina, celebrated the spontaneity of the performance of artistic creations and their uncalculated, organic delivery. However, given the contested portrayals of the heated relationship between them, Lorca might have tried to attract the attention of the Catalan artist.[11] Regardless, Lorca's letters tell us that New York had what these young, eager, artists needed to advance their work and make their mark on literary and cultural history.

Since Lorca's monumental collection of verses is frequently the point of departure for most discussions about Iberian and Latin American writing in New York City, attention to the extra-textual circumstances of its making as well as Lorca's own descriptions of his book also provides a helpful perspective from which to consider the work of one of his contemporaries, José Moreno Villa. Moreno Villa visited the city about two years prior to Lorca, but his texts have never been published in their entirety for an anglophone readership. Nonetheless, Moreno Villa's comments about New York present similar interactions with a linguistic fabric that led him, like Lorca, to question his own language and to push it in new directions.

Like Lorca, Moreno Villa did not even spend a year in the city, but its fruits forever impacted his future. Thus, "useful" could also qualify Moreno Villa's U.S. travel. During his few months in the city, Moreno Villa wrote a series of articles and a book of poems which would come to be known as his best collection and launch him into his most innovative and productive period.[12] For this Málaga-born intellectual, travel to New York and all its implications was a potent experience paralleled only by the onset of the Spanish Civil War. In his autobiography *Vida en claro* (1944), Moreno Villa shares: "Para mí es indudable que la peripecia de Nueva York opera un cambio en mi

11 See the biographies on Dalí and Lorca by Ian Gibson. The film *Little Ashes* (2008), directed by Paul Morrison, gives an account of the relationship between the two young artists based on their correspondence and the work of historians.

12 Hughes also translated Moreno Villa, as Evelyn Scaramella (2014) points out.

poesía, como lo opera también más tarde la sublevación y guerra civil" [In my opinion, there's no doubt that the New York adventure brings about a change in my poetry, just like the uprising and civil war later on] (206). For both Moreno Villa and Lorca, New York is useful to the advancement of their writing and their careers not only because of the novelties that provided a backdrop for their writing and the people they met, but also because of the exposure to English and other languages, as well as the sounds of the city that accompanied them during their travels abroad.

Moreno Villa's and Lorca's assessments of their travels to the United States as useful to their creative writing parallel how literary translation enlivens language. While addressing the political and ethical concerns of translation in "Anonymous Sources (On Translators and Translation)" (2013), Eliot Weinberger says that "translation liberates the translation language, and it is often the case that translation flourishes when writers feel that their language or society needs liberating" (18). Thus, translation is beneficial in that it loosens established conventions of the translation language. For both Lorca and Moreno Villa, who journeyed out of Spain during Miguel Primo de Rivera's almost seven-year dictatorship, which ended in 1930, travel invigorated their Spanish and moved them to remarkable periods of productivity. The dynamic city that they heard, lived in, and wrote about provided the Spanish language with new sounds, new rhythms, new poetry, and new prose. Contact with this city and its languages gave Moreno Villa and Lorca a path to avant-garde voices while at the same time granting their readers access to something more than a visual representation of New York.

Moreno Villa's New York texts lack the international visibility that Lorca's enjoy. *Poet in New York* is one of the most important literary works of the twentieth century. What is more, Lorca in general is one of the two most frequently translated European poets, along with Rainer Maria Rilke (Mayhew, "Reading Poetry"). In contrast, Moreno Villa's texts are unknown to English-speaking audiences. Given Moreno Villa's peripheral status within literary history, the second part of this book portrays his role in twentieth-century intellectual life in order to create awareness of his place among some of the major writers and artists of the earlier half of the last century. A discussion of his two New York book publications, *Pruebas de Nueva York* (1927) and *Jacinta la pelirroja* (1929), follows, contextualizing their beginnings and arguing that their brilliance lies in how their strategies for surpassing predictable notions of travel writing manifest themselves in the visible traces of translation throughout their prose and poetry. These texts represent the city in a way that relies on the burgeoning urban sounds associated with not only languages but also music and the discourses of

Fig. 2.2 Salvador Dalí, José Moreno Villa, Luis Buñuel, Federico García Lorca, José Antonio Rubio Sacristán. Pabellón Transatlántico, Residencia de Estudiantes, 1926.

other artistic media such as photography. The presence of these sounds offers readers more than description of the visual landscape of a distant city; they are also engaged in the contemporaneous artistic climate and a sense of its linguistic texture, expanding the way in which the city can be experienced through reading.

A Portrait of José Moreno Villa

Lorca and Moreno Villa both lived in the Residencia de Estudiantes in Madrid for at least nine years. The Residencia, founded in 1910 by Alberto Jiménez Fraud, was a center of artistic and scientific work and exchange bringing together international artists and scholars, welcoming avant-garde ideas, and promoting modernity. Many of the contributors to U.S. and European avant-garde cultural practices were familiar with the activities and events fostered by this unique institution. Individuals such as Albert Einstein, Le Corbusier, Alexander Calder, Luis Buñuel, Salvador Dalí, Victoria Ocampo, H.G. Wells, Miguel de Unamuno, Gabriela Mistral, and Marie Curie, all of whose scientific and artistic contributions forever marked the course of history, each visited the Residencia during their career. Jiménez Fraud, director of the Residencia for 25 years, recruited Moreno Villa, his friend and fellow *malagueño*, to join the Residencia in 1917, where he would become a permanent fixture for the next 20 years.[13] Spending a little less than one third of his life there, Moreno Villa was exceptionally active as he led trips to the Museo del Prado and other destinations and collaborated with the in-house publication *Residencia*, among other tasks that enriched the overall objectives of the institution.[14] Moreno Villa's attachment to the Residencia was so intense that he only left it twice for a notable amount of time: once for Gijón, on the Asturian coast, and another time for New York City, before evacuating Madrid for Valencia along with other intellectuals in late November of 1937, during the Spanish Civil War (Ballesteros and Neira 11).[15] He then began his exilic journey, which would take him to back to the United States and shortly thereafter to Mexico, where his life would come to an end almost 20 years later in 1955.

Given the multiple operations promoted by the Residencia de Estudiantes and its impressive roster of visitors and residents, it is no surprise that Moreno Villa would become a poet, painter, critic, historian, essayist, editor, enthusiastic promoter of the arts, and translator, a role overlooked in discussions of his intellectual activity.[16] Moreno Villa embodied the spirit of the Residencia in all its diversity and energy, not

13 Moreno Villa's affection for the Residencia de Estudiantes is shown in *Vida en claro*: "Pero aquella institución ejemplar y única en España me fué seduciendo insensiblemente, y me retuvo durante veinte años, desde 1917 a 1937 (otra vez los sietes). Hasta la guerra civil acabó con ella. (La fecha exacta de mi salida fué la del 29 de noviembre de 1936) [...] Yo trabajé hasta el último momento, mientras encima de mi cuarto los aviones defensores de Madrid contra de los alemanes e italianos" [But that exemplary and unique institution in Spain was imperceptibly seducing me, and it kept me there for 20 years, from 1917 to 1937 (sevens once again). Until the civil war did away with it. (The exact date of my departure was November 29, 1936 [...] I worked up until the last minute, while above my room there were defense planes from Madrid against German and Italian planes)] (*Vida en claro*, 101, 103). See Chapter X, "En presencia de la eterna juventud," for more details on his stay there.

14 See *La Residencia de Estudiantes 1910–1936* by Margarita Saenz de la Calzada for more on the Residencia de Estudiantes and *Residencia*. *Residencia*, founded in 1926, was published every four months quite regularly between 1926 and 1934 (Crispin 64). Also, see Crispin for a panorama of the content of the publication.

15 Ballesteros and Neira claim that he left on November 19, 1937, while other sources say he left on November 29, 1937 (Fajardo 39).

16 Moreno Villa's Spanish translation of Heinrich Wolfflin's *Conceptos fundamentales de la historia del arte* was commissioned by Ortega y Gasset (*Vida en claro* 114). His other translations from the German include *Contribuciones a una crítica de lenguaje* by Fritz Mauthner, *Lucinda: novela* by Friedrich von Schlegel, and *La señorita Elisa* by Arthur Schnitzler. He also illustrated Rafael Sánchez Mazas's translations of Giambattista Basile: *Las siete palomas* and *El archipámpano de las pulgas*.

to mention the fact that his autobiography provides invaluable details regarding its history. His importance not only lies in his connection with this unique center; many leading literary figures of twentieth-century Spanish writing, including Juan Ramón Jiménez, José Ortega y Gasset, and Pedro Salinas, have praised the quality of his work. More recently, Moreno Villa inspired one of the characters of Antonio Muñoz Molina's historical romance *La noche de los tiempos* (2009), translated into English by Edith Grossman as *In the Night of Time* (2013), whose protagonist is based on Pedro Salinas, his social and intellectual circles, and in particular his transatlantic journey to the northeastern United States, leaving behind his wife and children.

Despite Moreno Villa's intimate involvement in a rigorous intellectual exchange and his lasting impact on artistic representations of that era, he has not yet received widespread recognition for his role in twentieth-century cultural production. The critical tendencies that dominated Iberian literature of the early twentieth century placed writers in the Generation of '98 or the Generation of '27.[17] Moreno Villa did not neatly fit into either: he was too young to be part of the earlier generation and too old to be considered part of the later (Fajardo 67).[18] Moreover, although Moreno Villa was a practitioner of many arts, he is primarily labeled a poet and occasionally a painter, which hinders a more complete image of his versatile career (Valendar) and creates a flawed sense of his achievements. Finally, Moreno Villa did not subscribe to any of the -isms that peppered the early part of the twentieth century. In an effort to give proper recognition to Moreno Villa, literary critics have suggested moving beyond classifications based on genre or time period, and recommend studying him as a unique individual, well versed in the many artistic movements and trends of his time, but committed to none.[19]

17 David Miranda-Barreiro carefully lists the following critics' work as being central to attempts to break down these divisions: Helen Graham and Jo Labanyi (1995), David T. Gies (1999), Anthony Geist and José B. Monleón (1999), Carlos Blanco Aguinaga (1999), Mary Lee Bretz (2001), Susan Larson and Eva Woods (2005), Elena Delgado, Jordana Mendelson and Óscar Vázquez (2007), and Christopher Soufas (2007, 2010) (11).

18 In "Recuperación de Moreno Villa" (1977), Guillermo Carnero discusses the debate about Moreno Villa's inclusion in the Generation of '27 and addresses other failed attempts to place Moreno Villa. This insistence on the placement of his work says little about his work *per se*, but does emphasize its uniqueness and position in a league of its own.

19 See Francisco Calvo Serraller (1987) for the different dimensions and magnitude of the work of Moreno Villa. See Juan Pérez de Ayala's *José Moreno Villa [1887–1955]* for an overview of his work as well as a display of his paintings and drawings.

These critical efforts agree on Moreno Villa's versatility and singularity but lack a consideration of Iberian literature within a transnational framework in which travel and thus other sites or outposts of cultural production play a major part in artistic creation. Given the movement undertaken by the writers and artists who populated the past century, this is a major oversight. Moreno Villa concluded an extremely interesting seven-year period, 1920 through 1927, at the Residencia shared with Lorca, Dalí, Emilio Prados, Buñuel, and Pepín Bello, to name but a few, with a trip to New York City accompanied by his then-fiancée, Florence Louchheim, whom he had met in Madrid, in hopes of receiving her parents' consent for their planned marriage.[20] Unfortunately, her family did not approve and the couple split. Moreno Villa left the hotel where he was staying and retreated to the Morningside Heights neighborhood, where he could be close to his friend Professor Federico de Onís and other professors of Spanish at Columbia University.[21]

Moreno Villa visited the city during a notably vibrant time for all things Spanish, as noted in Part I. From the 1890s until the early 1930s, the United States felt the effects of a Spanish craze, as the historian Richard Kagan has labeled it, and New York was one of its centers.[22] Moreno Villa had contact with this craze and even contributed to it. He wrote an article about Miguel de Unamuno, gave two lectures on new Spanish painting at Columbia, presenting Dalí for the first time to the United States, and published a couple of long articles about modern painting in U.S. journals (Carmona Mato 18). He also gathered enough material for two book projects: *Pruebas de Nueva York*, a series of 11 articles, and *Jacinta la pelirroja*, a collection of poetry. Having had an experience that left a lasting imprint,[23] Moreno Villa said goodbye to New York a few months after his arrival to return to Madrid a

20 The couple left for New York on February 16, 1927, Moreno Villa's fortieth birthday. "El 16 de febrero—fecha republicana y de mi nacimiento—, me embarqué para América el año 1927, y el 16 de febrero llegué a Nueva York el año de 1937" [On February 16—the date of the republic and of my birth—of the year 1927, I embarked for America, and on February 16, 1937 I arrived in New York] (*Vida en claro* 72). Ballesteros and Neira reconstruct the start of Moreno Villa's relationship and its stages in the introduction to their edition of *Jacinta la pelirroja*. They also provide descriptions of Florence and what little biographical information is known about her.

21 For Moreno Villa's own account of the relationship, see Chapter XI, "Segunda vez la manta a la Cabeza," of *Vida en claro*.

22 Also see Fernández, "Poets, Peasants, Painters, Professors and Performers in New York."

23 See Ballesteros and Neira for a discussion of the lasting effects of this relationship on Moreno Villa and his work, as well as the effects of Moreno Villa's own *Vida en claro*.

"poeta recién soltero" [newly single poet], as his friends called him, alluding humorously to the title of Juan Ramón Jiménez's New York book, *Diario de un poeta recién casado*, known to English-speaking audiences as *Diary of a Newlywed Poet*, published ten years earlier in 1917 (Ballesteros and Neira 27). This short but intense visit did not allow him to benefit from all the city had to offer in terms of artistic collaboration. We can only imagine what might have happened if his stay had coincided with Lorca's sojourn a couple of years later.

Most importantly for the path of literary history, Moreno Villa's trip to New York invigorated him intellectually. Rafael Ballesteros and Julio Neira, editors of *Jacinta la pelirroja* and authors of the Castalia edition's scholarly introduction, point out that once Moreno Villa returned from New York, "y se asienta de nuevo en la Residencia, su actividad como escritor, pintor y también como conferenciante, articulista e investigador, se acentúa extraordinariamente" [and settles down again at the Residencia, his activity as a writer, painter and also as a lecturer, columnist and researcher is extraordinarily accentuated] (13). Moreover, his artwork circulated on the western side of the Atlantic, although it is unclear to what extent.[24] An English translation by an unnamed translator of a selection from *Pruebas de Nueva York* was published in the July 1929 issue of the short-lived, New York-based journal *Alhambra*, possibly marking the first time Moreno Villa's work was disseminated in a language other than Spanish.[25] Thus, shifting the critical lens of the period places Moreno Villa among the major figures from the Iberian Peninsula to whose artistic and intellectual development the city of New York was critical, and places him among the ranks of some of the most discussed poets of twentieth-century Iberian literature.

The New York publications of Jiménez and Lorca forever changed their careers as well as the landscape of national and international literature. Jiménez and Lorca arrived in a New York that was eagerly awaiting their arrival. The Camprubí family, who had ties in the United States, Puerto Rico, and Barcelona, was anticipating the marriage of their daughter Zenobia to the 35-year-old Jiménez, whom she had met in 1913. At the end of 1915 Zenobia and her mother left Spain for New York City to take care of family

---

24 Carmen Mato notes that Moreno Villa's work was exhibited at the Museum of Modern Art (18), although the Museum of Modern Art in New York does not have a register of his work being exhibited there.

25 *Alhambra* was published by Alhambra Press in New York. The single volume includes four numbers published from 1929 to 1930. I thank Evelyn Scaramella for bringing this translation to my attention. Dorothy Peterson translated for *Alhambra* although there is no indication that she translated Moreno Villa for the journal (Scaramella 65).

matters, and within weeks Jiménez impatiently boarded a transatlantic vessel taking him to the city to marry her on March 2, 1916. The newlyweds left New York about three months later. Michael P. Predmore tells us that Jiménez "recorded this transatlantic experience in an intimate diary, an intense work of highly symbolic poetry, which was to dramatically change the landscape of twentieth-century Hispanic lyric poetry" (21). *Diario de un poeta recien casado* was published no more than a year later and, as Jiménez himself has said, "a new life in Spanish poetry began" (Predmore 21).[26]

About ten years later, Zenobia's father, newspaper owner José Camprubí, the poet and translator León Felipe, graphic designer Gabriel García Maroto, and professors Federico de Onís and Ángel del Río stood on the West Side docks of Manhattan ready to greet Lorca as he disembarked from the transatlantic vessel. During Lorca's stay, he received no lack of attention, as he was "surrounded and affectionately cared for by Spanish-speaking friends, old and new" (Maurer x) and "seemed to constantly 'run into' or re-encounter friends he had made in Spain" (Fernández 55). Lorca himself describes all these positive interactions with the city in his letters to his family back in Andalusia. Although similar to Jiménez, in that sentimental relations and the prospect of marriage were tied to his trip, Moreno Villa was uncertain about what to expect upon his arrival in the city, as the purpose of his journey was to be introduced for the first time to his fiancée's New Yorker parents. It was later, after being rejected by them, that the focus of Moreno Villa's New York shifted and expanded:

> dejé el hotel donde me hospedaba y alquilé un cuarto barato, de once dólares a la semana, cerca de la Universidad de Columbia y de la casa de Onís [...] Allí me pasé sólo no sé cuántos días, dibujando, visitando el Museo Metropolitano, y conviviendo bastante Onís y con algunos otros profesores. También escribí dos largos artículos sobre la pintura moderna española y sobre Unamuno, a petición de un profesor que me dijo los traduciría y publicaría en buenas revistas. Por mi cuenta, además comencé la serie que luego publiqué en "El Sol" y reuní más tarde en un folleto titulado "Pruebas de Nueva York." (*Vida en claro* 129)

> [I left the hotel where I was staying and rented an inexpensive room, eleven dollars per week, close to Columbia University and Onís's home (...) I only spent I don't know how many days there (*sic*), drawing, visiting the Met, and spending a good amount of time with Onís and with some other professors. I also wrote two articles on modern

---

26 *Diario de un poeta recien casado* was translated by Hugh A. Harter and published in 2004.

Spanish painting and Unamuno, at the request of a professor who told me he would translate and publish them in good magazines. On my own, I also started the series that I later published in *El Sol* and collected later on in a leaflet titled "Pruebas de Nueva York."]

These dissimilarities in initial contact with the city resonate in each poet's writing representing the city. Even though the verses of *Diary of a Newlywed Poet* and *Poet in New York* have little in common, written more than ten years apart with a two-decade publication gap, Jiménez and Lorca both produced a remarkably fresh New York literature while often identifying recognizable locales such as Coney Island, Long Island, Wall Street, Broad Street, Battery Park, and the Chrysler Building. In other words, the fact that they were greeted in the city by personal contacts who willingly became their local guides is reflected in the sightseeing tours of New York that their texts provide readers. In contrast, Moreno Villa's work is unlike that of his compatriots, in that his prose and poetry are guided by the sounds, rhythms, and other media of the urban experience, thus providing close-ups of the city that take the reader beyond what might already be an iconic New York. Although *Jacinta la pelirroja* and *Pruebas de Nueva York* were inspired by a quick trip, and were published less than two years apart, critical work on these texts deals with each book individually or uses *Pruebas de Nueva York* to access greater detail about the speedy rise and sudden fall of a fascinating love story poetically rendered in the pages of *Jacinta la pelirroja* (Ballesteros and Neira, 2000; Díaz de Castro, 1989). Recently, in *Spanish New York Narratives 1898–1936: Modernization, Otherness and Nation* (2014) David Miranda-Barreiros studies the image of New York developed in *Pruebas de Nueva York* as "not a mere reflection of Moreno Villa's relationship with Florence or simply his personal circumstances" (21). Instead he examines Moreno Villa's view of New York and U.S. society to "provide insight into the contradictions brought about by modernization in both Spain and Europe" (21). These approaches overlook the ways in which the journey itself and the contact with the new environment shaped his New York writing. Although his trip was brief, travel granted Moreno Villa the opportunity to immerse himself in a new atmosphere where firsthand exposure not just to English and other recognizable languages, but to the various implicit languages of the city, acted as a motive for literary production and experimentation.

Photography in Writing

Pruebas de Nueva York was the first of Moreno Villa's two New York publications to reach a wide audience. There is no doubt that a curious reader in 1920s Spain would have read it and felt closer to a city an ocean away. The volume brings New York City to its readers via observations and details of urban life, from apartment interiors, construction projects, and fire escapes to meals, universities, automats, and work culture. At the same time, contemporary readers have much to gain from the pages of Moreno Villa's collection. Much as photographers' social documentation in Spain during the interwar period "provides valuable information about the folklore, work and leisure of certain communities" (Zelich 161), the descriptions found in *Pruebas de Nueva York* diversify extant narratives of New York's cultural history. A reading of this collection of texts in light of a relationship with photography is not solely inspired by what the texts choose to portray, but rather by the mode of portrayal. Written in the city, during the return voyage, and back in Madrid, the essays of *Pruebas de Nueva York* first appeared periodically in *El Sol* between May 19 and July 24 of 1927 and at the end of the same year as a collection with the addition of a prologue.[27]

While *Pruebas de Nueva York* might come across as a straightforward title, the several meanings of *pruebas* in Spanish suggest different potential readings of the book's content that are illuminated by considering its possible English translations. Still unknown today in its entirety to a monolingual English audience, the book's title alone has been translated on a few occasions as *Evidence of New York* or *Trials of New York*. *Pruebas* as "evidence" is a choice that speaks to those readers interested in finding out more about the mechanics of the city. *Trials of New York*, on the other hand, emphasizes the conflicted contact that an individual might have with a city that was advancing technologically and transforming socially like never before. Understood as referring to "trials," the title could have drawn a smirk from those familiar with the personal motives for Moreno Villa's transatlantic trip: instead of being tested by the city, he was being tried by Florence's family. Reflecting on his trip to New York and his encounter with Florence's parents, Moreno Villa later commented in *Vida en claro* that "No me agradaba ser invitado como a prueba" [I didn't like being invited for a test] (127). Here, of course, *prueba* is used to express his uneasiness with the pending visit and its unpleasant motives. But however one might read *pruebas*, neither "evidence" nor "trial" grasps the collection's objective, opting for the more common definitions of *pruebas*, and consequentially

---

27 A facsimile edition including the prologue was printed in 1989.

careless translations of the title could have contributed to this work's marginality within literary history.

When the New York-based magazine *Alhambra*, unknown to many readers given its limited circulation, published an English translation of a short fragment of Moreno Villa's work, the title was *Snap-shots of New York*, a choice that more accurately approaches what the Spanish title does as it adheres to the language of photography, but lacks the nuances involved in the process of making photography. As a translator from German to Spanish, not to mention the exposure he must have had to the multiple languages passing through the Residencia de Estudiantes, Moreno Villa's sensitivity to the use of language and the power of a single word must not be neglected. It is no minor detail, then, that his prologue to *Pruebas de Nueva York* appeared in the periodical *La Gaceta Literaria* on March 1, 1928, as part of the volume's advertising campaign since the opening paragraph clarifies the kind of *pruebas* found among the pages and delineates Moreno Villa's strategy for writing New York:

> De ningún modo pretendo hacer el libro de Nueva-York, pero tampoco me gustaría que resultasen las páginas que siguen como "mis impresiones". Estamos ya muy lejos de todo "impresionismo"; nos recreamos mucho más con el detalle concreto y la rápida consecuencia intelectual que con una mancha colora, por muy gentil y cargada de aire ambiente que sea. Mi propósito está más cerca del término fotográfico "prueba". Quiero enseñar unas pruebas de Nueva-York. Y sin caricatura, ni deformación. Con el mayor espíritu de justicia que pueda. He mirado a la "niña violenta" como quien mira un mecanismo, con afán de comprender su lógica y su funcionamiento. (8)

> [I am in no way trying to write the book of New York, but nor would I like for these following pages to come across as "my impressions." We are now very far from all "impressionism"; we take much more pleasure in concrete details and rapid intellectual conclusions than with a stain of color, regardless of however pleasant and filled with atmosphere it may seem. My objective is closer to the photographic term "proof." I want to show some proofs of New York. Without exaggerating, without distorting. Being as fair as I can be I've watched the "violent girl" like someone who watches a mechanism, with the desire to understand her logic and performance.]

On the one hand, Moreno Villa underlines that the collection of articles is not a definitive book on New York, thus granting access to writing's developmental stages. On the other hand, he does not hesitate to declare a break from tradition, as he does not want his work to be seen as his "impressions" of the city. Since impressions are a way of talking about travel, especially common in the nineteenth century, Moreno Villa wishes to avoid repeating anything that is artistically out of fashion. Michael Cronin outlines how, in order to endure, travel writing, like translation, must be "reworked and/or reinvented for a new generation of readers" (23). He notes that "the shift in travel writing from travel log to travelogue is the shift from fact to impression, the movement from the bald description of physical phenomena to the interpretive luxuriance of emotion and opinion" (Cronin 23). In furthering this movement that aligns with the times and the trends in reading culture, Moreno Villa strives to develop his writing from impressions, a word he associates with the nineteenth century, to a new way of interpreting the culture through which he travels, which is up to speed with modernity. Although a reading of *Pruebas de Nueva York* that does not see beyond a failed romantic relationship is insufficient, Moreno Villa's desire to emancipate his writing from previous origins and to write a New York free of any reaction charged by his feelings or mood is also of profound personal significance given that the trip to New York marks the beginning of his future without Florence. In the prologue, Moreno Villa establishes how he plans to detach himself from his work and modernize his writing.

Maintaining a dialogue with contemporaneous artistic tendencies, Moreno Villa turned to photography, a topic of intense discussion and exploration throughout the interwar period. During these years photography reached maturity and gained independence as a form of visual expression (Foncuberta 25). Photography was, as Joan Foncuberta explains, "the most suitable and direct medium [...] to scrutinize the world carefully, to register every detail with precision, to inventory every object and to marvel at each element of its construction, to emphasize its internal structure, to highlight its texture, to manifest its general context" (39). It was during the 1920s that these ideas about photography, as echoed in Moreno Villa's prologue, coincided with the transformation of photography's relationship with the individual as more people had access to the roll films and small portable cameras along with faster films and lenses (Trachtenberg xi). These advances in particular gave rise to new ways of considering photography as a means to document and, for Moreno Villa, as a new way to conceive of the (re)presentation of space through writing.[28] Given the artistic and historical climate, it is fitting that Moreno Villa should label his attempt to write New

---

28 Salvador J. Farjado studies the connection between Moreno Villa's sense of self and space, especially in his exilic writing.

York in a new way, as *pruebas*: he uses photography to immerse himself in an artistic dialogue and to limit the delicate emotional forces that might interfere with writing the city. In a sense, the pages of *Pruebas de Nueva York* are Moreno Villa's contribution to the period discussion on photography as well as an occasion to renew ways of writing. Further, his use of *prueba* takes authorial control over a word that suggests his victimization in New York. In claiming ownership of his trip as a strategy to get over the personal trouble he encountered, he turned to photography as a novel writing companion—a medium that was criticized during the same years for using impersonality as a means of expression (Gili 133). Thinking photographically, Moreno Villa attempts to remove himself from the personal obstacles set before him in New York.

Though Moreno Villa has never been labeled a photographer, he was not a stranger to the medium. Among his numerous roles at the Residencia de Estudiantes he was supervisor, along with Jiménez Fraud, of the Residencia's journal. Descriptions of *Residencia* note the large percentage of scientific compared to literary or artistic articles, while two sections titled "Guía de Madrid" and "Guía de excursiones" offered subject matter of a more cultural and poetical nature (Crispin 71). However, beyond its actual content, the artistic worth and impact of *Residencia* can also be assessed by focusing on the object itself. For example, each number generously printed illustrations including drawings by Moreno Villa and Dalí, to name a couple of contributors, as well as photographs.[29] Photography's ability to inform, interfere with, or expand the way texts are read and the interaction between reader and the object itself were explored in the pages of *Residencia*.

Eliminating the possibility that *pruebas* could refer to anything other than photographic proofs—a sheet of printed material in a non-final state—the prologue prioritizes Moreno Villa's approach to writing New York over definite conclusions about the city, thereby speaking to the benefits of his New York visit as a way to consider how and what it means to write a city that was so vastly new to him in so many ways. According to Moreno Villa, concrete details delivered with precision and efficiency in a way that transports the reader through the city are granted by engaging theories of photography. Besides the ways of thinking about photography's methods for artistic production discussed in the two-page prologue, other instances of how an individual interacts with the city throughout *Pruebas de Nueva*

---

29 In 1927, the same year Moreno Villa first traveled to New York, Dalí published "Photography, Pure Creation of the Spirit" in *L'amic de les Arts*. Exposure to the medium is not lacking, and photography was easily on his mind as Moreno Villa stepped onto the streets of New York.

York contribute to a better understanding of the writing that preoccupied Moreno Villa. Metaphors of photographic methods in writing not only kept Moreno Villa connected to contemporaneous discussions about art but also came with ease given the very nature of the city in which he found himself.

In his discussion of the culture of New York commerce, Moreno Villa states that there is a trepidation on the streets that "es pecado pararse a contemplar; anda, que no podrás volver si no tomas el ómnibus que pasa" [it's a sin to stop and look; go on, you won't be able to get back if you don't take the bus that's coming] (32). A haunting feeling—that the city negates contemplation and that speed, mobility, and the passage of time shape the urban experience—suggests that the writer needs something similar to what Edward Weston calls an "instantaneous recording process" in the essay "Seeing Photographically" (1943). This trait, which Weston identifies as unique to photography, concurs with Moreno Villa's ways of thinking about writing that moves away from delivering impressions for he sought to bring New York into focus by offering "detalle concreto" [concrete detail] followed by "rápida consecuencia intelectual" [rapid intellectual consequence], as expressed in his prologue. Further, Weston's description of the photographer's recording process does not encourage stationary observation:

> The photographer's recording process cannot be drawn out. Within its brief duration, no stopping or changing or reconsidering is possible. When he uncovers his lens every detail within its field of vision is registered in far less time than it takes for his own eyes to transmit a similar copy of the scene to his brain. (172)

An emphasis of precision, motion, and the lack of emotionally charged accounts of the city is available to Moreno Villa via the metaphor of photography but, as Weston indicates, the camera records much faster than a human. As such, writing photography is not about achieving a comparable final result but rather about a particular attraction to a strikingly new *process* of artistic production and a way of bringing New York to Moreno Villa's readers that exceeds mere description but reaches them through the very language they read. The dependence on an outside medium and its properties allows Moreno Villa to unleash a subtle perspective of the city and keeps him writing.

There is a sense of speed in New York that transforms the urban experience which Moreno Villa strives to communicate by including the language of photography. Speed can provoke unexpected, new, and different experiences, according to Jeffery T. Schnapp in "Crash: Speed as Engine of Individuation" (1999):

> Speed is the medium that ensures that the conjunction between human
> and mechanical individuals will engender not relaxation and tedium,
> but bigger living: quickened senses, aroused faculties, expanded powers
> of vision; acts of heroism, improvisation, and innovation; spectacular
> crashes and catastrophes; eruptions of laughter and glee. (34–35)

Speed, motion, and a rapid recording process, instead of long, unhurried
periods of contemplation, are what attract Moreno Villa to the photographic
method, as it will not only give him the exact detail of New York he is
looking to share with his readers but also renews his craft and cultivates
a relationship between text, image, and artistic innovation in general. In
short, translating photography into a written language set a new strategic
path for Moreno Villa's writing while simultaneously emphasizing his
interest in process as opposed to a complete picture.

Marking up the Text

Integration of the non-verbal medium of photography exemplifies just one of
the ways that *Pruebas de Nueva York* demonstrates a heightened sensitivity to
expression, documentation, and language. Given the personal circumstances
surrounding the motives for his transatlantic journey, anxieties about Moreno
Villa's limited knowledge of English could not have been a secondary concern.
In fact, upon receiving a letter from Florence's parents while in Barcelona,
already en route to New York, Moreno Villa and his fiancée anticipate the
linguistic situation that awaits them in New York: "Yo le respondía que no
sabiendo el idioma toda persona pierde personalidad y hasta hace el ridículo.
Ella me contestaba que a mi edad no se hace el ridículo" [I told her that when
you don't know the language, you lose your personality and even make a fool
of yourself. She answered that at my age one does not make a fool of oneself]
(*Vida en claro* 126). Although he is accompanied by his fiancée, a native New
Yorker, Moreno Villa finds that entering a new city surrounded by a new
language is no small thing; indeed it is one that would forever imprint
his memories of his days with Florence—this conversation is mentioned
twice in *Vida en claro*.[30] How would he speak to Florence's parents? What did
his conversations with her even sound like? How would these interactions

---

30 Earlier in *Vida en claro*, Moreno Villa wrote: "Hablando una vez, con mi amor
yanqui, del triste papel que haría yo en Norteamérica sin saber el idioma, lo cual anula
casi por completo la personalidad, me respondió: 'A tu edad no se hace el ridículo'"
[Once when I was talking with my Yanqui love about the sorry role I would play in
North America without knowing the language, which completely does away with
one's personality, she responded: "You can't embarrass yourself at your age"] (26).

and other contacts with the city be represented in Spanish for readers in Madrid? How do the linguistic negotiations of Moreno Villa's visit to New York appear in his text? Among the many poignant questions about travel and translation addressed by Michael Cronin in his discussion of interlingual translation in travel accounts, the overarching one is this: "Does the Traveller feature also as Translator or does the Translator once again become invisible, overshadowed by the solar presence of the Traveller as Author?" (39). The direction established by Cronin encourages textual analysis that goes beyond depictions of space and time in travel writing as it calls attention to cultural and linguistic exchanges and how they unearth innovative ways of critiquing a text. What does Moreno Villa do in Spanish with a travel experience that was tinged with anxieties about linguistic deficiency even before setting foot in the United States? How does Moreno Villa represent a city where Spanish only partially enters the urban soundscape?

The most obvious resources available to writers with which to signal the foreignness of a word are the addition to or alteration of the look of the text with the use of quotation marks and italics.[31] In a text written in Spanish, for example, words in languages other than Spanish or are most often italicized, and Spanish words surrounded by quotation marks ask to be read with special attention, as they have a visual impact on the surface of the text. Their presence—or, in some cases, absence—cautions the attentive reader and provokes contemplation of their very use. In *Pruebas de Nueva York*, quotation marks hug individual words or phrases while others stand out in italics. As mentioned earlier, in the prologue to *Pruebas de Nueva York*, quotation marks surrounding "mis impresiones" [my impressions] and "impresionismo" [impressionism] (8) signal that these terms allude to a kind of travel writing that was widespread in the nineteenth century and an influential artistic movement that flourished during the same century. Likewise, "prueba" (8) set in quotation marks guides the reader beyond the most immediate meaning of the word. Both examples test readers' linguistic horizons, just as New York challenged Moreno Villa.

In *Pruebas de Nueva York*, quotation marks not only indicate that words' multiple definitions should be considered but also introduce literal translations of American expressions for which there are no equivalents in the Spanish language. In a discussion of the dynamics of romantic

---

31 This is not to say that all writers who incorporate foreign words that have not yet been adopted by the language in which they write use italics or quotation marks. For example, contemporary writers who write in English, like Junot Díaz and Francisco Goldman, sometimes do not italicize foreign words that clearly have not been adopted into English. Eliminating italics gives the sense that the two languages are not foreign to each other.

relationships, the agency of the woman surprises Moreno Villa, and he notes that "consecuencia de esto es la frase americana de 'cincuenta y cincuenta' (*fifty, fifty*), que quiere decir: seamos partes iguals, tengamos el cincuenta por ciento en todo" [the result is the American saying "fifty, fifty," which means: let's be equals, let's go 50 percent each in everything] (17). Besides destabilizing the text's surface, the quotation marks around the literal Spanish translation, followed by the English expression in italics and an explanation, make this expression accessible and comprehensible to readers of Spanish because Moreno Villa is aware that "nuestra media naranja" (18), as Miranda-Barreiro points out, "alludes to the perfect sentimental match, which, however, does not imply the equality of both sexes in social and economic terms" (77–78). While a single explanation would have set straight the dynamics of romantic relationships perceived by Moreno Villa, the inclusion of a literal translation gives readers of *Pruebas de Nueva York* a feeling of the calculated approach to relationships in the New York context and how this is revealed in the very words used to describe that relationship. Further, the thorough presentation of this phrase to the Spanish-language reader underlines and maximizes the cultural difference between Moreno Villa and his fiancée, as the heightened attention suggests greater distance.

In *Pruebas de Nueva York*, quotation marks also surround English words in the text that would not be unfamiliar to a monolingual Spanish reader. "Metro" (16, 27), "cafeteria" (16, 27), "taxi" (16, 28), and "bus" (28) are always placed in quotation marks and at times receive an explanation. Unlike a *cafetería* in Madrid, a New York "cafeteria" is a "restaurante barato donde uno se sirve a sí mismo" [cheap restaurant where you serve yourself] (16) or, as later described, "el restaurante barato es lo que llaman 'cafeteria'" [the cheap restaurant is what they call a *cafetería*] (27). This strategy reduces the reader's comfort level by visually indicating that these urban fixtures are not similar to what might be found in Madrid. Quotation marks repeatedly appear as a reminder to the reader that this is a New York taxi, metro, or cafeteria, thus bringing attention to the very experience of travel, its surprises, and cultural differences. Just as *Pruebas de Nueva York* asks readers to leave behind comfortable definitions of certain terms, it also underlines one of the fundamentals of translation that all translators know too well: regardless of how similar or related they may be, "languages are never identical" (Bassnett, *Translation* 3). *Pruebas de Nueva York* takes the reader beyond the layman's idea that translation is a straightforward process in which one language transfers into another.

In the pages of *Pruebas de Nueva* York, readers are not disappointed to find the jazz-age image of the city that was most likely familiar to them.

"Snobs"[32] (32), "flapper" (47), "jazz" (66), and "cabaret" (67)[33] all appear within the collection without an immediate explanation. While the text resists incorporating these already familiar terms into its language by offsetting them with quotation marks, it does continue one of the objectives shared by both travel and translation to expand linguistic and cultural horizons. The addition of "business" (37) augments Moreno Villa's readers' New York vocabulary and knowledge. It is accompanied by with the Spanish *negocio* in Roman type and a relatively lengthy explanation:

> Como las Universidades tienen mucho de "business", de negocio (otra herejía para oídos españoles), ni el rector ni los presidentes de las Facultades, se oponen jamás a lo que puede constituir ingreso para ellas. Si el público solicita mañana otra enseñanza y paga por ella, buscan locales y profesores. (37)

> [Since the universities have a lot of *negocio*—"business" (another insult to Spanish ears)—neither the vice chancellor nor the department heads ever oppose what could be profitable for them. If tomorrow someone asks for another subject and pays for it, they find the space and the professors.]

Not only is "business" incompatible with the university structure in the Spanish context, but the sound of the word is also portrayed as disturbing. Again, this gesture not only emphasizes the cultural difference between New York and Spain, but also nudges the reader away from gaining a sympathetic view of New York. Thus Moreno Villa, as a traveler, writer, and translator, overtly displays his interpretation of the scene.

The university atmosphere of the city was familiar to Moreno Villa, as that is where he retreated after his separation from Florence. As quoted earlier, he sought the company of compatriots resident in New York, most of whom were professors at local universities. Through the "business" of the university or the entrepreneurial characteristics of the U.S. university system that continuously sought ways to expand its curricular offerings, he was able to return to his art and writing with a productive revitalization and the opportunity to reach a non-Spanish-speaking audience through the assistance of a U.S. university professor and his translation work. This

---

32 "Snobs" is a word that Moreno Villa uses in *Vida en claro* to describe Dalí's life in the United States: "Hoy vive en los Estados Unidos dedicado a pasmar a los *snobs* con sus extravagancias y payasadas" [Today he lives in the United States dedicated to amazing the "snobs" with his extravagances and slapstick] (112).

33 "Cabaret" is not italicized or in quotation marks in *Vida en claro* (126).

demonstrates the complexities of Moreno Villa's relationship with the city in that the benefits of his connection to the university milieu are slighted or portrayed negatively by his inability to produce a Spanish word to adequately describe the dynamics of university life. As words are not injected neutrally into language, translation is an opportunity to sculpt opinions about another language and culture.

In general, the preference for quotation marks, as opposed to italics, calls attention to the sound of a word coming from an English speaker or the foreignness of the word as pronounced by a native Spanish speaker. Both techniques give a sense of orality to the text and validity to Moreno Villa's experience as a witness of New York. In addition, it adds humor for readers who understand both Spanish and English. Moreno Villa is not alone in his initial concern about embarrassing himself because of his deficiency in English. Language is a frequent preoccupation for most conscientious travelers who are well aware that "speaking the language of others is enormously enriching but it can also be deeply humiliating" (Cronin 3). Like other texts that form part of Iberian literature in New York, knowledge of both English and Spanish offers another level of appreciation. Throughout *Pruebas de Nueva York*, English words appear misspelled in quotation marks or italicized. According to Moreno Villa, most writers from Spain did not cross the Gulf Stream but rather the "goof stream" (8) and use a "map" (26) for cleaning instead of a mop. These examples are not only notable for their humor but also because the sounds of Spanish in English are accentuated if read aloud as English words pronounced according to Spanish phonetics. In addition, in a discussion about the homes of New Yorkers, the standard Spanish word "confort" (21) is placed within quotation marks to call attention to the Spanish pronunciation of the English "comfort." Further on the topic of New Yorkers' dwellings, *Pruebas de Nueva York* lists them as "apartement" (18) and "apartements" (20). Some readers might identify "apartement" as the French word, while others might detect Moreno Villa's reluctance to use the widely accepted Spanish word *piso*, which refers, but is not limited to, urban apartments. Moreover, *apartamento* in Spanish often describes a small *piso* or a vacation home. On the other hand, "apartement" could have simply been an attempt to humorously add a Spanish flair to the English word. Later the inclusion of "apartments" (52) perhaps demonstrates Moreno Villa's progress with the English language while still indicating the difference between New York urban dwellings and in Madrid by the use of italics.[34]

34 In *Vida en claro* the Spanish word is used surrounded by quotation marks: "Llegamos a Nueva York. La familia tenía dos "apartamentos" en Park-Avenue" [We arrived in New York. The family had two "apartments" on Park Avenue] (*Vida en claro*

These choices visually mark up the text and phonetically emphasize Moreno Villa's foreignness and distance from the English language. They highlight his Spanishness, show his bumpy experience in New York, and justify his initial concerns about the linguistic situation. His translation of New York bears traces of his romantic separation from Florence. *Pruebas de Nueva York* maintains Moreno Villa's role as an outsider by leaving foreign pronunciation in the text, while showing his readers a glimpse of what happens to language when one moves beyond the comforts of one's own. The essays bring readers more than just descriptions of New York through showing how much is at stake linguistically in travel via a marked-up text. Even though there is a distance from the English language, there is also a reliance on or an attachment to English in writing Moreno Villa's New York for Spanish readers, highlighting his role as both Traveler and Translator, which should come as no surprise given his enduring tendency to work between several media.

In the preface to *Pruebas de Nueva York*, Moreno Villa surrenders his command over the direction of his New York by fusing his methodological approach with the use of photographic language that highlights the draft stage of production. Marking up the text with excessive quotation marks and italics gives readers access to Moreno Villa's concern for the meaning of words and produces an underlying anxiety that the words used are a forced choice calling attention to the tension between the narrator and language. Jorge Luis Borges, a writer deeply dedicated to translation, said that we publish in order to stop writing drafts. These words ring particularly true for translators, many of whom are hesitant to claim that they ever reach a final version of a translation. The lack of commitment to *Pruebas de Nueva York* as a final version speaks to Moreno Villa's awareness of the complexities of language, especially in travel writing, and recalls the narrative technique of Felipe Alfau's *Chromos* (1990), in which the writer character García has plans for the first-person narrator to translate his novel that unfolds in New York into English in order to publish: "but what I was really thinking is that you might help me with the English translation. I will show you some other parts I have already written out, even if they still need a little polishing" (34). What is striking about this proposal is that the first-person narrator, as translator of García's novel, is to be also an editor or

127). The alternation between italics and quotation marks for certain words such as "flapper" and "good sport" (40) underlines the constant negotiation still underway as to how Moreno Villa wants to accept these unique English terms in his writing while at the same time providing a seamless text. In doing so, he is making the reader aware of his work as a translator of New York.

even co-author, as he will assist in the making of the novel. Whether their time in the city lasts for weeks or a lifetime, the writing of both Alfau and Moreno Villa thrives on translational contexts that derive from the unique dynamic between New York and the Spanish language. The situations experienced by them or their characters surface as the tensions between languages emerge, especially when what they experience in one language tries to come through in another. The dominant presence of English in Spanish or Spanish sprinkled with English advances thoughts on language and how it works especially in multilingual situations. Consequently, the work of Moreno Villa and Alfau shies away from claiming a finalized product, suspending writing at the processional draft stage so familiar to translators and their literary activity.

Beyond Spanish and English

In addition to his relationship with a New Yorker, Moreno Villa's conversations with friends who had been professors at Columbia University for some time might have offered him a magnified idea of what it is like to live in an environment in which Spanish and English intertwine. As noted earlier, translations of texts about Iberian intellectual and cultural figures would be one example of the collaboration between Moreno Villa and the Columbia group. The dynamics of language could have also been on his mind given that he visited New York City when many languages flooded the streets and many of the city's residents were foreign-born. A glance at the table of contents of the 1924 publication *Around the World in New York* by Konrad Bercovici provides a sense of the multiple languages of the city during the decade. Observations of how these populations navigated the city, combined with Moreno Villa's own contemporaneous experience, do not overwhelm the pages of *Pruebas de Nueva York* as the text attempts to offer quick and concise statements about the city. Moreno Villa succinctly comments on the distinguishing factor that the migrant population brought to North America: "civilización de emigrados: ahí debe buscarse el secreto de la civilización norteamericana" [emigrant civilization: that's where the secret of the North American civilization should be sought] (42).

Although *Pruebas de Nueva York* frequently returns to the conflicts between the Spanish and, as Moreno Villa calls them, "Yanqui" spirits, the multilingual environment of New York City streets impacts his writing. Its most meaningful contribution is not necessarily as subject matter but rather as a provocation for Moreno Villa to portray a multilingual environment by engaging the languages of his own repertoire. Moreno Villa notes: "He conversado con puritanos, con anglosajones de cara limpia y espíritu democrático, con obreros españoles, franceses, italianos; con intelectuales de todos los países" [I've talked with Puritans; with Anglo-Saxons with clean faces and democratic spirits; with Spanish, French, and Italian workers; with intellectuals from every country] (45). Whether or not these conversations actually took place and in which language they were conducted is unknown; exchanges with several national groups would not be foreign to Moreno Villa since the Residencia de Estudiantes hosted visitors from several countries during his time there. He was ready to thrive in such a diverse environment, primed by his four-year stay in Germany as a student at the Universität Freiburg.

More than 20 years after his studies abroad, Moreno Villa repeatedly asks in *Vida en claro*, "¿Qué sentido tiene dentro de mi vida la estancia en Alemania?" [What does my stay in Germany mean for my life?] (69). He traveled there to study chemistry in preparation to work for his family's wine business; however, this pursuit became less of a priority as he was seduced by humanistic interests. He arrived in Freiburg with no knowledge of German, but within three months he was able to speak the language and understand the lectures at the university (*Vida en claro* 60).[35] Learning a language is of course one of the immediate outcomes of his stay abroad, as Moreno Villa himself notes:

Por lo pronto, adquirí un idioma. Y no un idioma de mozo de hotel o de cicerone, sino de Universidad, es decir, de profundidad, que me reveló un mundo muy distinto del español y me permitió traducir, esto es, introducir en España algunas finas manifestaciones de ese mundo. (*Vida en claro* 69)

[For one thing, I learned a language. And not the language of a bellhop or a guide, but rather a university language. In other words, a profound language, which revealed to me a world that was very different than the Spanish one, and allowed me to translate, that is to say, to introduce Spain to some fine publications of that world.]

---

35 Here is an account of Moreno Villa's initial encounter and adaptation in Germany: "Todo era desconocido: la lengua, el carácter de las gentes, sus costumbres, sus comidas, hasta sus camas. Palabra por palabra, gota a gota, fuí tragándome materialmente aquel idioma de estampidos ensartados y garabateos hiperbáticos, entre sorbos de té, mordiscos a las salchichas y unturas de mermelada al pan mantequillado. La mesa de comer fué mi primera clase de idioma" [It was all new: the language, the people, their habits, their food, and even their beds. Word by word, drop by drop, I physically swallowed that language of strung booms and hyperbaton scribbles, between sips of tea, bites of sausages, and spreads of jam on buttered bread. The dining table was my first language class] (*Vida en claro* 59–60).

While he would eventually translate a number of books from German into Spanish—such as *Der Abenteurer und die Sängerin* [The Adventurer and the Singer] by Hugo von Hofmannsthal, which he handed over to the Valencian writer Federico García Sanchiz (*Vida en claro* 64)[36]—it could be argued that German was just part of the new language that Moreno Villa acquired during his time away from Spain. In *Vida en claro* he confesses to having detached himself from Germans to spend most of his time with people from England and countries other than Germany (*Vida en claro* 65). This international group of students from other European cities, such as Prague and Davos, as well as from Canada and England, prepared him for the intellectual environment he would eventually encounter at the Residencia de Estudiantes. Together they read and discussed the great works of notable writers, such as Omar Khayyam, Johann Wolfgang von Goethe, Heinrich Heine, Friedrich Schiller, Ludwig Uhland, Miguel de Cervantes, Charles Baudelaire, Paul Verlaine, Edgar Allen Poe, Novalis, Gerhart Hauptmann, Leo Tolstoy, Stendhal, and Gustave Flaubert, Gabriele D'Annunzio, Giacomo Leopardi, and Anatole France. To accompany their syllabus, they listened to the music of Beethoven, Wagner, and Strauss.

All serious translators know that the demands of translation require one to have knowledge that exceeds the acquisition of two separate languages. Thus, although he clearly identifies work on actual translation projects and the benefits they would have for readers of Spanish, the absence of the word "alemán" [German] from Moreno Villa's assessment of the fruits of his trip to Germany is significant; instead, he uses the more general term "idioma" [language] (*Vida en claro* 69). This gesture coupled with his withdrawal from the locals and subsequent immersion in an international community engaged in readings of humanistic texts suggest that he too understood the complexities of translation and the way in which his travels not only brought him to the German language but also to a body of knowledge that would guide his future. Moreno Villa later expressed his dissatisfaction with his initial assessment: "Lo que quiero es saber si Alemania ha influido en mi destino, en mi vida. Y a esto respondo categóricamente que sí. Ya lo veremos" [What I want to know is if Germany has influenced my destiny, my life. I categorically answer "Yes." We'll see] (70).

About 17 years after his stay in Germany, in 1927, on his return voyage across the Atlantic, Moreno Villa used the words "Estados Unidos" to creatively explain to Spanish readers the fundamentals of the characteristics

36 A Spanish translation of this title does not figure among those published by Moreno Villa.

that drive the United States. The "E" stands for "ENERGÍA, ESFUERZO, EFICIENCIA" [energy, effort, efficiency] (47). The "U" stands for the concepts of "UNIFORMIDAD, UNIVERSALIDAD" [UNIFORMITY, UNIVERSALITY] as well as the German "UMGESTALTUNG," which Moreno Villa explains to mean "transformación, reorganización" [transformation, reorganization] (48): "No podía faltar la palabra alemana en este triángulo de conceptos radicales, como no faltan raíces germanas en el idioma ni en las costumbres de Norteamérica" [The German word must be in this triangle of radical concepts, just as German roots are in North American language and customs] (48). The multilingual environment of New York leads him to rely on his own multilingualism within a text intended for a Spanish-speaking audience. German vocabulary helps him to articulate the concepts that unite the North American conglomeration of people from all over the world:

> El yanqui tenía que trasformar todo lo recibido. Tenía que voltearlo, revolverlo y hasta ponerlo del revés (*umkchren*); tenía que rehacer (*umschaffen*); tenía que trasegar y refundir (*umgiessen*); tenía que talar, destroncar (*umhauen*); tenía que derribar, tumbar (*umstossen, umstürzen*); que cambiar (*umwälzen*), etc. La U alemana era indispensable en sus cifras y en la trinidad de sus conceptos. (48)[37]

> [The Yankees had to alter everything they got. They had to turn it, return it, and even put it upside down; they had to do it again (*umschaffen*); they had to switch it around and transfer it (*umgiessen*); they had to cut it down, chop it off (*umhauen*); they had to knock down, knock over (*umstossen, umstürzen*); change (*umwälzen*), etc. The German U was essential in their initials and the trinity of their concepts.]

Although the German reader would note the mistakes in Moreno Villa's use of the language, the incorporation of German, in writing about an environment in which many languages populate the soundscape, transports Moreno Villa's readers to a multilingual text while at the same time defining what unites a vastly diverse group of people. Moreover, this example shows that Moreno Villa's writing of New York exceeds the communication of detailed descriptions of a fascinating city by expressing how the language itself can also portray this environment.

---

37 Moreno Villa misspells some of these German words. They should be spelled *umkehren* instead of *umkchen*, *umschaffen* should be *umschiffen*. *Umgiessen* and *umstossen* should also be *Umgießen* and *Umstoßen* but this could be due to printing issues.

Pruebas de Nueva York does not assign a single national language to reign over the city. The operations of the city do not rely on a specific verbal language though there is a language that leads to success: "Poco a poco va viendo luego que el acento principal de la ciudad es eso: poderío comercial" [Little by little it becomes apparent that the dominant accent of the city is that: business power] (31). Such defiance of a national language extends to other examples:

> Se nota que los americanos tienen una facilidad enorme para retener cifras y detalles prácticos. Sin ser un detective se llega a concluir que se debe a los muchos números de calles, casas, *apartments* y teléfonos que han de utilizar al día. (52)

> [You can tell that Americans have an enormous ability to retain numbers and practical details. You don't have to be a detective to come to the conclusion that this is due to the many numbers of streets, houses, *apartments*, and telephones that you need every day.]

On the one hand, the substitution of numbers for what carefully selected words do in Spanish is striking to Moreno Villa. On the other, while facilitating everyone's successful navigation of the city, this accommodation also separates city dwellers in that they need not communicate with one another in order to locate a specific site (*Pruebas de Nueva York* 52).

Numbers are not the only aspect of New York life that make the city accessible and navigable to its residents and visitors. In the absence of a national language, Moreno Villa looks for other factors that unite New Yorkers. In doing so, he returns to the first sounds that would eventually lead him to New York:

> No puedo figurarme cómo serían los Estados Unidos sin "jazz". Creo que es una de las cosas que más unifican su fisonomía. Es posible que este sello que pone la raza negra a las múltiples razas de los Estados Unidos sea momentáneo, transitorio; pero nadie sabe las derivaciones que trae una influencia momentánea si es fuerte. (66)

> [I can't imagine what the United States would be like without "jazz." I think it's one of the things that best brings together its appearance. This stamp that the black race puts on the multiple races in the United States might be momentary, temporary, but you never know what kind of derivations a momentary influence can bring about if it is powerful.]

Music constitutes the fabric that brings together the diverse population of the United States. The accessibility of jazz penetrated the poetry that

Moreno Villa would write as a result of his trip to New York and would likewise introduce Spanish verse to new sounds. If one of the main tasks of translation is to "allow readers to have access to texts that would otherwise be incomprehensible to them" (Bassnett, *Translation* 169) and to expand readers' ideas about language and the uses of their own idiom, then Moreno Villa, as a traveler and translator, gave his audience a New York through the very sounds of language. Jazz gave him access to New York and the confidence to boldly inject his verse with incomparable spontaneity and intensity.

Poetry Notes

An author of more than ten books of poetry, José Moreno Villa first published his verse in book form in 1913. *Jacinta la pelirroja*, his sixth and best collection of poetry and one of the major works of Spanish avant-garde literature, not only receives more critical attention than his other poetry collections but also more than *Pruebas de Nueva York* (Huergo 17).[38] Each of the two parts of *Jacinta la pelirroja* contains 20 poems accompanied by scattered black-and-white line drawings. The two parts differ in tone. In the first, the language is fiery and full of action, and the poet addresses his lover Jacinta directly. In contrast, the second part, "Jacinta es iniciada en la poesía" [Jacinta is Initiated into Poetry], is contemplative and unhurried, and Jacinta is absent until the final poems, sealing the collapse of the love affair.[39] *Jacinta la pelirroja* is most often read as "la crónica poética de la relación amorosa que Moreno Villa mantuvo con una joven norteamericana" [a poetic chronicle of the amorous relationship that Moreno Villa had with a young North American woman] (Ballesteros and Neira 17). This statement, although not inappropriate, flattens the linguistic vivacity of the text in favor of biographical notes. Moreno Villa's writing, as seen in *Pruebas de Nueva York*, not only tests the language of a visual medium that was enjoying intense vitality, but also an

---

38 Miranda-Barreiro also speaks about the attention given to Moreno Villa's poetry (20).

39 In *Vida en claro*, Moreno Villa identifies three sections: "Está compuesto de tres partes: una, dedicada a los encuentros y descubrimientos con Jacinta; otra, a iniciarla en la poesía mediante algunos poemas difíciles, y la última, al rompimiento. Todo ello alegremente, es decir, sin melancolía. El verso es bastante quebrado y con tendencia a ser hablado, no cantado" [(The book) has three parts: one dedicated to the encounters and discoveries with Jacinta; another to her initiation into poetry with some difficult poems; and the last to the breakup. All of it happily, in other words, free of melancholy. It is a verse that is quite broken up and with a tendency to be spoken, not sung] (154).

audible one that invigorates his poetry. These poems, enlivened with the dynamism of jazz, brought new sounds and energy to the Spanish language, marking "una innovación signifitiva" [a significant innovation] in Iberian poetry (Ciplijauskaité 53).

While Moreno Villa's New York prose tried to eliminate excess words and unnecessary reflection, his poems, as José Francisco Cirre observes, are free of any kind of "sensiblería idealizante y los tortuosos vericuetos de la cursilería. La niebla retórica ha sido barrida del horizonte y las cosas surgen con la hermosura de su luz original sin tópicos enfermizos ni acrobacias virtuosistas" [idealizing sentimentality and the tortuous intricacies of affectation. The rhetorical fog has been erased from the horizon and things come out with the beauty of their original light without sickly clichés and virtuoso acrobatics] (66). This time, the abrupt endings of poems and the reduction of words to their dominant sounds slim down language and break all the traditions of Spanish poetry (Ciplijauskaité 49). Where *Pruebas de Nueva York* offers a guide to Moreno Villa's approach to writing the essays that follow, it is not until the publication of *Vida en claro* that Moreno Villa offers reflection on this collection of poetry: "quise apariciera algo del espíritu y la forma sincopada de 'jazz', que me embriagó en Norteamérica" [I wanted to do something with the spirit and syncopated form of "jazz," which fascinated me in North America] (354). An explicit reference to the sources of inspiration does nothing more than confirm for readers the reliance on another artistic medium that is clearly present in the verses themselves. Biruté Ciplijauskaité suggests that, in order to achieve such celebratory innovation in the verse of *Jacinta la pelirroja*, Moreno Villa utilizes Cubist techniques as several of the poems present "un solo elemento visto desde ángulos diferentes que recuerdan el nuevo procedimiento de pintura" [a single element seen from different angles that recall the new painting process] (54). Reading these poems as Cubist fits the contemporaneous artistic climate and Moreno Villa's role as a painter and his commitment to several art forms, but the language of yet another medium shines through these poems as demonstrated in the compact and swift opening poem "I. Bailaré con Jacinta la pelirroja" [I. I'll Dance with Jacinta the Redhead]:

> Eso es, bailaré con ella
> el ritmo roto y negro
> del jazz. Europa por América.
> Pero hemos de bailar si se mueve la noria,
> y cuando los mirlos se suban al chopo de
> la vecina.
> Porque, —esto es verdad—

cada rito exige su capilla.
¿No, Jacinta?
Oh, Jacinta, pelirroja, peli-peli-roja
pel-pel-peli-pelirrojiza.
Qué bonitos, qué bonitos, oh, qué bonitos
son, sí, son, tus dos, dos, dos, bajo las tiras
de dulce encaje hueso de Malinas.
Oh, Jacinta,
bien, bien mayor, bien supremo.
Ya tenemos el mirlo arriba,
y la noria del borriquillo, gira. (77–78)

[Oh yes, I will dance with her
broken and black jazz
rhythm. Europe for America.
We dance if the Ferris wheel spins,
and when the blackbirds fly up the neighbor lady's
                                                 black poplar.
Because—it's the real thing—
each rite needs its chapel.
Right, Jacinta?
Oh, Jacinta, redhead, red-red-head
Rah-rah-red-reddish head.
How pretty, how pretty, oh, how pretty
they are, yes, they are, your two, two, two under the straps
of sweet lace Malinas's bone.
Oh, Jacinta,
good, greater good, supreme good.
We now have the blackbird up above,
and the little ass's Ferris wheel, spins.]

In the poem's first line, the use of the future tense in the verb *bailaré* [I will dance] expresses the poet's energy and determination to have fun with Jacinta, to become part of the landscape, and leave behind Europe for America via the "ritmo roto y negro del jazz" [broken and black rhythm of jazz]. Leaning on this new music communicates a playful love as the poet teases Jacinta in a moment of intense emotion. Repetition and alliteration contribute to the musicality of the poem, inspired not only by the sounds of jazz, but also by the heightened passion of their love. The poet refers to her "dos, dos, dos" [two, two, two] but leaves the rest to the reader's imagination. The ascending flight of the "mirlo" [blackbird] as the poem progresses is a metaphor for the lovers' rising passion. This flood of emotions leaves the poet susceptible to subsequent transformations and is the vehicle that moves him forward. Likewise, years later in *Vida en claro*, Moreno Villa speaks to the impact of jazz on his poetry and uses it as a metaphor to describe the relationship between Europe and the United States:

"Bailaré con Jacinta la Pelirroja" indica un desenfado voluntario, un elocuente ¡basta ya! a los trémolos del coleante romanticismo, pero, además, confirma que toda Europa, frenéticamente entregada al "jazz", pide que la rapte América. Tal cosa puede tomarse hoy por un presagio. Europa está siendo raptada. (156)

["I'll dance with Jacinta the Redhead" shows a voluntary freedom, an eloquent "basta, basta" to the tremolos of nagging romanticism, but also confirms that all of Europe, frenziedly devoted to "jazz," is asking to be kidnapped by America. Such a thing would be considered an omen today.]

As with his relationship to photography, Moreno Villa was never known to be a musician, but music had a central role in his surroundings. At the Residencia de Estudiantes, it was not unusual to hear his "discos de fox y de zarzuelas antiguas" [foxtrot and old opera records] playing in his room (Saenz de la Calzada 114). In "El Arte Nuevo y el jazz: el cifrado del siglo XX" (2005), Juan Herrero-Senés collects and discusses articles on jazz that appeared in contemporary periodicals, many of the same ones that published the work of Moreno Villa and his peers. Music, too, was central to Moreno Villa's relationship with his fiancée Florence. On the night they first met, she later went to look for him at his place and brought him to an apartment where an international group was listening to music (*Vida en claro* 123–24). For Moreno Villa, music became a language that would define not only New York but also their relationship, which is revealing, given the fact that he was not fluent in English.[40] As a result, in his poetic rendering of their time together, the poet uses the sounds of jazz to communicate with his lover.

As the incorporation of an iconic New York sound sculpts the verses, the poet maintains a proximity to Jacinta that isolates the two lovers and

---

40 Moreno Villa offers details about how he and Florence managed English and Spanish: "Ella sabía bastante de español y me traducía las palabras de los demás o las mías al inglés" [She knew a good amount of Spanish and translated for me what the others were saying or what I said into English] (*Vida en claro* 124). He adds: "Quiso enseñarme inglés y todas las noches nos reuníamos en su casa para leer" [She tried to teach me English and every night we got together at her house to read] (125). These details are significant in that they provide a look at what might have been the soundtrack of Moreno Villa's New York and encourage new readings of his work.

rejects others. For example, in "IV. Y el chofer volvía la cara" [IV. The Taxi Driver Turned Around] the poet and his lover share a nocturnal cab ride in "Parque central de Nueva York, / cinco minutos cruzando la noche," [Central Park New York, / five minutes crossing the night], a frolicsome moment comes to an abrupt end when the "curioso y rabioso" [curious and furious] taxi driver turns around (82). This poem, like many others in the first part of *Jacinta la pelirroja*, creates distance from the reader, receiving its inspiration from situations that only Jacinta and the poet fully understand. This mystery deepens as the poet retreats deeper into himself as the collection progresses.

The poems of the book's second half lack the excitement and motion of the first part and explore instead the feelings of the aching poet. He is alone with his words, trying to make sense of his lost love. Jacinta is gone and the only thing that remains is poetry. For example, "III. Causa de mi soledad" [III. Why I'm Lonely] discusses how the poet compensates for this loss:

> No es afán de apartamiento
> sino atención al secreto.[41]
> Soy yo mi miedo.
>
> No es orgullo ni desdén,
> sino hambre de conocer.
> Soy pico y pared.
>
> La solución de los otros
> no me basta; siendo asombro.
> Soy mi piloto.

41 Moreno Villa explains this line in *Vida en claro*: "Atención al secreto, es decir, estar alerta para entrar y descubrir lo que las cosas y el mundo espiritual tienen oculto a la vista corriente, pasajera. Por eso digo que quisiera haber tenido esos varios oficios o actividades. Me aparto, pues, para llegar a la intimidad de las cosas. En primer término, a la de la poesía" [Pay attention to secrets. In other words, be alert to enter and discover what things and the spiritual world are hiding from the normal, passing view. That's why I say that I wanted to have had those several trades or activities. I separate myself to get to the intimacy of things. First of all, to that of poetry] (*Vida en claro* 204–05). Moreno Villa's openness is notable and an ideal attribute that translators should possess. In the following paragraph, Moreno Villa connects the ability to be accepting of new outlooks with the circumstances that present themselves: "Otro aspecto que no traté antes al hablar del libro es su absoluta dependencia de las circunstancias. Si no hubiese conocido a Jacinta y no hubiera hecho el viaje a Nueva York, no existirían los poemas que lo integran" [Another thing that I didn't deal with before when talking about the book is its absolute dependency on the circumstances. If I hadn't meet Jacinta and I hadn't gone to New York, the poems that make up the book wouldn't exist] (205).

Quisiera morir habiendo
sido poeta, carpintero,
pintor, filósofo, amante y torero.

¡Ay! y cantor negro
de un jazz que siento
a través de diez capas del suelo. (112)

[Not for the sake of departing
but for caring for the secret.
I'm my own fear.

It's not out of pride or disdain,
but of hunger for knowledge.
I'm the pick and the wall.

What fixes the others
isn't enough for me; being amazed.
I'm my own pilot.

I'd like to die having
been a poet, a carpenter,
a painter, philosopher, lover, and bullfighter.

Ah! and a black jazz
singer who I feel
through ten layers underground.]

In an effort to persevere, the poet takes control of his feelings—"Soy mi piloto" [I'm my own pilot]—and shares that he would like to end his days having been a poet, a carpenter, a painter, a philosopher, a lover, and a bullfighter, ending with a jazz singer. Unlike these other occupations, that of the jazz singer embodies the true emotion which the poet seeks in order to leave a lasting impression. Arturo del Villar suggests that the poet chooses the jazz singer in order to "dejar boquiabiertos a los españoles" [shock Spaniards] (6). Besides reinforcing the typical images of New York shown abroad, this proposal fails to scrutinize the reasons for which the jazz singer would be the true expression of the poet's emotion. Moreno Villa portrays New York as a city that is heavily saturated with a calculated numerical language, one that in its efforts to give an opportunity to all individuals ultimately isolates them from one another. Jazz, a music that constantly renews itself through improvisation, however, is the language that unites New Yorkers and gives coherence to Moreno Villa's New York experience.

The poet eventually realizes that his verses are the only thing by which to remember this affair. The short poem "VI." reads:

Ya no vuela, ya no canta,
ya no es pájaro siquiera.
No es negro, pardo ni blanco,
no es sombra ni es entelequia.
Si es pájaro, es mi pájaro
insensible a la escopeta,
inmortal, porque su cuerpo
es espíritu, mi letra. (116)

[It no longer flies, nor sings,
nor is it merely a bird.
It's not black, dark gray nor white,
it's not a shadow nor an entelechy.
If it's a bird, it's my bird,
numb to any shotgun,
immortal, because its body
is spirit, my script.]

This time, the bird is a metaphor for a fleeting love. Although the love affair
is gone, what remains is an unvanquishable memory. That memory is his
script, his word, his poetry. The poetry itself becomes memory contained
in its very verses. And unlike an identifiable image that so often guided
visions of New York, for Moreno Villa, the city turns out to be a memory and
the feeling provoked by that memory is his poetry. As a result, New York is
pure emotion in the same sense that, only a few years after Moreno Villa's
New York trip, Sebastià Gasch would speak of jazz as a "ritmo primario y
puro, descarnado, virgen de la hojarasca y reducido a lo esencial" [basic
and pure rhythm, thinned down, virgin of the fallen leaves and reduced to
what's essential] (qtd. in Herrero-Senés 322). In his discussion of *arte nuevo*
and jazz, Juan Herrero-Senés states that "lo caractéristico del jazz residiría
en que es sólo música" [what's characteristic of jazz resides in the fact that
it's just music] (322). Thus, confronted with the emotional struggles of a
failed relationship and an unfamiliar setting, jazz, a form of rebellion,
allowed the poet to determine that the experience transformed would
only be poetry to the extent that Moreno Villa himself, years later, felt a
distance from his New York verses and their originality: "Al cabo de los
años, mirando esta poesía como si fuera de otro, la considero más directa,
fresca, libre, juvenil y jugosa que la de todos los poetas de mi tiempo"
[After all these years, looking at this poetry as if it belonged to someone
else, I consider it more direct, fresh, free, youthful, and juicy than that of
any other poet of my time] (*Vida en claro* 157).

New York in a Few Words

The intensity of Moreno Villa's New York experience unleashed numerous possibilities for his writing. On the one hand, his determination to write New York for an audience in Spain was an opportunity to recover travel writing and poetry from Impressionism and Romanticism, artistic movements of the previous century. In an effort to distance himself from his work, through the influence of jazz and photography, he pushed his writing into a new era that was in sync with contemporary artistic discourses. On the other hand, his slim knowledge of English put him in tune with the other sounds of New York, leading in some cases to the invocation of his own multilingualism. Through the play of these dynamics in writing, readers of *Pruebas de Nueva York* and *Jacinta la pelirroja* encounter much more than mere descriptions of the city. They are turned on to the artistic climate of New York and the city's many languages during their journey through the pages of the book. Thus, the traces of these techniques in the text reveal Moreno Villa himself not only as a traveler but also as a serious translator who remained open to the possibilities that presented themselves to him.

Reading *Jacinta la pelirroja* as a lyrical autobiography would not be off-target, but such an approximation of the text should not conceal the value of the verse as writing that has much to say about a significant turn in poetry and ways of depicting a city, and a deep impact on Iberian literary production. In fact, Moreno Villa himself speaks to the autobiographical nature of the poems:

> "Jacinta la Pelirroja" es un libro auténtico porque brota de una experiencia absoluta concreta y personal; la de mis amores con Jacinta. Pero no por esto sólo, sino por el tono empleado en él, sin parecido con el de ningún otro poeta conocido. Ya he dicho que lo sacado por mí de aquella aventura fué mi liberación de la melancolía romántica. Me levanté a un plano vívido, confiado, por encima del abatimiento en que pude caer. Me situé como en una tribuna de hipódromo, al aire libre y al sol, o como en el interior embriagante de un cabaret de Harlem, el barrio neoyorkino de los negros. (*Vida en claro* 145)

> [*Jacinta the Redhead* in an authentic book because it comes from an absolute concrete and personal experience: my love affair with Jacinta. But that's not the only reason, it's also because of its tone, which is nothing like any other known poet. I have already said that what I got out of that adventure was my escape from romantic melancholy. I rose to a lively, confident level, above the depression into which I could have fallen. I situated myself in the grandstand at the racetrack, in the

open air and sun, or in an intoxicating cabaret in Harlem, the black
neighborhood of New York.]

Referring to Florence as Jacinta further problematizes the divisions between
his life and fiction. Using her poetic name in his autobiography does not
confirm that the poems of *Jacinta la pelirroja* tell a true story, but rather
speaks to Moreno Villa's ability to overcome the heartbreaking loss of a
lover by crystalizing her in a writing that relies on the memory of a defined
moment. Being able to write and tame the pain liberated Moreno Villa from
personal hardship while at the same time giving the Spanish language new
sounds.

While Moreno Villa's poetry encapsulates the development and end of
a relationship with the aid of jazz, in *Pruebas de Nueva York* he was able to
suspend the finality of his New York by consciously employing a number
of tactics to discourage his personal experience from interfering with his
writing. But, since the translator is never neutral and acts of translation
are determined by interpretation, choices, and other motives, the distancing
efforts ultimately failed and Moreno Villa could not untie the attributes of
his fiancée which he intuited were the reasons why her family vetoed their
plans to marry.

In an effort to gain the support of Florence's father for the proposed
marriage, Moreno Villa invites Professor Federico de Onís to mediate one of
their meetings, as a translator. Through the play of at least four languages,
it was during this meeting that a major factor contributing to Florence's
father's opposition of their marriage was revealed:

> Yo intervine alguna vez en alemán, que la familia medio entendía por
> hablar el *yiddish*. No sabiendo por dónde salir el padre de Jacinta, se
> agarró a lo de la nacionalidad mía, y al lugar común de que los judíos
> no podían olvidar lo que hicieron con ellos los españoles. Onís contestó
> que aquéllos eran otros tiempos y que los españoles de hoy no tenían
> aversión al judío, como lo demostraba mi caso. Que en España no era
> como en Alemania. (*Vida en claro* 131)

> [I intervened once in German, which the family partially understood
> because they spoke Yiddish. As a last resort Jacinta's father went for my
> nationality, and the old chestnut that the Jews could not forget what
> the Spaniards did to them. Onís answered that those were other times
> and that today's Spaniards didn't have any problem with Jews, as my
> case showed. Spain wasn't like Germany.]

Although little is known about the biography of Florence, she has been
described as "una joven norteamericana, judía, pelirroja, rica, 'moderna',

interesada en Picasso" [a young, North American, Jewish, a redhead, rich, modern, interested in Picasso] (Pérez de Alaya III). Throughout *Pruebas de Nueva York*, Moreno Villa mentions the Jewish presence in the city, but seldom mentions his own religious affiliation. The fact that he was Spanish carried enough weight to make her parents oppose the marriage.

How does Moreno Villa then respond to his rejection by Florence's father? *Pruebas de Nueva York* repeatedly mentions the Jewish accent of the city. New York is labeled "la metrópoli judía" [the Jewish metropolis] (30), or "una ciudad judía y negociante" [a Jewish and business-minded city] (31). He further explains:

> Siempre he creído que la inquietud es una de las más profundas virtudes y defectos de la raza judía, y por eso veo en Nueva York el prototipo de la ciudad hebrea. Como español y como europeo, rechazo este dinamismo, a pesar de lo conveniente que pueda ser para mí, para el otro y para la Humanidad. (33)

> [I have always thought that restlessness is one of the most profound virtues and defects of the Jewish race, and that is why I see in New York the prototype of the Hebrew city. As a Spaniard and a European, I reject this dynamism, despite how advisable it might be for me, for others, and for humanity.]

Moreno Villa thus detects the dominant Jewish traits of New York and uses them to explain his incompatibility with the city, while simultaneously emphasizing his Spanishness. Instead of refuting the notion put forth by Florence's father, his writing highlights it. Translations are never neutral in that the translator's own views inevitably infiltrate the text and shape the image of the translated culture.

Playing with the struggles within his own relationship, Moreno Villa's essay "X. La niña violenta" [X. The Violent Girl] in *Pruebas de Nueva York*, discusses the women of New York. Referring to them as "niñas" [girls], he attaches the adjective "violentas" [violent] to describe their confidence, intellect, strength, rebellion, intrepidity, physical beauty, liberated dress, and fear of fidelity and motherhood.[42] Most salient is their ability to live carefree in the present (64). The "niña violenta" becomes Moreno Villa's metaphor for New York:

---

42 See Miranda-Barreiro's chapter "Images of the Modern Woman: The Challenge to the Patriarchal Nation" for a lengthy discussion of Moreno Villa's reading of the modern woman of New York in contrast with her Spanish counterpart. Miranda-Barreiro concludes that "the ambiguity of this image reveals the contradictory attitudes towards modernization conveyed" in *Pruebas de Nueva York* (83).

"Pienso en la niña violenta, en la niña violenta que es Nueva York toda, y toda América del Norte" [I'm thinking about the violent girl, about the violent girl that is all of New York, and all of North America] (63). In imagining New York in this way, he is able to exercise control over the city: "Yo lo que hago es incorporar ese concepto; llamarle 'niña' y 'niña violenta' para luego bautizar así a la metrópolis más inquietante y violenta del mundo actual" [What I'm doing is incorporating that concept; calling it "girl" and "violent girl" to then name as such the most disturbing and violent metropolis in the world today] (63). The choice of the verb "bautizar" [to name] is obviously significant in that gives Moreno Villa power over the city from which he was rejected. One way he is able to overcome the disintegration of his relationship, due to presumed religious incompatibility, is through the act of writing and ultimately the play of religiously decorated vocabulary. It is only in the image of the city that he is able to triumph. Writing New York, translating his experience into literature that would crystalize his affair, leads to a victory over his grief and becomes a source of renewal.

Anticipating Lorca

Moreno Villa concludes *Pruebas de Nueva York* with an essay titled "Puntos Negros." Once again, playing with the expectations of his readers and the multiple meanings of this title, "Puntos negros" could indicate obscure things about New York; a revelation of compromising points about the city; physically dark dots, such as a period used in punctuation; or a type of music. An array of choices confronts the reader, just as when the translator brings a text into another language. Moreno Villa asks his readers to be active in their participation and interpretation of the text. The subject of this section is the black community of New York:

> Sin saber por qué, le adjudicaba yo a todo negro que ví el conocimiento del español y, con ello, un cierto parentesco; pero esta falsa emoción, que sin duda tiene su raíz en que Cuba fué nuestra, y que de niño vi negros que castellanizaban y hasta influían en el cante "jondo" con sus "habaneras," "rumbas" y demás, no acaba de seducirme. (65)

> [For no particular reason, I automatically thought that all black people whom I'd see spoke Spanish and because of that I felt a certain kinship with them; but this false emotion—which is undoubtedly is rooted in the fact that Cuba was ours and that as a child I saw black people who spoke Castilian and even influenced the *cante jondo* from Andalusia with their *habaneras*, rhumbas, and more—continued to seduce me.]

Besides Moreno Villa's friendships with professors from Spain who teach in New York City, identification with the black population is the only other moment in *Pruebas de Nueva York* in which he feels camaraderie. This is facilitated, if only momentarily, by the conception that they share a language and musical roots.[43]

After so much displeasure, disgust, agony, revelation, and protest, the poet of Lorca's *Poet in New York* also expresses relief when he reaches Cuba. The line "Iré a Santiago" [I'm going to Santiago] is repeated 19 times in "Son de negros en Cuba" [Blacks Dancing to Cuban Rhythms], the last poem of Lorca's collection (174–77). The frequent use of the future tense in the poem hints at the poet's enthusiasm for his arrival on the Caribbean island. The poem lightens up the deep and dark themes traced throughout the volume. In Cuba the young poet found great relief from the oppression and depression of New York, as noted by his biographers and critics. Like Moreno Villa, Lorca identifies with the blacks in Havana and their musical rhythms, and they remind him too of his home in Andalusia.

What is more, Lorca's poem "King of Harlem" expresses how the New York blacks retain the wisdom of the world. While for Moreno Villa the blacks provided the answer for unifying people of various origins in the United States through jazz, jazz also stood in for the language that was not accessible to him. It gave him the language for his poetry and an outlet for dealing with loss. Moreno Villa's peripheral place within his New York visit is understood through the cultural production of another community in the margins. Jazz as a unifying factor led him to consider the concepts that brought together the amalgam of people in New York. For Moreno Villa, as for the poet of *Poet in New York*, encountering a powerful speck of hope in the black community leads to an uplifting voice that suggests a desire to integrate after so much isolation. As such, the dark spot that concludes the collection is the last period of Moreno Villa's proofs of New York and his affair.

Final Shot

Although his westward transatlantic journey brought an end to his lively romantic relationship, for Moreno Villa this trip and the geographical, cultural, and linguistic divisions it presented ultimately led to imaginative

---

43 In 1925, before to his trip to New York, Moreno Villa wrote about the origins of modern art and the link with Negro art in "Temas de arte. El arte negro, factor moderno" in *El Sol*. See David Miranda-Barreiro's article "Primitivist Modernism and Imperialist Colonialism" (2013) for a broader discussion about primitivist modernism and Iberian authors at large.

beginnings. Jazz, besides being part of the soundtrack of these years, filled the silences between English and Spanish, giving shape to the memory of a love affair, while photography suggested a methodology for showing space through writing in an economical way. As a practitioner and supporter of several artistic media, Moreno Villa carried within himself multiple traditions and their discourses, which provided him with the resources to maintain, rejuvenate, and strengthen his work in trying times. He could have easily uttered the same words that Lorca did when he referred to his New York stay as the most useful experience of his life. A little over 15 years after his visit to New York, Moreno Villa states in his autobiography that: "una gran cosa obtuve de esta verdadera aventura: el triunfo sobre el romanticismo" [I got something big out of this real adventure: a victory over Romanticism] (135). In New York he could play with the languages he knew, and with the new ones that came his way, to find his avant-garde voice. Finally, New York introduced Moreno Villa to the "concepto inglés intraducible, llamado *good sport*" [untranslatable English concept called *good sport*] (*Pruebas de Nueva York* 17), or, as he explained it years later, "la saludable norma de poner buena cara al mal tiempo" [the healthy habit of looking at the good side of something bad] (*Vida en claro* 135). Rafael Ballesteros and Julio Neira believe that the necessity and the difficulty of explaining what had happened in New York forced Moreno Villa to adopt this attitude and to move forward with his work (28). Being a good sport could have aided the kind of self-transformation required to motivate him to write after emotional hardship, but travel and attention to the sounds of New York came to mean translation in a broad sense as a way of writing, through media, with the city as a catalyst for new beginnings. Just as the acquisition of new languages forces us to see the familiar in another way, after his transatlantic voyage, Moreno Villa saw things in Spain in another light (49): "Mi visión de España en América no era ésta; puede que cambie a su vez ahora mi visión de Nueva York desde aquí. ¿Cuántas caras tiene la verdad?" [This wasn't my vision of Spain while in America; perhaps my vision of New York from here will now change. How many sides are there to the truth?] (*Pruebas de Nueva York* 49).

PART III

Travel in Translation:
Julio Camba and Josep Pla
Write for a Home Audience

Reading from a Distance

In 2012 Antonio Muñoz Molina began the article "Paisajes del idioma" in *El País* with the question: "¿Cómo sería encontrar en el periódico de la mañana un nuevo artículo de Julio Camba, de Josep Pla?" [What would it be like to find an article by Julio Camba or Josep Pla in the morning newspaper?]. It would not be odd for Muñoz Molina's readers to imagine that he is referencing a travel piece by one of these writers. After all, between them, the two writers traveled to well over 20 countries and cities during their careers, and wrote for over a dozen newspapers, often about their visits to places throughout the Iberian Peninsula and beyond.[1] Although Muñoz Molina's article appears in an Iberian daily, a reader in the know might wonder whether he asked this question from Madrid or from New York. Since around 2001 Muñoz Molina has been dividing his time between the two cities, all the while contributing regularly to *El País*. Was he simply wondering what it would be like to read a Camba or Pla article as would, say, a Spanish-language reader in Madrid reading about New York, of which he had only seen a few images, if any? Or was Muñoz Molina overhauling the initial way in which these articles were experienced publicly and imagining a reader in New York, like himself perhaps, waking up to lay eyes on a New York article by Camba or Pla in the day's paper?

The first situation is straightforward; the latter uproots the reader and the text to reduce the distance between the reader and the context of the text's

---

1 His fifth trip to the American continent was to Peru in 1924. Camba wrote for the best-known periodicals in Spain, such as *Diario de Pontevedra*, *España Nueva*, *El País*, *El Radical*, *El Mundo*, *La Tribuna*, *La Vanguardia*, *El Imparcial*, *ABC*, and *El Sol*. He covered the First World War and the stock market crash of 1929. At one point, he was considered the best-paid journalist in Spain.

creation. In other words, the second situation shifts the reader to a place different other than where the texts were first read publicly, but minimizes the distance between the reader and the place read about, bringing the texts back to their place of origin. Muñoz Molina might have also been lamenting the fact that the book form in which we now find Camba's and Pla's texts alters the original context in which they were generally experienced: as periodically published articles leaving their faithful readers eager to receive the arrival of their next words. Nonetheless, Muñoz Molina's words encourage a consideration of a central issue: was he going back in time to the initial context in which these texts were made available to readers? Or was he bringing the texts to the present and wondering how they would be experienced by a readership in a new location? Regardless, Muñoz Molina longs to recuperate the experience of reading a Camba or a Pla text for the first time.

As Theo Hermans reminds us, "translations normally address an audience which is not only linguistically but also temporally and/or geographically removed from that addressed by the source" (qtd. in Polezzi 58). The questions that Muñoz Molina proposes are also asked of translated texts. They speak to the age-old predicament associated with translation: Does the translation bring the text to the reader or the reader to the text? Such circumstances recall Lawrence Venuti's discussion about the strategies of domestication and foreignization: domestication means making the text conform to the culture of the translation language; foreignization means preserving as much of the source text even if it means disregarding conventions of the translation language.[2] Thus, an unpacking of Muñoz Molina's seemingly straightforward question uncovers the relationship between travel texts and translation.

Both Camba and Pla traveled to the predominantly English-speaking New York, although other languages and accents were scattered across the city. In addition, on their journeys and while in the city, they were not completely cut off from Spanish nor Catalan. Their experiences, however, have been transferred to the page in what is visibly Spanish or Catalan and read without consideration for how much translation work their texts present to their readers. In this third and final part of *Translating New York*, I address how Camba's and Pla's writing on New York negotiate between Spanish, Catalan, and English. As representatives of the multilingualism of the Iberian Peninsula and world travelers, Camba and Pla exhibit independence in manners of language in the texts they wrote from abroad for a readership

---

2 Venuti's widespread discussion of domestication and foreignization is largely based on the U.S. perspective of translation, or translation in the anglophone sphere.

of newspapers and books. By contextualizing and examining the strategies, manipulations, struggles, and brilliances of their attempts to write the city, I study what these New York texts say about Camba's and Pla's understanding of the languages in which they wrote and the culture to which they belonged. In this part, I propose that travel writing, like literary translation, has the potential to transform and innovate the translation language, here Spanish or Catalan, in immediate and long-lasting ways, contributing to a new and deeper understanding of Camba's and Pla's work and the significance of this travel opportunity.

From the Iberian Periphery

On December 16, 1884,[3] Julio Camba Andreu was born in Vilanova de Arousa, close to the Atlantic Ocean, in the northwest corner of the Iberian Peninsula. He died a little less than 80 years later in Madrid, on February 28, 1962, after a life that led him to Buenos Aires, Istanbul, Paris, London, Berlin, New York, and several other cities. About 13 years after Camba's birth, on March 8, 1897, Josep Pla i Casadevall was born on the opposite side of the Iberian Peninsula in the town of Palafrugell close to the Mediterranean Sea. Like Camba, Pla also saw much of the world beyond his hometown. He spent his university years in Barcelona, and then traveled to Paris, Madrid, Portugal, Berlin, Great Britain, the Soviet Union, Marseille, Rome, Israel, Cuba, New York, the Middle East, South America, Russia, and many places in between. He died on April 23, 1981, in Llofriu, not 5 kilometers inland from his birthplace.

Both Camba and Pla remained single and childless, leading lives intensely dedicated to writing.[4] They are not widely known as authors of fiction or poetry, but works of this kind are not absent from their *œuvres*. They were authors of life and travel narratives, and each had an incomparable ability to transfer the world around them to the printed page. Of course, this is not to dismiss the role which fiction plays in travel writing. Loredana Polezzi writes

---

3 Silvia Novo Blankenship states that Julio Camba was born on September 16, 1882 (1).

4 This is not to say that they did not enjoy the company of romantic companions. At 24, around 1908, Camba "sufre un grave desengano amoroso" [suffers a serious broken heart], rejected by a woman named Andrea who opted for a "heredero de profesion banquero" [an heir in the banking profession] (López García 78). Alfonso Camín says that "Camba vive solo. No tiene vínculos de familia. No los quiere. Es un gran discípulo de Epicuro. Comer y beber" [Camba lives alone. He doesn't have family ties. He doesn't want them. He's a great disciple of Epicurus. Eat and drink] (qtd. in García Martín, "New York" 12). For a study of Pla's amorous relationships see *Les dones de Josep Pla* by Xavier Febrés (1999).

in *Translating Travel: Contemporary Italian Travel Writing in English Translation* (2001) that "Just as travel crosses boundaries, cultures and languages, so travel writing produces texts which are marked by alterity, by distance, and by multiple allegiances, crossing fact and fiction, autobiography and description, ordinary life and extraordinary adventure" (1). Thus, in travel writing, places are not only described but also reconstructed, reimagined, and interpreted for a distant community of readers, much like literary translation.

Critics and readers alike have generally admired Camba and Pla for their journalistic writing. Just as travel writing is a dynamically hybrid genre, Camba and Pla, too, transcend the restrictions of any generic classification. In fact, Pla himself says that "Camba escriví en els periòdics—gairebé la totalitat dels seus llibres no són res més que articles aplegats en un volum—però periodista, no hou fou mai" [Camba wrote in newspapers—almost all of his books are just articles gathered in a volume—but never ever was he a journalist] (358).[5] Pla's own contributions to literature exceed the limitations of any categorization. In discussing the "impossibility of conventional classification," Monserrat Roser i Puig has noted that for Pla, "the greatest difficulty remains the classification of his peculiar genre: a constant use of first-person accounts of events that paradoxically corresponds neither to reality nor to fiction" (554). Speaking to the dimensions and quantity of Pla's work, Valerie Miles writes that "a political and cultural journalist, travel writer, biographer, memoirist, essayist, novelist, and foodie, whose collected works clock in at more than thirty-thousand pages and thirty-eight volumes—[Pla] was more than just a writer" (2014).

Camba and Pla are also from regions of the Iberian Peninsula where Spanish coexists with other languages. Camba spoke Galician. In 1900, at the age of 16, he wrote his first verses in Galician and Castilian Spanish (López

5 Francisco Fuster García points out that "el gallego fue un escritor vocacional, de formación autodidacta, que no creyó jamás en facultades ni escuelas de periodismo; un superviviente de la pluma que—no lo olvidemos—empezó como 'redactor de mesa' en esas efímeras publicaciones de Madrid de principios de siglo en las que firmar los artículos era todo un privilegio (cobrarlos, un milagro), y al que el éxito sólo le llegó cuando, después de muchos intentos, halló la 'fórmula mágica' en ese género híbrido entre la información y la opinión—la crónica—al que logró llevar a su máxima expresión" [the Galician was a vocational, self-educated writer who never believed in journalism departments or schools. He made a living as a writer who—we mustn't forget—got his start as an "desk editor" on those short-lived publications in Madrid from the beginning of the century in which putting your name on an article was a privilege (getting paid for it, a miracle). He only became successful when, after many attempts, he found "the magic formula" in a hybrid genre somewhere between information and opinion—the chronicle—of which he took full advantage] ("Yo, periodista" 8–9).

García 211) and published them in regional newspapers. However, according to López García, that was the extent of his writing in Galician (208). Nonetheless, Camba's beginnings as a published writer were bilingual. Pla, of course, presents an entirely different case, as he was published in Catalan or Spanish depending on the venue and the year. According to Luisa Cotoner Cerdó, Pla "sólo firmó sus versiones en castellano durante los años de la primera postguerra" [only signed his Castilian versions during the first postwar years] (160). These works were first conceived in Catalan but published in Castilian for obvious reasons (Cotoner Cerdó 160). In some cases, Pla dedicated time to translating his own works, such as *Un senyor de Barcelona*, first published in Castilian in 1945 and later in Catalan in 1951.[6] Pla rejected being referred to as a bilingual writer. Cotoner Cerdó states that he "sólo domina el catalán y que, si escribió en castellano, lo hizo por 'raons alimentàries', es decir, como ganapán" [only mastered Catalan and that if he wrote in Castilian, he did so for "alimentary reasons," in other words, as an odd job in order to eat] (160). Keeping each writer's linguistic profile in mind, not to mention the way in which they might have negotiated through and in other languages while traveling beyond theit native peninsula, a sensitivity surfaces in terms of reading their work. This is especially true of the works they produced while traveling beyond the Iberian Peninsula in situations in which they must have had to use a range of linguistic resources, even if the resulting text appears to be monolingual. At the same time, this linguistic sensitivity is coupled with the creative possibilities that writing new places might ignite. In other words, their travel experiences continuously sensitized them to the nuances of language and the capabilities or shortcomings of their own written language.

Camba and Pla visited a myriad cities, and many of the same cities, and wrote most of them in some form or other. A rapid glance at their respective bibliographies shows that each produced at least one title based on a trip to New York, an honor not extended to all the other places they visited. Camba traveled to the city three times and lived there for more than a year. In contrast, while Pla did not even spend a week in the city during his initial trip, he produced an approximately 200-page book on New York. From Madrid, Camba reached New York twice prior to 1930, when individuals had significantly less access to images of distant places than they do today. Enric Bou, in his chapter "In Transit: Exploring Travelogues" in *Invention of Space: City, Travel and Literature* (2012), reminds us that "those

---

6 See Luisa Cotoner Cerdó's essay "Ética y estética de la autotraducción: una cala en las versiones al castellano de Josep Pla, Joan Perucho y Carme Riera" (2004) for an analysis of Pla's versions of these two texts.

images had to be provided by paintings, travelogues, or public exhibitions (panoramas, World Fairs, etc.)" (169). Thus, Camba wrote for his audience about something vastly unknown. Pla wrote New York years later, when access to images was generally much easier. He traveled to New York in the 1950s, the decade during which "rich and vivid layers of information from foreign lands became readily available and permeated Western societies through picture books, movies, film, and TV documentaries, which provided specific images from distant and idealized landscapes that made the exotic familiar" (Bou 169). Pla's first pages on New York even comment on this accessibility to the city: "les [les imatges] ha [el viatger] vistes moltes vegades en una innombrable quantitat de documents gràfics" [(the traveler) has seen (the images) many times in numerous graphic documents] (*Week-end* 22). Although Pla's text specifically refers to the narrator-traveler, as opposed to a general public, having previously seen images of New York, it should be remembered that throughout the 1950s the circulation of such images might have been less extensive than Bou implies, especially in the postwar Iberian Peninsula where many homes did not yet have refrigerators or televisions (Obiols). Thus, though they wrote decades apart, Camba and Pla provided views of New York for audiences that had possibly never seen a wide array of visual representations of the city.

At the same time, they not only wrote against a lack of visual images of New York, but also against other existing narratives of the city that had been published by Iberian writers before them, not to mention New York texts produced by writers from beyond the peninsula. Whether or not their readers were familiar with these texts, as writers Camba and Pla demonstrated an awareness of the fact that they were contributing to an emerging tradition, that they were in some way writing versions of a common text. Camba first set sail for New York in 1916, the same year that Juan Ramón Jiménez crossed the Atlantic to marry Zenobia Camprubí (1887–1956). Camba's first New York collection, *Un año en el otro mundo*, was published in book form in 1917,[7] as was Jiménez's book of poems *Diario de un poeta recien casado*. Camba's second New York stay in 1929 coincided with Federico García Lorca's visit. Camba even gave a talk at Columbia University on July 17, 1929, a month after Lorca arrived. Other versions of New York that Camba and Pla could have very well known about include, but are not limited to, those of José Moreno Villa, Ramiro de Maeztu, Ramón Pérez de Ayala, and Joaquin Belda.[8] Camba alludes to Jiménez's poem "La luna" from his

---

7 All quotes from *Un año en el otro mundo* are from the 2009 edition.

8 See Leslie Stainton's "Oh Babilonia!" (1992) and Pelayo H. Fernández's "Norteamérica vista por Ramón Pérez de Ayala y Julio Camba" (1981).

New York volume in the prologue to *La ciudad automática* (1932), his second
New York volume: "decía un poeta español que, en Nueva York, las estrellas
le parecían anuncios luminosos. A mí, en cambio, los anuncios luminosos
me parecen estrellas" [a Spanish poet said that, in New York, he thought
the stars looked like illuminated signs. I however think the illuminated
signs look like stars] (6). For Camba's readers, this example presents another
version of an original to which they do not have access. It also speaks to the
tensions at play in the development of Camba's and Pla's texts, which would
give shape to the making of a city, in writing that would eventually leave a
notable mark on their respective careers.

New York's impact on both men's writing was not limited to a single
volume. Camba's articles, like the essays of José Moreno Villa's *Pruebas de
Nueva York*, were initially delivered periodically to readers. Shortly after
their initial appearance, they were gathered and published in two book
volumes: *Un año en el otro mundo* (1917) and *La ciudad automática* (1932). Even
then, as James Shearer notes, Camba's interest extended beyond those two
volumes, as every collection after 1917 "contains articles with substantial
dependence on American themes, either as the basis of the articles, or in
the use of American material for comparative purposes" (Shearer xxiii). Pla
first traveled to New York aboard the *Guadalupe* in 1954. Leaving from the
southern port city of Cádiz, the journey took 13 days, longer than he would
spend in the city (Capdevila 240). Less than a year later, in the spring of
1955 he published the book *Week-end (d'estiu) a New-York*. In 1963, Pla made
his third trip to New York. During that decade and the following, his articles
about New York continued to appear in Spanish in *Destino* and *El Correo
Catalan*.

The short amount of time between visits and the production of the
resulting New York texts means reader and writer share the immediacy of
encountering the city. While the writer navigates his way by writing the city,
readers navigate their way by reading it. Moreover, for irregular lengths of
time and to varying degrees, because Camba's and Pla's articles appeared
in newspapers, they comprised a part of their audiences' routine reading
practices. The frequent contact, coupled with publication not long after the
actual trips, or even while the authors were still abroad, contributes to what
Susan Bassnett has called "the collusion of writer and reader in a notion of
authenticity, that is, the reader agrees to suspend disbelief and go along with
the writer's pretence" ("When Is a Translation" 35). For Bassnett, this "is one
of the bases upon which travel writing rests" (35). There is, however, a huge
disconnect between writer and reader in terms of language. The reader is
constantly in a position of uncertainty about language, even if the question
never appears. Bassnett subsequently adds: "Readers are asked to believe in

the veracity of the traveller's tales, but the question of linguistic competence is thus carefully obscured. We collude with the idea that travellers can talk to anyone, anywhere in the world and record their conversations in the form of direct speech" (36). Thus, in the collusion of writer and reader, the idea that the traveler does a great deal of translating in order to bring foreign experiences to readers becomes even more submerged. What is more, as Cronin has pointed out, the relationship of the traveler to language is a fundamental aspect of travel that "[c]ritical writing on travel and tourism has largely neglected" (Cronin, *Across* 2). Travel writing, then, is a translated text that also has its own relationship to invisibility under such terms.

Camba and Pla, as writers from regions of the geographic and linguistic Iberian periphery, were attuned to the nuances of language. This factor, and the stakes involved in being among the writers who traveled to New York to bring the city back to a home readership, render even more complex the multiple layers of translation already present in the complex genre that is travel writing.

None of the writers in this book were born in New York; they traveled there. Felipe Alfau had a one-way ticket. José Moreno Villa received a sorrowful return ticket. Camba and Pla held return tickets and were assigned to write the city. Even so, this is neither to be understood solely as an obligation nor an obstacle for them, as travel was always a central part of their writing. With respect to Camba, María Dolores Costa observes that even when his "articles [...] do not ostensibly constitute travel literature, they are impregnated with the idea of travel" (154).[9] Similarly, Joan Ramon Resina asserts that Josep Pla, "[t]he indisputable shaper of modern Catalan prose and its most prolific representative[,] was pre-eminently an author of travel books" (225). These statements on their work serve not only to underline travel as an essential part of Camba's and Pla's development as writers, but also to defend literariness as a quality that should not be denied to travel writing, especially that of writers who had to contribute to newspapers in order to achieve financial stability. The fact that *Un año en el otro mundo*, *La ciudad automática*, and *Week-end (d'estiu) a New-York* all hold a certain weight in

9 In her article "The Travel Writing of Julio Camba," Costa claims that "Camba creates for us the image of the clever mordant Spaniard as tourist throughout the early part of this century" and shows "how Camba forges this identity in relation to both the reader and the places visited, and how, by assuming this identity, the narrative voice regards itself as superior to all the groups framed by the text" (154). To do this, she reads his travel literature through the framework of Hunter Lewis's six values system, elucidated in *A Question of Values: Six Ways We Make Personal Choices That Shape Our Lives* (1990). She claims that Camba's ideal reader is the "cultivated Madrid intellectuals" (155).

their respective author's bibliography creates an impetus to read these texts with a consideration for what it means to travel to this North American city and write it for Iberian audiences of the early to mid-twentieth century. In order for this city to merit its own place on their bookshelves, the resulting texts must possess something beyond mere informative descriptions of the place that make them shine.

The frequency of their travel provided Camba and Pla with multiple perspectives that needed to be communicated in a language that was not always that of their experiences, thus transforming their language and maintaining its vitality and uniqueness. In a discussion on Camba, Pla states that

> Els articles de Camba i en general la seva producció, no tenen precedents en la literatura castellana. Si més no, jo no els conec. Ni pel seu estil no pel seu temari, no per la seva manera de desplegar-lo, no és poden citar precedents de Camba. (359)

> [Camba's articles and his production in general have no precedents in Castilian literature. At least, I'm not familiar with them. Regarding his style, subject matter, and way of putting it all together, Camba has no precedents.]

Camba's originality could have been largely based on the fact that, as a traveler, his sources were constantly shifting. Enric Bou underlines that travel writing is a "literary genre under construction" (181). Moreover, given that travel writing has dominated the work of Camba and Pla as well as that of many other major Iberian authors throughout the twentieth and twenty-first centuries, it should not be considered an isolated genre but rather understood as a major part of the construction and inspiration of Iberian literatures in general.

On Julio Camba

According to Gustave W. Andrian, Camba was not only "the most distinguished Spanish humorist of the twentieth century, but also Spain's most widely traveled journalist" (1). Even before newspapers started paying him to travel, he set off on his own to see the world. In 1900, at the tender age of 16,[10] he traveled to Argentina on a boat full of emigrants, stayed

---

10 Some sources, such as Gustave Andrian (1) and James Shearer (xi), say that Camba was 13. Novo Blankenship says that he sailed off to Buenos Aires when he was "barely thirteen" (2).

with a friend of his father, met the writer Alberto Ghirado (López García 28), joined a group of anarchists, and wrote newspaper articles. After two years in Buenos Aires, he was deported for his supposed link to anarchist acts.[11] He sailed back to Barcelona, and then from Barcelona he crossed the Iberian Peninsula to return to Galicia. He was handed over to his father. These short years traveling across the Atlantic and over the peninsula were "muy importantes para la formación de su personalidad y temperamento, de su ideologia como escritor" [very important for the development of his personality and disposition, and his ideology as a writer] (López García 31). By 1903, he made it to the largest city on the peninsula, Madrid, and two years later Camba started to become known for his writing (López García 59). Then, in 1908 *La Correspondencia de España* sent him to what was then Constantinople to report on political change. In 1916 he made his second transatlantic trip as a correspondent for the newspaper *ABC*. This was his first trip to New York. A year later, he published *Un año en el otro mundo* (1917), his first volume on New York. He would travel to the United States twice more, in 1924 and in 1929.

Julio Camba's name appears on about 14 volumes, if we count only first editions.[12] His writing was published in at least ten different newspapers fairly regularly for 40 years in cities throughout the Iberian Peninsula. Like José Moreno Villa, Camba was a solid fixture on the Madrid literary scene. He frequented the city's literary locales and participated in *tertulias* [literary social gatherings]. Pío Baroja and his brother Ricardo, José Martínez Ruiz (better known as Azorín),[13] Ramón del Valle-Inclán, and Miguel de

---

11 Sagahun notes that Camba was there for four years and wrote the book *Recordos*, which is "muy difícil de encontrar" [very difficult to find] (89). Camba's experience from this trip is fictionalized in the book *El destierro* (1907). This edition was published along with *El matrimonio de Restrepo* in a collection titled *Dos novelas bastante cortas* by Ediciones del Viento in 2007. Allones explains that *El destierro* presents Camba's life as a youth in the anarchist circles of Buenos Aires. López García is not sure if Camba was deported (31). Additionallly, Federico de Onís gives two versions of Camba's deportation (Novo Blankenship 3).

12 Shearer divides Camba's work into three parts. The first, dealing with articles that were later grouped into books, includes: *Alemania*; *Londres*; *Playas, ciudades y montañas*; *Un año en el otro mundo* (1917); *La rana viajera* (1920); *Aventuras de una peseta* (1928); *La ciudad automática* (1932). The second part is "the miscellanies" (Shearer xv): *Sobre casi todo* (1928) and *Sobre casi nada* (1928); *Esto, lo otro y lo de más allá* (1945); *Etc... Etc...* (1945); *Mis páginas mejores* (1956), and *Millones al horno* (1958).

13 Little is known about the writers that influenced Camba. Azorín is one of the few contemporary writers whom Camba admired (López García 60). López García comments that Camba "prefiere la conversación con pintores y escultores antes que con sus compañeros de profesión, siempre envidiosos y pedantes" [prefers to talk

Unamuno, with whom he exchanged letters, were all friends (López García 52). Camba was also a friend and correspondent of the Nicaraguan poet Rubén Darío (1867–1916), who introduced him to the Parisian literary scene, even though Camba supposedly preferred not to spend his time with these writers, "gente de una vanidad insoportable" [unbearably vain people] (López García 85). Camba eventually wrote about Darío's death, in 1916, in "Recuerdos de Rubén Darío" [Memories of Rubén Darío], the nineteenth chronicle of *Un año en el otro mundo*.[14] What is more, during his lifetime, notable contemporaries such as Benito Pérez Galdós, José Ortega y Gasset, and Ramón Pérez de Ayala, to name but a few, all situated Camba among the most influential writers. The scholar Pedro Ignacio López García calls him "uno de los escritores más interesantes [...] de la literatura española del siglo XX" [one of the most interesting writers (...) of twentieth-century Spanish literature] (12). At the same time, Camba was favorably recognized by a general readership who were in touch with his writing almost daily for some years. Across the Atlantic, Federico de Onís, a foundational participant in the making of U.S. Hispanism and Columbia University professor of Spanish, published an anthology of Camba's articles titled *La rana viajera* (1928). A little over three decades later, Professor James Shearer, who also served as chairman of the Graduate Spanish Department at Columbia University,[15] found Camba's writing of particular interest for the U.S. student of the Spanish language and literature. In the year of Camba's death, Shearer published a collection of 47 of Camba's *crónicas*—"short prose pieces descriptive of the author's impressions" (Shearer xii)—in *Países, gentes y cosas* (1962), complete with an introduction and pedagogical exercises to facilitate the comprehension and appreciation of Camba's work.[16]

to writers and sculptors more than colleagues in his profession, who are always envious and pedantic] (150).

14 This chronicle includes a question in French—"*C'est bon pour moi?*"—with no Spanish translation (85), a nod to the fact that Camba first met Darío in Paris.

15 For more on Shearer as a professor see Francisco Jiménez's *Taking Hold: From Migrant Childhood to Columbia University* (2015).

16 It is interesting to note that a tape recording of the selections along with other supplementary material of this textbook was available from the publishers. The book also features illustrations by Lorenzo Goñi (1911–92), who supplied the drawings for Camilo José Cela's *Viaje a U.S.A. o el que la sigue la mata* (1967). Camba seems to have been a popular choice for inclusion in U.S. textbooks teaching Castilian. The second edition of Gustave W. Andrian's *Modern Spanish Prose: An Introductory Reader with a Selection of Poetry* begins with three selections of Camba's prose from his New York writing, complete with a variety of exercises tailored to the anglophone learner of Castilian. This volume also includes the literature of Julio Cortázar, Pio Baroja, Jorge Luis Borges, Ramón Gómez de la Serna, and Octavio Paz, among others. Camba's

The year 2012 marked the fiftieth anniversary of Camba's death, and the surrounding years saw new publications of his work.[17] For example, the publishing house Rey Lear printed a new edition of *Un año en el otro mundo* (2009); new editions of *La ciudad automática* appeared with Alhena Media in Barcelona in 2008 and with Renacimiento in Sevilla in 2015, complete with a prologue by José García Martín and the addition of articles that had previously been published in newspapers; and in Madrid, Fórcola published *Crónicas de viaje: Impresiones de un corresponsal español* (2014), edited by Francisco Fuster and introduced by Muñoz Molina. Apart from this publication surge, however, critical work on Camba's writing has been scarce since his death. Familiarity with the biography and bibliography of the man who was once the best-paid journalist of the Iberian Peninsula during the first half of the twentieth century makes it difficult to believe that he is seldom studied (López García 12).[18] The attention and enthusiasm from both sides of the Atlanic did not persist; he is not an author who is extensively read, discussed, and studied in contemporary Iberian literary studies, either on the peninsula or in the United States (Llera 16). Llera, who has studied Camba's work, finds it disconcerting that literary history has paid him so little attention, and that there are few detailed readings of his articles (Llera 16, 18).[19]

Camba's absence from critical discussion is compounded by the fact that his work has not been widely translated, especially into English, despite the two books dedicated to New York City; this lack of translation

work is included in yet another compilation published in 1939, *Cuentos hispánicos* by John A. Crow, featuring the short stories of Spanish-language writers from Spain and Latin America. This volume also includes vocabulary and exercises for the language learner.

17 López García speaks to the possibility he sees in Camba's reception: "Lograr una primera edición de Camba será dentro de unos pocos años tan difícil como conseguir las primeras ediciones de Valle-Inclán, de Azorín o de Baroja" [Within a few years, to get hold of a first edition of Camba will be just as difficult as finding a Valle-Inclán, Azorín, or Baroja first edition] (13).

18 López García points out that the work of Socorro Girón, Almudena Revilla, José Antonio Llera, Arcadi Espada are exceptions (12).

19 When Llera's book was printed in 2004, he noted that "aparte de necrológicas, recensiones y memorias de personajes coetáneos, la magra bibliografía sobre el escritor se reduce, practicamente, al libro de Diego Bernal (1997), al sucinto ejercicio biográfico de Benito Leiro Conde (1986) y a los trabajos de Socorro Giron (1981) y de Almudena Revilla Guijarro (1999)" [apart from obituaries, reviews, and memoirs of contemporaneous characters, the meager bibliography on the writer is more or less limited to Diego Bernal's book (1997), Benito Leiro Conde's succinct biographical exercise (1986), and the works by Socorro Giron (1981) and Almudena Revilla Guijarro (1999)] (17).

has curtailed his audience to that delimited by the Spanish language.[20] Furthermore, considerations of Camba mostly as a journalist—even though his journalism alone merits an outstanding place in literary history— have perhaps dissuaded scholars from incorporating his work into literary studies. Additionally, much of Camba's *œuvre* comprises texts that he wrote about places beyond the Iberian Peninsula, an important point to remember when noting, as Resina does, that "some national literatures pivot around authors whose masterworks include travel abroad" (225).

If that were not enough, while he was an active participant in the cultural scenes of the cities he visited, Camba, like Felipe Alfau, struggled to embrace his position as a writer to the extent that at some point he even abandoned the act. In fact, he did not even like being called a writer, nor was he interested in any classification (López García, 116). According to López García, "Él escribía para vivir, no vivía para escribir, y hubo un momento, a mediados de los años cuarenta, en que este gran perezoso decidió que el esfuerzo no valía la pena" [He wrote to live, he didn't live to write, and there was a moment, in the mid-1940s, during which this great idler decided that the effort was not worth it] (14). In other words, Llera describes Camba as an "escritor y viajero más por profesión que por vocación" [a writer and traveler more by profession than by vocation] (19). This attitude could have stemmed from the fact that he was a self-taught writer who received no formal education beyond elementary school. Attesting to the importance of travel for Camba's profile, Novo Blankenship remarks that his "classrooms were the nations of the world, and he was a diligent student" (6). Camba

---

20 There is a 1941 Italian translation of Camba's work by Carlo Boselli and published in Milan by Sperling & Kupfer titled *Come un giramondo prende il mondo in giro.* In 1949, the American historian and Harvard professor Oscar Handlin (1915–2011) compiled a volume entitled *This Was America: True Accounts of People and Places, Manners and Customs, As Recorded by European Travelers to the Wester Shore in the Eighteenth, Nineteenth, and Twentieth Centuries.* A selection from Julio Camba's *Un año en el otro mundo* is among the 40 selections featured in the volume, in the fourth part titled "The Burdens of Maturity." Handlin's introduction to the book only mentions in the final paragraph that he is mainly responsible for the English versions of the texts. He writes: "The translations are free. For the purpose at hand, I have not felt it necessary to preserve archaic inelegancies or awkwardness of style. I have also taken considerable liberty in editing, transposing whole sections to eliminate repetition and to add coherence. But I trust I have been faithful to the meaning of the original. I have used older translations when available, but in such cases have checked against the original and made changes as I found them necessary" (4). Since Camba's *Un año en el otro mundo* has not been translated into English in its entirety, it is assumed that Handlin himself translated his Camba selection. Handlin's "Iberian Sketches" is the only English translation of Camba that I have been able to locate.

was not known to be a voracious reader, nor were his sources known to be classic works of literature or sanctified cultural production. Llera tells that:

> en él son más importantes las fuentes orales y ambientales que las librescas. Nuestro autor no es Goethe: en Italia le fastidia la consigna tacita de que haya que visitar el mayor número posible de museos. Prefiere las calles y los cafés. (147)

> [what he heard or picked up from his surroundings was more important to him than what he got from books. Our author is not Goethe: in Italy he was bothered by the unspoken rule that you had to visit as many museums as possible. He preferred the streets and cafés.]

Camba was interested in some of the city's most transitory spaces, in which the faces, voices, smells, sounds, and ambiance quickly change. He was also known to find inspiration in "las bulliciosas reuniones, los bares y cabarets, las tabernas, [y] las tiendas" [noisy gatherings, bars, cabarets, taverns, and stores] (Sagahun 91). It is not the urban environment *per se* that inspired him, but more so these defined city spaces where many people gather for brief periods of time—spaces that are aurally and visually in constant transformation, in which the sounds and voices, noises, and music can be just as interesting as or even dominate the visual. These are the places where Camba rooted his writing. Spaces such as these that are constantly renewing themselves, just as travel does for the individual, keeping the individual on edge given the unpredictability as to what they may contain.

Other than travel *per se*, an additional aspect of Camba's roots as a writer worth noting is his work as a literary translator. Little is known about his translation work, and the early twentieth-century translations he produced, including those of Émile Zola and Victor Margueritte for the publisher Salvá in Barcelona, are not even attributed to him (see López García). López García notes that when he did these translations, Camba hardly knew French (51).[21] Despite the lack of details about Camba's secretive translation work, his practice as a literary translator would have further exposed him to questions of language beyond those already acquired through travel.

---

21 López García says that Camba also translated "algunos libros y folletos de propaganda anarquista para la Editora Moderna, que dirige Francisco Ferrer Guardia. Es Mateo Morral, a quien Julio ve por primera vez en el Café Oriental de la Puerta del Sol (se lo presenta Pío Baroja), quien le escribe proponiéndole esas traducciones" [some books and anarchist propaganda pamphlets for Editora Moderna, directed by Francisco Ferrer Guardia. Mateu Morral, whom Julio met for the first time at Café Oriental in the Puerta del Sol (Pío Baroja introduced them), wrote to him to suggest that he do those translations] (López García 51).

The year 1907 marked the start of Camba's collaboration with newspapers. First, he contributed to *El Mundo*, which would soon include his sought-after column "Palabras de un mundano" [Words of a Worldly Person]. Camba would eventually be recognized for his writing in three periodicals other than *El Mundo*: the conservative *La Tribuna*, the liberal and intellectual *El Sol*, and the royalist *ABC*.[22] While most of Camba's writing reached his first readers via periodicals, to label him a journalist is to fail to acknowledge his contributions to literary history. Because of Camba's brief involvement with literary translation, his early poetry and other literary texts, and the coincidence of travel with his genesis as a writer, Felipe Sagahun notes that "[s]us comienzos [...] fueron más literatos que periodísticos" [his beginnings (...) were more literary than journalistic] (90). Most, if not all, of his articles are written in the first person.[23] In an article written in Germany, he refers to himself as an author of "crónicas literarias" [literary chronicles] (Llera 39). Thus, despite his resistance to associating himself with a literary tradition or tendency, Camba places his work in dialogue with "un género con amplia tradición en España, que alcanza su apogeo a finales del siglo XIX, y que tiende a integrar la descripción, la narración y la exposicion argumentativa" [a genre with an extensive tradition in Spain, which reaches its peak at the end of the nineteenth century, and which tends to integrate description, narration, and argumentative exposition] (Llera 39).

Camba's travels to and within several cities prior to his first trip to New York mark pivotal moments for his development as a writer, moments that would prepare him for that city, for rendering it into memorable words that would impact readers as well as his own career. Camba's first piece of travel writing from abroad was composed in Constantinople on December 4, 1908 (López García 81).[24] As a result of his experience in Turkey, he became

---

22 Early on, Camba worked for anarchist publications such as *El Porvenir del obrero* and *El Rebelde*. Later he wrote for *El País* (1905–07), *España Nueva* (1907), *La Correspondencia de España* (1908–09), *El Mundo* (1907–12), *La Tribuna* (1912–13), *El Sol* (1917–27), and *ABC* (Llera 31).

23 Llera divides Camba's journalistic writing into two large blocks: (1) the chronicles, including the ones he wrote as a correspondent from abroad (Turkey, England, Germany, France, Portugal, New York) and the local ones from within the Iberian Peninsula; and (2) the "columnas personales" [personal columns] published in *El Sol* and *ABC*.

24 Camba's writing is often referred to as *crónicas*. Shearer notes that Camba's writing could also be called *correspondencia*, as it is "expressive of the real nature of [Camba's] articles, *i.e.*, an informal exchange or communication between the author and his readers, reaching them through the medium of popular diffusion, the newspaper. They are running commentaries, very close in spirit, word and idiom to the spoken language, spontaneously and impressionistically produced in reaction to

convinced of the benefits of learning languages: "ve ahora la necesidad de aprender idiomas y de hablar con todo tipo de gentes" [now he sees the need to learn languages and to speak with all kinds of people] (López García 82). Soon after his trip to Turkey, he moved on to a 14-month stay in Paris, a period that "han hecho de él un hombre y un escritor diferente" [had changed him as a man and a writer] (López García 90). Three short days after leaving Paris, Camba traveled to London, the first English-speaking city he would write about. Having lived in at least three vastly different cities and among speakers of at least three languages other than Spanish, his popularity increased by 1911 to the point that he was now one of the most-read Iberian chroniclers (López García 96), and consequently "uno de los mayores escritores en periódicos que ha dado la literatura española contemporánea" [one of the greatest newspaper writers of contemporary Spanish literature] (Fuster García, "Yo" 13).

Thus, for Camba traveling not only meant the opportunity to write cities, but also the chance to learn new languages. After seven years abroad, Sagahun writes that "[c]uando volvió a España, en 1916, era un políglota: hablaba alemán, francés, inglés, italiano, un poco de griego, un poco de turco y un poco de ruso. Cuando se fue no sabía más idioma que el propio" [when he returned to Spain, in 1916, he was a polyglot: he spoke German, French, English, Italian, a bit of Greek, a bit of Turkish, and a bit of Russian. When he left, he had known only his own language] (Saghun 92). Camba's knowledge of seven languages, in addition to Spanish and Galician, coupled with the fact that most of what he experienced while writing for an Iberian readership was in a language other than Spanish, indicates the close associations between travel and language, and travel as an event that perpetuates writing.

However, the complexities of Camba's situation might have been less apparent to his readers. After all, in line with Bassnett's discussion of the collusion between the reader and writer of travel writing, Cronin argues that "interlingual translation is often disguised by writers and critics to create the illusion of linguistic transparency" (*Across* 3). In a summation of Camba's vast *œuvre*, Fuster García writes:

> Como ningún otro periodista de su época, Camba supo ganarse al público empatizando con él y haciéndole partícipe de sus filias y de sus fobias, de sus alegrías y miserias cotidianas. Desde este punto de vista, el lector fue para él un "igual", un confidente y un amigo al que

his surroundings" (xiii). I like to maintain "travel writing" as a way to speak about Camba's work since it features the action that made the writing possible.

convenía respetar y mimar y al que, por purito profesional y obligación moral, no se le debía ocultar nada. ("Yo Periodista" 10–11)

[Like no other journalist of his time, Camba knew how to win over his audience by empathizing with his readers and making them participants in his loves and hates, in his daily happiness and misery. From this point of view, his reader was an "equal," a confidant and a friend, who should be treated with respect and indulged and, out of professional obsessions and moral obligation, should not be kept in the dark about anything.]

The success of Camba's writing speaks to his ability to navigate several cities, negotiate among several languages, and to write his experiences in a way that attracted and included instead of isolating and excluding readers. His example celebrates the outcomes of the challenges presented by travel and the act of translating that experience.[25]

The year 1916 was pivotal in Camba's life. He returned to the Iberian Peninsula after seven years away. Not only did he have nine years of experience writing for newspapers, presenting at least seven cities to Spanish readers, but he could also now speak English, French, German, Italian, a little Turkish and Greek, and even Russian (López García 118). With nine languages on his résumé, at the age of 31, Camba traveled to New York City on the *Antonio López* as a correspondent for *ABC*. While in New York, he received a letter from Gregorio Martínez Sierra, the director of the Iberian publishing company Renacimiento, suggesting a collection of Camba's works (Novo Blankenship 9). Soon after, his chronicles from previous trips were collected and published in book form as *Londres: Impresiones de un español* (1916), *Alemania: Impresiones de un español* (1916), and *Playas, ciudades y montañas* (1916), this last a collection of essays on Galicia, France, Switzerland, and Belgium.

He returned to Madrid in April of 1917, when the United States entered the First World War, and later that same year *Un año en el otro mundo* was published. Camba's book on New York reached readers on the Iberian

---

25 Camba went on to publish his travel chronicles in book form *Un año en el otro mundo* (1917), *La rana viajera* (1920), *Aventuras de una peseta* (1923), and *La ciudad automática* (1932). Some of his miscellaneous articles were published in *Sobre casi todo* and *Sobre casi nada* (1928), *Esto, lo otro y lo de más allá* and *Etc... Etc...* (1945), and *Millones al horno* (1958). Besides his travel chronicles, his best-known work is *La casa de Lúculo o El arte de comer* (1929). In 1943, he published *Haciendo de República*. A good part of his work was collected posthumously, in *Caricaturas y retratos* (2013) and *Crónicas de viaje* (2014). There are plans to publish *Constantinople*, which will feature his travel writing on Turkey.

Peninsula around the same time as some of the most monumental texts associated with Iberian literary production in New York City: Jiménez's *Diario de un poeta recien casado* (1917) and García Lorca's *Poeta en Nueva York* (1940). Camba's writing, although critically less well-known, prepared an Iberian readership to receive his contemporaries' New York writing. He offered his fellow writers and intellectuals access to a place of decisive importance in world politics and the evolution of modern society.

Despite praise from his peers and the connection he could make with his readers beyond intellectual circles, Camba's writing in book form did not sell as widely:

> Los artículos de Camba son muy celebrados a leerse en el periódico, pero luego, reunidos en volumen, parece que no tienen importancia, que es una literatura fácil y amena, para leer mientras se viaje en tranvía. (López García 134)

> [Camba's articles are very well known when read in the newspaper, but then, when gathered in a volume, they are not important. He writes an easy and enjoyable literature for reading while traveling via streetcar.]

He was a writer who spoke best to the city dweller on the move, a reader who, because of demands on his or her time, sought short, fast, satisfying pieces that could be easily read during the daily commute in a format that reflected the fleeting moments of engagement with their own city. When Enric Bou writes that "[t]ravel literature explores freedom from the limitations imposed by the traveler's own culture" (179), he references Michel Butor's essay "Le voyage et l'écriture," in which Butor pays attention to "passengers on the subway who read, or the act of reading as an act of escape from everyday life" (Bou 180). The connections that Bou and Butor draw between travel, reading, and the city speak to travel and reading as offering the individual the necessary opportunity to transcend the restrictions of regular, everyday established paths. In doing so, their work gives an increased significance to the weight of Camba's work for his readers.

Camba lived in and wrote several cities, and, published in newspapers, his actual writing was part of the Madrid cityscape. Camba himself observes that his work could be found "en los ándenes del Metro; está en la librería de todas las estaciones" [on metro platforms; it's in the bookstores in all the stations] (López García 134). Not only was his work found on newsstands in places frequented by the city's masses, but also in the hands of "[t]axistas, funcionarios, comerciantes, carpinteros, intelectuales, barrenderos, hombres y mujeres de todos los pueblos y ciudades de España" [taxi drivers, civil servants, businessmen, carpenters, intellectuals, street sweepers, men and women of every town and city in Spain], who "diviertieron y aprendieron mucho leyéndo" [had fun and learned a lot from reading] Camba's chronicles (Allones 159). Thus, it is not only Camba's writing that makes him part of an urban landscape that was literally in motion, but also Camba himself who, when not traveling abroad, was a significant part of Madrid's cultural and literary scene because of time spent in the city's iconic places:

> Dedica las tardes a pasear los alrededores de la Puerta del Sol o a jugar al *jiley* con los caricaturistas Sancha, Bagaría y otros amigos en la cervecería famosa de la Plaza de Santa Ana. [...] Todos los taxistas de las madrugadas madrileñas conocen a Julio Camba y sus amigos. Pasean la calle de Alcalá desde la Puerta del Sol hasta alguna cervecería cercana la antigua Plaza de Toros, enfrente del Retiro. El edificio de Correos es el lugar donde a las cuatro o cinco de la madrugada, a veces más tarde, se despiden los amigos. (López García 140)

> [He spends the afternoons around the Puerta del Sol or playing *jiley* with the caricaturists Sancha, Bargaría, and other friends at the famous bar in the Plaza de Santa Ana. (...) All the early-morning taxi drivers in Madrid know Julio Camba and his friends. They walk down Alcalá from the Puerta del Sol to some bar close to the old Plaza de Toros, across from El Retiro. At four or five in the morning, sometimes later, the friends go their separate ways when they get to the Correos building.]

The extra-textual circumstances surrounding Camba's position as a writer—his travel record, his urban lifestyle, and the format of publication of his writing in relation to its content and readership—surface as rather informative and influential for a careful examination of his city writing, especially at its peak with the New York texts. Camba's commitment to writing chronicles stems not only from the fact that this is how he made his money, but also because the chronicle is the most appropriate format for the literature of the city, which is intended to reach city dwellers on the move, people living the city.[26] What is more, in "Un sitio para escribir artículos"

26 Camba is often compared to the French-born author Paul Morand (1888–1976), who made four trips to New York City between 1925 and 1929 and wrote *New-York* (1930). Umbral writes: "Camba viajaba por cuenta de los periódicos y hacía un periodismo costumbrista, sociológico y literario que iba bien para los suplementos dominicales. A Morand le pagaba el Ministerio de Asuntos Exteriores. A Camba le pagaba algún periódico madrileño que había comprendido la necesidad de servirse de aquel periodismo ameno, personalista y literario. De acuerdo con la diferencia de sueldo, Morand mandaba unas crónicas líricas, sabias y cosmopolitas. Camba mandaba unos artículos cortos e irónicos, con una ironía de clase media" [Camba

[A Place to Write Articles] in *Maneras de ser periodista*, Camba writes about his disagreement with writers who want a peaceful writing retreat by the sea or in the mountains, attesting to the centrality of the city in his work at large and the city as his inspiration:

> Esto nos decimos todos, y, sin embargo, yo, por mi parte, nunca he trabajado más a gusto que en plena redacción, ante un compañero que hace chistes y pide pitillos, o que en un antrillo sórdido, debajo de una teja, en el quinto piso de una calle de mucho tráfico, llena de bocinazos, de pregones y de toda clase de ruidos. En plena Naturaleza soy hombre muerto. (61)

> [That is what we all say. In my experience, however, I've never worked more comfortably than deep into writing, in the presence of a friend who tells jokes and asks for cigarettes, or in a measly little dive, under a tiled roof, on the fifth floor of a traffic-filled street, full of honking horns, street cries, and all kinds of noise. In the middle of nature, I am a lifeless man.]

Camba and New York

Julio Camba traveled to New York in 1916 as a correspondent for the newspaper *ABC*.[27] This was the first of two trips to the city. His next would be about 15 years later, still before the outbreak of the Spanish Civil War, again as a correspondent for *ABC*, to report on the outcomes of the stock

traveled because of his newspaper work and practiced a *costumbrista*, sociological, and literary journalism that worked well in the Sunday sections. The Ministry of Foreign Affairs paid Morand. Some Madrid newspaper that had understood the need for that enjoyable, personal, and literary journalism paid Camba. In line with the difference in their salaries, Morand would send in lyrical, intelligent, and cosmopolitan chronicles. Camba would send short and ironic articles, with a middle-class sense of irony].

27 Carlos Allones states that Camba's first trip was in 1918. In his article "Las crónicas norteamericanas de Julio Camba. Una nueva lectura" (2012), he is interested in the sociological aspect of Camba's work: "Y llamar la atención de los de nuestro oficio sobre esa mina de oro sociológico que es Julio Camba, que permanece abandonada (cuando no ignorada) por los sociológicos ibéricos e iberoamericanos que deberíamos explotarla" [And calling the attention of those in our field to Julio Camba's sociological goldmine, which remains abandoned (if not ignored) by Iberian and Iberoamerican sociologists who should exploit it] (160). Allones selects some passages from Camba's trips to New York and analyzes them for their sociological value.

market crash of 1929. Francisco Fuster published what he considered the best of these chronicles about New York in *Crónicas de viaje: Impresiones de un corresponsal español* (2014). A chapter of this collection is dedicated solely to Camba's words on New York, while the others contain writings from his stays in Constantinople, Madrid, Paris, London, Milan, Rome, Naples, Florence, Geneva, and Berlin. Besides dedicating an entire chapter to Camba's New York writing, the role of New York in Camba's work receives special attention in the volume's prologue by Antonio Muñoz Molina, which provides a deep connection between Camba's work and that of contemporaneous New York artists, such as the iconic composers and songwriters Irving Berlin (1888–1989) and Cole Porter (1891–1964). Just in terms of the quantity of the songs they produced, Berlin and Porter resemble the impressive output of Camba's chronicles. Berlin wrote more than 1,500 songs, while Porter wrote just under 1,000, and much like Camba's prose, their songs are immediately recognized by large audiences. Furthermore, the choice of Muñoz Molina, an Iberian writer with a close link to New York City, to write the prologue further emphasizes the impact of this city on Camba's work while placing him in the lineage of Iberian writers who connected with New York in a major way.

When Camba first went to New York, he was a little over 30 years old and already had a wealth of travel and work experience behind him. By then he had been working for seven years as a correspondent in Paris, London, and Berlin. He moved freely in at least seven languages besides Spanish and Galician, and was among the highest-paid journalists on the Iberian Peninsula. As such, he was fully equipped to confront the multilingual, rapidly changing U.S. city. What is more, he would find there an established and influential Iberian community. In 1917, he met Federico de Onís and "en seguida [se hicieron] amigos" [they immediately became friends] (de Onís 167). About 12 years later, de Onís would invite Camba, just as he had Moreno Villa, to visit Columbia University. On July 17, 1929, a month after García Lorca arrived in New York, there was a reception in Camba's honor at the Instituto de las Españas,[28] during which "Camba puede saludar a dos de sus más fervientes admiradores literarios, Federico de Onis and Angel del Rio" [Camba could say hello to two of his most devoted literary admirers, Federico de Onís and Ángel del Río] (Lopéz García 154). To further establish de Onís's relationship with Camba and Camba's participation in U.S. Hispanism, de Onís also edited and published *La rana viajera: Artículos humorísticos* in the United States in 1928 with an introduction, notes, vocabulary, and illustrations by an artist named

---

28 Today the Instituto de las Españas, founded in 1920, is called the Hispanic Institute for Latin American and Iberian Cultures.

Usabal. *La rana viajera*, which includes excerpts from Camba's published works, is part of a series called Contemporary Spanish Texts which "present[s] to students of Spanish the works of the outstanding figures in contemporary Spanish literature" (de Onís iii).

Considering the great acclaim that Camba received for his writing and his unique embodiment of the international Iberian literary and cultural scene, his travel writing received superficial critiques. In a 1933 review of Camba's second New York book, *La ciudad automática* (1932), published in *Books Abroad: An International Literary Quarterly*, Marjorie L. Crandall criticizes Camba for "fall[ing] into the pitfall, so common in all travelers, of too sweeping generalizations" (350). Evaluations like Crandall's imply an expectation of travel writing to deliver a certain type of information, thus limiting the range of possible readings of the city, in this case, by prioritizing the message: Does Camba deliver a specific and accurate portrait of New York? This narrow focus on reading travel writing for according to a prescribed notion echoes discussions of literary translation in terms of fidelity or faithfulness. However, fidelity has been understood and interpreted in a wide range of ways by translators, translation critics, and theorists. On the one hand, fidelity can denote a word-for-word transmission of the message of what is deemed to be the original in the translation language; on the other, a faithful translation can also be one that takes notable liberties, regarding word choice, for example, in order to emphasize a certain aspect of a text. Overall, to whom or to what this so-called fidelity pertains is a central question that should be addressed before engaging in a critique of fidelity in a translation. A narrow approach to fidelity or faithfulness ultimately limits engagement with the complexities of travel writing. Shifting the emphasis to Camba's actual writing and broadening the approach to what might be considered the fidelity of his New York opens new considerations of the significance of his texts.

What is more, within Iberian literary studies there is a tendency to speak about whether writers liked New York. In the introduction to his anthology *Geometría y angustia: Poetas españoles en Nueva York* (2012), Julio Neira remarks on the dichotomy of attraction to and repulsion by the city:

> la atracción por la monumentalidad y la belleza de las grandes realizaciones de la ingeniería urbanística (rascacielos, puentes, avenidas, etc.) y el rechazo por la inhumanidad del sistema capitalista que la sustenta y por la vida alienante para las personas que la fundamenta. (10)

> [attraction to the monumentality and the beauty of the great developments of urban engineering (skyscrapers, bridges, avenues,

etc.) and rejection because of the inhumanity of the capitalistic system that supports the city and because of the alienating life for the people that provide its foundation.]

Regarding Camba's relationship with the city, the editor of the 2009 edition of *Un año en el otro mundo* says: "A Camba no le gustan demasiado los Estados Unidos, pero al mismo tiempo le atraen poderosamente" [Camba does not like the United States too much, but at the same time the country exercises a powerful attraction on him] (20). Camba himself said of New York: "Nos atrae porque uno no puede vivir al margen del tiempo y nos rechaza por la estupidez enorme del tiempo en que le ha tocado vivir a uno" [It attracts us because we cannot live on the margins of time, yet it rejects us because of the enormous stupidity of the time in which it is our turn to live] (*Ciudad* [2008] 13). A contemporary version of this split appears in the opening poem of J. M. Fonollosa's collection *Ciudad del hombre: New York* (1990): "No hay nada bueno en ti. Por eso te amo" [There's nothing good about you. That's why I love you] (19). Neira discusses this tension of emotions as "un dilema de difícil salida" [a difficult dilemma to get out of] (10). Although this may initially appear to be a situation requiring remedy, it should be acknowledged that the complexity of the experience puts the temporary or permanent city dweller on edge, leading to creative possibilities, to writing, which in itself can be thought of as the way out. After all, Josep Pla noted that "Nova York—és necessari repetir-ho—és la ciutat dels contrastos continuats" [New York—it's necessary to say it again—is the city of continuous constrasts] (117). Thinking of the writer's relationship with New York as being caught between the torturous extremes of attraction and rejection, we are also reminded of how literary translators negotiate the material with which they work, continuously being attracted to and rejected by language and searching to discover solutions for the text they are writing in another language. Moving between attraction and rejection could accompany the existing dualities that surround discussions on literary translation: the results are often discussed in terms of impossibility versus possibility, and gain versus loss. The state of fascinating, prolonged wavering between two different linguistic or emotional places is often found in Iberian writing related to New York and translation.

Another point worth mentioning with regard to the critical reception of Camba's travel writing concerns readers' expectations when confronted with travel writing. In María Dolores Costa's article "The Travel Writing of Julio Camba" (1996), she says that Camba's

negative portrayals of the places he visits leave the reader wondering why anyone would want to go there. The point in reading these essays cannot be to become acquainted with the places they describe, since that will not occur here. But even though the locations Camba puts before us seem largely inhospitable, we do not want to occupy the privileged perspective of the narrative voice in these texts. (155)

Costa's reading of Camba's writing negates the differences between the possible kinds of travel writing. Her essay makes no distinction between travel books and guidebooks, for example. Guidebooks, according to Paul Fussell, "are not autobiographical and are not sustained by a narrative exploiting the devices of fiction" (203). In addition, guidebooks are also for readers who may one day be travelers themselves. Thus, according to this principle and the literariness of Camba's work, his articles are excluded. On the other hand, travel books, as Resina indicates, "are addressed to readers who do not necessarily plan to abandon their armchairs" (226). Originally published periodically for a large newspaper-reading audience, Camba's travel writing functions more as a travel book, the form in which it was later republished. Beyond overlooking the variety in travel writing, Costa suggests that there should be something attractive or inviting about the place described that would make the reader want to travel there or at least do so via the narrator. Such a reading stresses a binary outcome for travel writing: readers do or do not want to travel either physically or imaginatively, while simultaneously shutting down the possibility of travel or reading in order to explore curiosities and potential for growth. In other words, the emphasis is on the result rather than the experience.

Costa further discusses Camba's work in the context of tourism, referring to him as a "tourist-narrator" throughout her essay, even though Camba was never a tourist writing for future tourists. Her reading does, however, shed light on the New York that Camba wrote for an Iberian audience: "For the most part Camba has a tourist's vision that frames more than it inhabits. There is no authentic mixing with the people, so there is no mutual influencing" (156). Rather than being the result of a "tourist's vision," this hints at the kind of writer and translator of New York that Camba was. In part, this detachment detected by Costa could be a result of the process in which Camba wrote the city.

Prior to his second visit to New York, his friend the painter Julio Romero de Torres died on May 10, 1930, and Camba found himself without much drive to write (López García 154). Luis Calvo, part of the new leadership of *ABC* and responsible for finding the best collaborators, proposed that Camba return to New York (López García 154). Camba was happy with this idea, and from December of 1930 to July of 1931 he wrote a long series of "nuevas y excelentes cronicas" [new and excellent chronicles] (López García

154). The terms of his contract stated that Camba was to submit ten articles per month. During the final week of the month, he would lock himself in his room at the Hotel Pennsylvania on Seventh Avenue across from Pennsylvania Station, ignore all phone calls, and write the ten articles. This method and sudden distance from the streets granted Camba plenty of time to enjoy the city, supporting his statement that a writer must participate in urban life in order to write it. The life of the city, however, does not transfer to the page, as the writing lacks the active participation of the narrator on the urban scene and instead presents a point of reflection. In other words, the narrator's participation in city life is limited and distant. This could also be attributed to the kind of writer he was, for Pla speaks to Camba's distance from the source of his writing:

> No fou, en cap cas, un escriptor que escrivís amb rapidesa fluent. No fou un repentista. Tot al contrari. Gairebé tot els seus articles foren llargament meditats i reflexionats. En el seu origen hi ha gairebé sempre un fet de la vida real que a través de donar-li voltes mentals s'esquematitzava en idees de caràcter general. Alguns dels seus articles els pensà durant molt de temps. Després, escriure'ls fou relativament fàcil, perquè ja els portava escrits en el seu procés mental. Si Camba hagués hagut de fer alguna cosa al marge dels seus articles no n'hauria pogut escriure ni un, per falta de temps per pensar-los. La vida de Camba no fou res més que una organització per a escriure articles. Tots estan basats en una absoluta falta de frivolitat. ("Idees" 360)

> [In no way was he a writer who wrote with fluent speed. He didn't improvise. He did the exact opposite. He thought about and reflected on his articles for a long time. Almost all of them start with something based on real life from which more general ideas were outlined over time. He thought about some of his articles for a long time. Then, writing them was relatively easy, because he already had them written in his mental process. If Camba had had to do something apart from his articles he wouldn't have been able to write even one of them, because of the lack of time he would have had to think about them. Camba's life was only organized to write articles. All of them are based on an absolute lack of frivolity.]

This incompatibility between being an active participant in city life and creating a literature that was equally active is further evidenced in Camba's Madrid writing. During the 1920s, Camba was writing less but, ironically, during this period he was one of the most popular figures of the literary scene in Madrid, frequenting the city's literary hotspots: "la cervecería El

Cocodrilo de la plaza de Santa Ana, en el Café del Prado, en el Ateneo, en Lhardy, en el Casino de Madrid, en el Círculo de Bellas Artes" [El Cocodilo bar in the Plaza de Santa Ana, the Café del Prado, the Ateneo, Lhardy, and the Casino de Madrid, and the Círculo de Bellas Artes] (López García 144).

Costa concludes that "[t]he city is for Camba a mechanical, cold-blooded place [...] In part due to this frigidity, the United States is an artless society [...] Adaptation to the U.S. is, not surprisingly, a disconcerting process" (159). Regardless of the veracity of this statement, it devalues New York in Camba's writing as well as the backstory which New York tells about his work and its ramifications for the Iberian artistic and intellectual scene of the twentieth century. A reflective narrator who does not present an entirely welcoming depiction of a place is no reason to disregard travel writing, especially writing with such widespread appeal. Rather, it suggests that other readings of the city in writing are yet to be uncovered. So, if the fast pace and participatory spirit is not a dominant characteristic of the narrator, we must look elsewhere, beyond the perspective of the narrator, to see how else the city enters the text: looking beyond what the narrator tells, at the text's very language.

Un año en el otro mundo

Since its first publication in book form in 1917, by Biblioteca Nueva in Madrid, *Un año en el otro mundo* has been printed five times, most recently in 2009, in addition to the selections that have been included in anthologies. Some editions give prominence to New York, as they include a typical image of the city (see Figs. 3.1[29] and 3.2), thus placing it at the center of readers' initial contact with the text. These covers diverge from the first edition, which presents a portrait of a young Camba (see Fig. 3.3). The choice to feature Camba on the 1917 cover acknowledges his contemporaneous popularity as a writer. The collection of cover illustrations reveals Camba's lost centrality and the growing interest in New York City among a general audience. Removing Camba from the cover is also paradigmatic of the reception of travel writing. With few exceptions, such as the work of Bassnett, Cronin, and Polezzi, critical readings commonly dismiss the work of the traveler and the intermediary stages of relaying the travel experience instead searching for descriptions of the place and often in evaluative terms.

Camba did not usually write an introduction to the collections of his chronicles published in book form. He did, however, preface the first edition

29 Rafael de Penagos (1889–1954) was an illustrator and painter working in the art deco style. He was widely known in Madrid's modernist scene.

Figure 3.1 Rafael de Penagos.
Cover of *Un año en el otro mundo*
by Julio Camba, 1934.

Figure 3.2 Jorge Arranz.
Cover of *Un año en el otro mundo*
by Julio Camba, 2009.

JULIO ~ CAMBA
UN·AÑO·EN·EL·OTRO·MUNDO
BIBLIOTECA ~ NUEVA

Figure 3.3 Cover of the first edition of *Un año en el otro mundo* by Julia Camba, 1917.

of *Un año en el otro mundo* with brief introductory words in which he offers his audience a gentle guide to reading the text. First, he discourages readers from looking for a true, faithful, or accurate account of the United States in his writing: "me entra una sospecha terrible: la de que todos, o casi todos [los artículos], sean fundamentalmente falsos" [I have the terrible suspicion that all, or almost all [the articles], are fundamentally false] (9). Next, he encourages readers to rule out comparisons between the United States and other countries because it is a waste of time, since the United States is different from Europe. Desire to release his writing on New York from the burdens of comparison, he seeks to liberate the text so that it is read on its own merits, much like translators prefer their work to be evaluated. Camba also demonstrates awareness of the negative stereotypes of the United States as a place burdened by "la técnica y la mecánica" [all that is technical and mechanical], and reminds readers that these very ideas carry a different meaning in the U.S. context than they do in Europe. By way of conclusion, Camba sets the reader up to explore his chronicles as transitory writing with questionable finality. Instead of presenting the reader with an impressive description of a landscape or cityscape of the United States, he instead opts for an approach that destabilizes the reader's expectations of travel writing and preconceived notions of the United States and of the book as a definitive text. Developing ideas about the United States is an ongoing process, as something incomparable takes place: "América me parecerá un país de posibilidades infinitas. El país, sencillamente, de donde puede surgir nada menos que una nueva humanidad" [It might seem to me that America is a country of infinite possibilities. The country, simply, from which nothing less than a new humanity can emerge] (13).

Un año en el otro mundo is divided into three sections. The first and longest, the focus of this chapter, is untitled and contains 31 chronicles about New York. Two other sections follow: "Unas elecciones presidenciales" [Some Presidential Elections] with ten chronicles and "La Guerra" [The War] with eight.[30] In one of the earlier chronicles of the book, Camba continues to offer his readers approaches to thinking about New York that push them away from lengthy descriptions of the physical space. For example, in the fourth chronicle, "La ciudad teoría" [The Theory City], he confidently claims, "Nueva York no es una ciudad. Es un sistema, una teoría. Para conocer Nueva York no hace falta habitarlo, ni siquiera estudiar una guía que lo describa. Se aprende la teoría y ya está" [New York is not a city. It is a system, a theory. To become familiar with New York it isn't necessary to live

---

30 Novo studies *Un año en el otro mundo* by concentrating on areas of contrast which she lists as liberty, sensitivity, materialism, and mechanism.

there, or to even study a guide that describes it. You learn the theory and that's it] (37). Of course Camba, a humorist, is not to be taken literally, and *crónicas* can be defined as "humorous and satirical short articles" (Andrian 1). Nevertheless, his message is effective as he elevates his text from the city streets, from the typical images that his reader might already know or expect, while also confirming that his text is far from a practical guide to the city. He puts readers on edge, eager to read him, as his text offers to all the possibility of learning about New York. In this sense, *Un año en el otro mundo*'s success is due to the fact that Camba made New York appear "cercano, comprensible y ameno" [close, understandable, and entertaining] to his readers, for many of whom New York was largely unknown and surprising (Carrión 15).

Camba is able to bring his faraway readers nearer to New York because his theory of the city surpasses a specific language as a necessity for getting to know the city. In "La ciudad teoría," like Moreno Villa in *Pruebas de Nueva York*, Camba highlights the fact that the streets are numbered instead of bearing the names of "hombres ilustres" [distinguished men] (37) as the streets of Iberian cities do. This feature creates a feeling that the city is accessible to anyone and everyone:

> Yo no puedo deslumbrar en Nueva York a ningún recién llegado. Todos se manejan aquí lo mismo que el más viejo nuevo-yorkino. Si, encontrádose en la calle 114, por ejemplo, un recién llegado quiere ir a la calle 120, este recién llegado sabe que todo consiste en cruzar seis calles. La 120 estará a continuación de la calle 119, y no se diferenciará de ella más que por el número. No es cuestión de haber visto jamás la calle 120. No es cuestión tampoco de haberse estudiado el plano de Nueva York. Es cuestión de saber un poco de aritmética rudimentaria. Nueva York, como digo, no es una ciudad. Es una suma. (37)

> [I can't dazzle any newcomer to New York. Everyone gets around here just like the oldest New Yorker. If a newcomer on 114th Street, for example, wants to go to 120th Street, this newcomer knows that it's a matter of crossing six streets. 120th will be after 119th Street, and it won't be any different except for the number. It's not a question of having ever seen 120th Street. Nor is it a question of having studied a map of New York. It's a question of knowing a bit of rudimentary arithmetic. New York, as I say, is not a city. It is a sum.]

As language does not come across as a barrier to physical navigation of the city, the role of Camba as translator and traveler is further occluded, while readers are meant to feel that they too can master the city. This further serves to launch a reading of the city that will be revisited throughout the chronicles: the significance of numbers and abundance. In many ways, numbers become more important than words and can even replace them.

The seventh chronicle, "El anhelo artístico" [Artistic Desire], opens with a list of diverse artists that becomes a call to come to New York: "Pintores, escultores, arquitectos, bailarines, actores, músicos, poetas ... Artístas del color y de la forma, de la cabriola y del gesto, del ritmo y de la rima ... Venid a América" [Painters, sculptors, architects, dancers, actors, musicians, poets ... Artists of color and of form, of jumping and gesture, of rhythm and rhyme ... Come to America] (47). This inventory of artists followed by ellipses, punctuation that pervades the chronicles, not only suggests the endless variety of artists in New York, but also offers readers a moment to imagine themselves or other artists in the city, evoking, perhaps, an entrepreneurial spirit in the reader, as a gesture to point out the possibilities of New York. This invitation is quickly conditioned, however, by the fact that "los americanos quieren traer aquí a los artistas mejores del mundo" [the Americans want to bring the best artists in the world here] (47), pushing the reader away by pointing out the competitiveness of the city.

In stressing the apparent inclusivity of New York in terms of quantity, variety, and quality, Camba's chronicles often omit details that personalize his experience. In other words, there is little information about what happened to the narrator *per se* during his trip to New York. For example, the same chronicle then introduces Charlot, a woman artist of some sort (47). Since no details are shared, the text leaves readers with the idea that numbers are the defining and motivating factor of the city's artistic pulse. This is all executed, of course, in a humorous tone. On occasion, the humor is heightened by the inclusion of fragments of dialogue:

> Se les pagará a la americana, como a *Charlot*, que gana mil veinticinco dólares semanales.
> —Los veinticinco—dice *Charlot*—son para vivir.
> —Y los mil, para qué los quiere usted, si vive con sólo veinticinco?
> —Los mil son para la categoría. Yo soy un actor de mil dólares por semana. No puedo cobrar menos ...

> They might pay an American woman, like Charlot, who earns one thousand and twenty-five dollars per week.
> —The twenty-five—says Charlot—cover living expenses.
> —And the thousand, why do you want that, if you can live on only twenty-five?
> —The thousand are for my status. I am a thousand-dollar-a-week actress. I can't charge less ... (47)

While giving dimension to the chronicles, these dialogues—all in Spanish, indicating that translation took place if only in the narrator's head—do not come across as actual conversations had by the narrator, nor do they act as proof of the narrator's interaction with New Yorkers; rather, they support the chronicle's subject. Whether they are costs, measurements, dimensions, or some other stream of numbers, *Un año en el otro mundo* continuously reminds its readers that numerical value is of utmost importance in New York's language, overshadowing any personalized details, a point made in nearly every piece and exaggerated in the later chronicle "La mecánica como civilización" [Mechanics as Civilization], which comments on the lack of leisure time or a way to "perder el tiempo" [waste time] (89). After humorously offering some advice to "las autoridades neoyorquinas" [the New York authorities] (90) on how to boost leisurely activities that include planting trees, installing benches, offering free concerts, and opening cafés, to name but a few suggestions,[31] New York's language of numbers appears:

> De este modo, dos o tres millones de personas llegarán a perder tres o cuatro horas cada día. Supongamos—a los americanos les gusta ver las cosas en números—supongamos ocho millones de horas dedicadas directamente al ocio—las horas, naturalmente, de muchísima gente—y supongamos esto durante cinco años. El total sería unos ciento cincuenta mil millones de horas que se habrían pasado sin hacer ningún esfuerzo físico, flaneando, curioseando, soñando, conversando o pensando en tonterías. Ciento cincuenta mil millones de horas de aislamiento, de inconsciencia y de libertad mental ... (90)

> [This way, two or three million people will be able to waste three or four hours each day. Let's suppose—Americans like to see things in numbers—let's suppose eight million hours dedicated directly to leisure—the hours, naturally, of very many people—and let's suppose this happens during five hours. The total would be some one hundred fifty billion hours that would have passed without making any physical effort, strolling, browsing, dreaming, chatting, or thinking about stupid stuff. One hundred fifty billion hours of isolation, of thoughtlessness and mental freedom ...]

31 José Luís García Martín notes that perhaps Camba exaggerates a little and reminds readers that in 1916, Central Park was already in existence as was the library on 42nd Street, "una de las primeras del mundo cuya intención era poner los libros—escritos en cualquier lengua que se hablara en la ciudad—al alcance de todos" [one of the first in the world whose goal was to put books—written in any language that was spoken in the city—within everyone's reach] (11).

In this passage, as in others, the exaggeration and humor of Camba's writing detracts from the actual trip or Camba's New York itinerary, instead reinforcing the strategy of representing in Spanish the defining pulse of New York and the value of a structure, individual, or activity. These examples are just some of those repeatedly offered to the reader throughout Camba's New York writing.

Beyond presenting New York's language of numbers, what about English, the dominant language of the city? Throughout the 232 pages of the first edition of the collection, based on an experience of less than one year, little English is used. Loredana Polezzi's *Translating Travel: Contemporary Italian Travel Writing in English Translation* (2001) examines the different uses of English in travel writing. According to Polezzi, English can have a distancing role depending on when the book was published (85), while at the same time its uses "highlight the fact that an analysis of the translation strategies adopted by travel writers cannot disregard the norms and expectations regulating the reception of the texts in the target culture" (85). Authors writing for a widespread audience in Spanish-language newspapers had to handle English with care. The chronicles of *Un año en el otro mundo* rely on a range of strategies regarding the use of the English language.

The first chronicle, "La llegada" [Arrival], reserves English for the proper names of buildings, such as the Adams Building, the Bankers Trust Building, and the Woolworth Building, as well the area surrounding those buildings, "Down Town" (28). The use of "Down Town," unitalicized and without quotation marks, stands out among the city's other landmarks, which appear in Spanish: "la estatua de la Libertad," "la isla del Gobernador," "el puente de Brooklyn" (27–28). What appear early in the text as "los gigantescos rascacielos del Bajo Manhattan," [the gigantic skyscrapers of Lower Manhattan] (27) later become "los rascacielos de la Down Town" [the skyscrapers of Down Town] (28). New York's "Down Town" then becomes a landmark, a unique city space, just like the skyscrapers that populate it. Likewise subsequent uses of "rascacielos" also accompanied by the word *skyscrapers* (36), suggesting a failure of equivalency in this context. Used throughout the chronicles to introduce readers to the city's local language, the strategy of offering a Spanish translation and then introducing English in subsequent instances avoids making the narrative cumbersome while requiring an extra effort by the non-English-speaking reader.

In a similar fashion, Camba's chronicles continue to expand his reader's urban lexicon. For example, in just two chronicles, Spanish-language readers in Madrid are introduced to five new words and one new expression. The text defines "el *subway* o ferrocarril subterráneo" (31), but thereafter "ferrocarril subterráneo" is eliminated, leaving it up to readers to remember the meaning of "subway." The first time the expression "*Hurry up!*" appears, the Spanish translation "(pronto, apresuradamente!)" (32) follows, only to be dropped the next time the expression is used. Additionally, by giving readers two Spanish options for "hurry up," the text shows the range of the expression's meaning and contrasts the brevity of English to the multisyllabic Spanish "apresuradamente," which also injects humor into the text, since such a drawn-out word would be ineffective in any situation that calls for what it singifies.

As to be expected, some words pertaining to the city's vocabulary remain in English, italicized, calling readers' attention to their use. At times these words are delivered without a Spanish translation or explanation— "*building*" (32), "*trolleys*" (32), "*fox-trots*" (53), "*cabarets*" (53), "*match*" (53), "*cake-walk*," and "*water-chuts*" (121), to name but a few examples—but do not isolate the reader, as their meaning can be deduced from context and their repetition throughout the chronicles in several contexts. Italics also indicate that the reading public should be familiar with these words from their use in other venues. In other instances, English words make up part of phrases like, for example, "algún *sport* violento: el fútbol, el boxeo, el *catch as catch can* ..." [some violent *sport*: soccer, boxing, *catch as catch can* ...] (33). A translation accompanies phrases that might not be as familiar to readers: "*He was chewing her gum.* (Él mascaba la goma de ella)" (68) and "*melting pot* o crisol de las razas" (69). The strategy of placing the translation in or outside parenthesis varies throughout the collection. Finally, a culturally specific term like *self-made man* is the subject of the twenty-first chronicle, "El «self-made-man»" (93). "Self-made-man," defined in the opening sentence as "el hombre que se ha hecho por sí solo" [a man who has made it on his own] (93), is repeated ten times throughout the brief chronicle, allowing the phrase to dominate the pages, making it unforgettable to readers.

Overall, Camba's "cercano, comprensible y ameno" [close, understandable, and entertaining] style (Carrión 15) has also been described as a "spontaneous, personal, and conversational" (Andrian 1). The incorporation of English does not isolate the reader, nor does it highlight Camba's cosmopolitanism as a differentiating factor between himself and his readers. In fact, he rarely mentions his knowledge of several languages and his travels to many countries, although readers would likely be aware of his biography because of his publications and public profile. Instead, the use of English reveals itself to readers as proof of Camba's visit and experience in the city as well as an invitation to join the linguistic journey of the narrator, as each chronicle develops a New York lexicon, encouraging readers to augment their knowledge of the city in the same way. Different strategies represent linguistic growth, instability, negotiations with the city and its residents, and so on, none of which are hidden from the reader. The repetition of English words and descriptions of the city in New York's dominating numerical terms, rendered in Spanish throughout the chronicles, offer a systemized way of thinking about the city that gives Spanish readers a new way of imagining urban-centric terms.

The penultimate chronicle of *Un año en el otro mundo*, "XXX. Fuego" [XXX. Fire], portrays a narrator who is part of the scene described in the present tense: the evacuation of a building on fire. The notable amount of dialogue gathers the translation strategies of the previous chronicles, ranging from fully translated statements to others left in English with Spanish translations or explanations. For example, "*Ladies first!*" is initially accompanied by the Spanish translation "(¡Primero las mujeres!)" (123). Later, a firefighter tells the crowd "Señoras y señores: Muchas gracias. Pueden ustedes volver a su trabajo. *It is all right*" [Ladies and gentlemen: thank you very much. You can go back to work. *It is all right*] (124). This is followed by the crowd's response: "¿Cómo *all right*? ... ¿Quiere usted decir que ya ha sido sofocado el fuego?" [How is it *all right*? ... Do you mean that the fire has already been extinguished?] (125). The meaning of *all right* is not given, but must be deduced from context, and at the same time marks a turning point in the chronicle in which the narrator discovers that this is nothing more than a fire drill. This exercise is shocking to the narrator but routine for New Yorkers. In this example, the narrator, who is first presented as part of the crowd, a development from previous chronicles, becomes alienated from the group by two words around which the chronicle is developed. Thus, translation becomes the foundation of the chronicle. Regardless of the veracity of this interaction between the firefighter and the crowd, or even the event, as one of the concluding chronicles of the collection, it is apropos to demonstrate the ebb and flow of language comprehension in travel situations. The chronicle denies the reader a succinct Spanish translation of *all right* in favor of one that contextualizes the phrase for readers, sharing the impact of a small linguistic utterance. In many cases, Camba's chronicles artfully inform a wide audience that translation does not happen effectively with the replacement of one word for another; rather they indicate that translation occurs through context and example. Camba's writing thus shifts the focus of New York as an image to an idea. Camba does not prioritize giving readers a description of how New York looks but rather the ways in which the city works. Those ideas about New York complemented his readers' and contemporaries' visions of the city.

Just as simultaneously reading two different translations of a single text illuminates different aspects of the translated text and the choices made by each translator, significant insight is to be gained by reading Camba's *Un año en el otro mundo* alongside Lorca's *Poeta en Nueva York*, an idea suggested by Muñoz Molina in his prologue, "El secreto de Julio Camba," to the collection of Camba's chronicles *Crónicas de viaje* (5–6). Camba's and Lorca's New York texts visit some of the same places, such as Harlem and Coney Island. When Camba's "XXIX. Coney Island" concludes that "Coney Island es lo mismo que Nueva York, sólo que reducido y concentrado" [Coney Island is the same as New York, just smaller and more intense] (122), how might that shift a reading of Lorca's "Paisaje de la multitud que vomita (Anochecer en Coney Island)" [Landscape of the Vomiting Crowd (Twilight at Coney Island)]? And then how might understanding that poem influence readings of the other poems? The most illuminating exchanges between the texts are not guided by specific urban places, but rather found throughout the chronicles and poems, surfacing in unexpected moments. For instance, Camba's third chronicle, "La fiesta nocturna" [Nocturnal Party], describes the city's nightlife:

> Y a la noche, cuando los detalles arquitectónicos desaparecen de nuestra vista y los *skyscrapers* se iluminan en toda su altura, entonces el espectáculo es real y positivamente hermoso. Dijérase que el mundo entero estuviese de fiesta. En las fachadas enormes resplandecen millares de algres ventanas. Las perspectivas luminosas se suceden y se superponen, y la ciudad parece infinita. Es una orgía que le embriaga a uno. Hay anuncios luminosos que son enormes serpientes, aspas girando sin cesar, bailarines escoceses que mueven brazos y piernas, gatos atrapando ratones, salamandras, relojes que van marcando las horas y los minutos ... (36)

> [And at night, when the architectural details disappear from our view and the *skyscrapers* are lit up in all their height, then the spectacle is real and positively beautiful. One might say that the whole world is partying. Millions of happy windows shimmer on the enormous facades. The luminous views follow one another and overlap, and the city seems infinite. It's an intoxicating orgy. There are illuminated signs that are enormous snakes, blades spinning constantly, Scottish dancers who move their arms and legs, cats catching mice, salamanders, clocks that mark the hours and minutes ...]

Camba's text invokes some of the same animal, reptile, amphibian imagery of Lorca's collection; concretely, the first stanza of what has come to be the opening poem of *The Poet in New York*, "Vuelta de paseo" [Back from a Walk]:

> Asesinado por el cielo.
> Entre las formas que van hacia la sierpe

y las formas que buscan el cristal,
dejaré crecer mis cabellos. (4–5)

[Murdered by the sky.
Among the forms that move toward the snake
and the forms searching for crystal
I will let my hair grow.]

Reading these passages together gives readers greater appreciation for the style of each writer while at the same time making their respective texts more accessible by expanding the imaginative possibilities of the New York behind the text.[32]

La ciudad automática

During the 1920s, Julio Camba's intellectual prestige grew. To close the decade and open the next, he was invited by the Carnegie Foundation to tour the United States along with ten other journalists from European countries. During this period, many personalities and friends of Camba, such as Concha Espina, Dámaso Alonso, Eulalia Galvarriato, Ignacio Sánchez Mejías, and the dancers known as La Argentina (Antonia Mercé) and La Argentinita (Encarnación Júlvez) traveled to New York. While Iberian writers and artists were visiting the city, Spanish-language literature about New York circulated on the Iberian Peninsula, including the prose of Ramiro de Maeztu, Ramón Pérez de Ayala, and Joaquín Belda,[33] not to mention Camba's earlier New York writing and the already published verse of José Moreno Villa and Juan Ramón Jiménez, as well as any which Lorca might have disseminated among contemporaries. As a result, during the

---

32 Other critics have made connections between Lorca and Camba. Benitez has said that "La estancia de Lorca en Nueva York bien podría haberse titulado como el primer libro de Camba, 'Uno año en el otro mundo', ya que fueron meses intensos, de profundo reencuentro con la vida, cargados de jovialidad y muy fertiles en cuanto a su capacidad creativa. Lo mismo podría decirse de Julio Camba, más viajado hasta la fecha que Lorca—habia huido a Argentina muy joven, pero también había ejercido de corresponsal en Turquía, Francia, Inglaterra, Alemania e Italia" [Lorca's New York stay could have very well been called "Un año en el otro mundo," the title of Camba's first book, given that they were intense months of deep reunions with life, full of cheerfulness and very fertile with regard to his creative ability. The same could be said about Julio Camba, who had by that time traveled more than Lorca—he had escaped to Argentina at a very young age, but he had also worked as a correspondent in Turkey, France, England, Germany, and Italy].

33 See the work of Leslie Stainton and Pelayo H. Fernández.

1920s and 1930s, New York captured the imagination of intellectual and cultural communities as well as that of the general public.

Not surprisingly, during this second trip to the United States, Camba wrote more chronicles for his readers back home, eventually leading to the 1932 publication of *La ciudad automática*. If *Un año en el otro mundo* made Camba's name, *La ciudad automática* was his best book, one that "culmina su trayectoria como cronista de viajes" [caps his trajectory as a chronicler of travels] (García Martín 11).[34] Following its publication, major literary figures such as the *novecentistas*—José Ortega y Gasset, Ramón Pérez de Ayala, Ramón Gómez de la Serna—"le consideran uno de los suyos y cuentan con la admiración, acrecentada por este libro neoyorquino, de los jóvenes que comenzaban a formar una generación pronto famosa" [consider(ed) him one of their own and count(ed) on the growing admiration for this New York book among the young people who were starting to form a generation that would soon be famous] (García Martín 12). Later José Ángel Mañas (1971), author of the Madrid-based novel *Historias del Kronen* (1994), would praise *La ciudad automática*, defining Camba as his "articulista preferido de todos los tiempos" [favorite article author of all time] (Mañas). All this is to say that the literary fruit of Camba's second visit to New York—a city in which Spanish is and was not the dominant language, despite being a major presence—was not only a highlight of his career but also an inspiration for other writers.

La ciudad automática consists of ten parts. The untitled first part, containing 21 chronicles, has received the most critical attention, while the others—"Rascacielos" [Skyscrapers], "Los Estados Unidos al detalle" [The United States in Detail], "Los Estados Unidos en conjunto" [The United States as a Whole], "Comunismo y capitalismo" [Communism and Capitalism], "El embrutecimiento por la cultura" [Brutalization for Culture], "Variedades americanas" [Americans Varieties], "El pistolerismo" [Gun Laws], "La serie" [The Series],* and "La mecanización" [Mechanicization]—vary from two to five chronicles. The first part and "Rascacielos" focus on New York, while the remaining shorter parts of the book deal with other U.S. cities,

34 After its initial publication in book form in 1932 by Espasa Calpe in Madrid, *La ciudad automática* was re-edited in 1934 and 1942 by the Austral collection and enjoyed several reprintings. Then in 1948 the collection was published by Plus Ultra in *Obras completas*. José Luis García Martín's recent edition includes an appendix with four articles that Camba left out when first putting the edition together, and a later article "Patología de un gran hotel" [Grand Hotel Pathology], in which he recalls his stay in New York. A second appendix includes an interview from November 1930, with Antoniorrobles in which *ABC* newspaper announced the beginning of Camba's New York chronicles.

and critics have noted that they are less successful than the rest, as they stress "the standardization and mechanization of American life in all its phases" (Crandall 350). Their lack of appeal, however, further emphasizes the importance of New York for an Iberian readership. When the chronicles that make up *La ciudad automatica* first appeared in *ABC*, an accompanying promotional piece about Camba's New York collaboration with the newspaper defined the author's intentions:

> Camba tiene el propósito de ir revelando, desde nuestras columnas, al público español, las intimidades, las grandezas y las servidumbres de la vida en los Estados Unidos. Nueva York representa, frente a las grandes capitales de Europa, una nueva organización material y espiritual. Sus tipos y costumbres tienen muy escasa relación con los tipos y costumbres europeas. La literatura yanqui empieza a descubrir esas diferencias fundmentales y radicales, y, por todas partes, la América del Norte dicta e impone la moda, buena y mala. Nueva York es la ciudad típicamente moderna, base de la ciudad futura. (qtd in García Martín 16)

> [Camba's objective is to reveal to the Spanish audience, through our columns, the intimacies, the grandeur, and the drudgery of life in the United States. New York represents, in opposition to the major European capitals, a new material and spiritual organization. Its forms and customs have very little to do with European forms and customs. Yankee literature is starting to discover these fundamental and radical differences, and North America dictates and imposes its style everywhere, good or bad. New York is the typical modern city, the basis of the future city.]

Although the United States is mentioned, the interest is clearly New York. As such, *ABC*'s advertisement also underlines Camba's earlier writing on the U.S. city, in which he encourages readers to forget comparisons of Europe and the United States in favor of embracing the novelty of the city and new ways of reading it. While readers are asked to prepare themselves for something new, New York prepared writers and other contemporaneous artists for innovations in their work, as the city has been described as "el mejor sitio posible para respirar libertad y recorrer sin miedo el camino de la experimentación" [the best possible place to breathe freedom and follow the path of experimentation without fear] (Benítez).

The context of Camba's second visit to New York was of course different. The city's potential continued to grow throughout the first three decades of the twentieth century, and then the crash of 1929 and subsequent economic

crisis ushered in a tense environment in which to write, offering a myriad
of material as a basis for representing the city. In *La ciudad automática*'s first
part, the New York section, Camba expands the physical space he covers in
the city, taking his reader to the city's streets, Harlem, cafeterias, automats,
Jewish neighborhoods, hotels, and Spanish-speaking areas, as well as
allowing space for representations of the city not guided by location. At the
same time, the narrative voice of these chronicles is confident, quick, and
comfortable in the city. How, then, has the treatment of language developed
throughout these celebrated chronicles as a result of a second trip to New
York? How has this trip fed into the visibility of Camba as a translator-
writer of New York? On the one hand, *La ciudad automática* presents a more
frequent and spontaneous use of English, an indication of greater ease in
New York. Some of the same strategies found in *Un año en el otro mundo*
reappear, such as including a phrase in English followed by a Spanish
translation in parenthesis—"*Unemployed: Buy Apples* (Desempleados: comprad
manzanas)" (14)—or directly after the English in a clause—"*speakeasies*,
o establecimientos donde se venden bebidas espirituosas" (16)—to name
two among numerous examples. Other words that refer to the city's unique
operators include "*gangsters*" and "*racketeers*" (52), which are defined or not
depending on the context. Camba's asks his readers to gather the meaning
of English words in italics from context, such as "*manager*" (16), "*bell-boy*"
(17), "*shimmy*" (24), "*docks*" (24), "*subway*" (33), "*standard of living*" (66), "*hall*"
(35), "*lobby*" (36), "*roastbeefs*" (39), "*ticket*" (38). The frequent inclusion of
these words does not alienate readers; instead, it gives them access to the
city by inviting them to figure out the city, as a traveler must do. Camba's
travel writing thus momentarily satisfies the reader's yearning for a mildly
cosmopolitan lifestyle.

Camba's writing also teaches readers of the linguistic surprises to be
encountered in words similar to those in the Spanish language. For example,
his description of a cafeteria carefully explains to readers not only that the
experience differs from that of being in a cafetería in Madrid, but that the
word itself does not follow the same pronunciation in New York. A "*cafeteria*,"
he explains is "una palabra indudablemente española, pero que ha viajado
mucho y que, después de pasar por México, California y el Middle West,
ha llegado a Nueva York en la forma fonética de *cafitíria*, con el acento en
la sílaba «ti»" [an undoubtedly Spanish word, but it has traveled a lot and,
after making its way through Mexico, California, and the Middle West,
arrived in New York in the phonetic form of *cafitíria*, with the accent on the
«ti» syllable] (38). Including the different pronunciation at the heart of the
chronicle, as in previous examples, maintains the humor of the text as it
shakes up a very familiar word for an Iberian audience. On the other hand,

it shows a wide readership that travel means change for language and thus requires an intralingual translation. Furthermore, Camba's text does not let readers forget this, as it subsequently reminds them of how *cafetería* sounds in the New York context: "Usted entra en la *cafitíria* o cafetería" [You go into the *cafitíria* or cafetería] (38). Likewise, "*Taxi*" (18), not an unusual word for an Iberian Spanish speaker, almost always appears in italics, marking the difference between the taxis of Madrid, for instance, and those of New York. Taxis in New York operate differently from those to which the readers might be accustomed. In short, in travel writing, as in literary translation, the translation strategies vary depending on the context. Overall, Camba's ease with and greater inclusion of English presents a narrator with a heightened knowledge of the city, and allows readers to access New York in a manner beyond description, expanding their linguistic possibilities related to the city's everyday beat.

As the more frequent use of English becomes an expected characteristic of this series of chronicles, so does the evidence of Camba's experience from travels to European cities, as in the chronicle "La ciudad del bueno vino" [City of Good Wine] (49–51) about Prohibition and homemade winemaking practices, for example. There has been widespread acknowledgment that *La ciudad automática* tackles more contemporary and cosmopolitan themes. At the same time, in the context of these chronicles, James Shearer has described Camba as a "provocative and entertaining spokesman for Spanish culture in his time" (xxiv). Camba's writing does not use his cosmopolitanism to alienate the widespread readership attracted to his work; rather, it reinforces the role he had in expanding his readers' imaginations of a world beyond the local. In doing so, his chronicles also take readers beyond instances of translation as a presentation of a linguistic conundrum to deeply cultural examples through the display of an interest in the Spanish-speaking areas of the city, as noted in the three chronicles "XVI. Sevilla Street," "XVIII. La España Negra" [XVIII. Black Spain], and "XIX. La Inquisicion y el Arroz Con Pollo" [XIX. The Inquisition and Chicken with Rice] (59).

Similar to the transformations which *cafetería* undergoes, not only in terms of pronunciation but also in definition, when moving from the Iberian Peninsula to New York City, Camba exposes readers to the shifts that occur when culture moves or is envisioned from afar. Based on these chronicles, Camba informs his readers that what is celebrated as "Spain" or "Spanish" in the New York context is in no way restricted to the Iberian Peninsula but rather has its origins in any Spanish-speaking cultural expression. Instead of contesting this definition or expression of Spain in New York, Camba guides his readers in understanding its development. He refers to the neighborhood from 110th to 116th Street between Fifth and Eighth Avenue as "España en toda su enorme variedad histórica. Es la España grande, la España donde nunca se pone el sol todavía, la España hispánica, en una palabra" [Spain in all of its enormous historical variety. It's the great Spain, the Spain where the sun still never sets, the Hispanic Spain, to sum it up] (56). Throughout the chronicles of *La ciudad automática* and *Un año en el otro mundo*, Camba effectively uses repetition and multiple means to explain the New York he wants his readers to remember. He remains faithful to that technique and further defines the enormously inclusive boundaries of Spain in New York to be "en pequeño, [...] una España muy grande" [in miniature, (...) a very great Spain] (57). In an effort to illustrate his point in specific terms, he concludes:

> Para Norteamérica, España resultará siempre una mezcla muy confusa de la Inquisición, el arroz con pollo, los Reyes Católicos, el general Sandino, Sevilla, Antofagasta, Salvador de Madariaga, la Pastora Imperio, los toros, la rumba, Cristóbal Colón y don Niceto Alcalá-Zamora. (61)

> [For North America, Spain will always be a very confusing mix of the Inquisition, chicken with rice, the Catholic Monarchs, General Sandino, Seville, Antofagasta, Salvador de Madariaga, Pastora Imperio, bullfights, rumba, Christopher Columbus, and Don Niceto Alcalá-Zamora.]

Through this example, Camba expands his reader's understanding of translation to be something beyond a purely linguistic experience, but a cultural one as well. Just as familiar words in new contexts work in different ways, New York's expression of Spain as something other than how it might be envisioned by his readers in a strictly Iberian context offers yet another opportunity for readers to see language's link to context.

One of the best chronicles of *La ciudad automática* is "IV. El Chrysler Building" [IV. The Chrysler Building] (74) in the final section, "Rascacielos," of the part of the collection dedicated to New York City. Here, referring to Jules Verne's short story "Une fantaisie du docteur Ox" [Dr. Ox's Experiment] (1872), Camba makes some general statements about the city:[35]

> Nueva York tiene también algo de ciudad oxigenada. Es una ciudad donde parece que todo el mundo está rascando ollas de barro de la mañana a la noche y de la noche a la mañana. Es una ciudad delirante,

---

35 A Spanish translation of Jules Verne's short story was published in 1925 in Madrid as part of the "Novela de la libertad" series. Camba, however, could have read Verne's original French version.

una ciudad exasperada y frenética. Paseando por sus calles uno va poco a poco saturándose de electricidad, y no es que uno pisotee deliberadamente a nadie, pero si por casualidad resulta que le dan un pisotón a algún transeúnte, se alegran de habérselo dado. (76)

[New York also has something of an oxygenated city about it. It is a city where it seems that everyone is working their fingers to the bone from morning to night and from night to morning. It is a delirious city, an exasperated and frenetic city. Strolling through the streets you get soaked with electricity little by little, and it is not that anyone deliberately trample someone, but if by chance it happens that they step on some passer-by, they are glad to have given it to them.]

Camba references a work of science fiction in order to make sense of the excitement and aggressiveness of the city streets. In an effort to momentarily escape, Camba climbs to the top of the Chrysler Building: "No hay más que un procedimiento para substraerse a la violencia ambiente y poder tener de Nueva York una visión desapasionada: subir al último piso del Chrysler Building" [There's only one way to get away from the violence of the atmosphere and get a dispassionate vision of New York: go up to the top floor of the Chrysler Building] (76). It is from there that one is able to leave the "hormiguero" [anthill], seek a respite from it all, "*au-dessus de la mêlée*" [up above the tussle] and "entender a Nueva York en su totalidad" [understand New York in its totality] (76). The perspective from the top of one of the tallest buildings in the city at the time offers Camba a vision that he has never known, "una anticipación de lo futuro" [an anticipation of the future] as well as "una reconstrucción de lo pasado" [a reconstruction of the past] (77).

This narrative gesture immediately recalls Lorca's "Grito hacia Roma (desde la torre del Chrysler Building)" [Cry toward Rome (from the Tower of the Chrysler Building)], in which the poet is also removed from the intense atmosphere of the city streets, including the masses of Coney Island, Harlem, Battery City, and Wall Street, to name but a few locales referenced in the collection's poems. The poet thus directs verses toward Rome from the top of the Chrysler Building, denouncing all the negativity that saturates New York, or at least that is found in the accompanying verses of the collection. This is not to say that this is the single poem that speaks out against the injustice, pain, and harshness of the city, but it is distinctive in that the poet's voice is strong, confident, and speaks from above the city streets while directed at the ancient city of Rome, adding, like Camba, an historical perspective to representing New York while engaging with

Rome. Once Camba returns to the city streets, "[l]a perspectiva histórica se desvanece, los detalles anulan el conjunto, y las hormigas, sin dejar de ser hormigas, crecen y adquieren la proporción espantosa de seres humanos" [the historical perspective fades, the details cancel out the ensemble, and the ants, without stopping being ants, grow and attain the atrocious proportions of human beings] (77).

Did Camba know about Lorca's poem when he wrote this chronicle? Had Lorca read Camba's text while he was developing his poem? The answer matters less than what reading the two texts together does for Iberian translations of New York. On the one hand, it speaks to the centrality of the Chrysler Building within the literary imagination of the time. As one of the tallest structures in the city, the skyscraper offers an imaginative respite from the city streets, making way for a more general, but not simple, assessment of New York as a whole. On the other hand, it underscores the tendency toward fragmentation that writing from the street provides. Camba writes that New York is attractive because "uno no puede vivir al margen del tiempo" [you can't live on the periphery of time] (*Ciudad* [2008] 13). From within, New York can only be talked about for its movements and for its moments. The city generates stories and keeps writing going because of the fragments of life that it offers its dweller-writers.

Final Note on Camba

As a correspondent for Spanish newspapers and a prolific writer of cities, Camba understood himself to be more of an interpreter than a reproducer of his subject, something for which he has been criticized, as mentioned earlier in the discussion of María Dolores Costa's analysis of his work. In one of the longest sections of *Un año en el otro mundo*, "'La España Consciente', de Ignacio Zuloaga" (79), Camba defends Zuloaga from the criticism his work received while exhibited at the Brooklyn Museum. Some critics felt that Zuloaga should have painted Spain in another way (79); others felt that "Zuloaga reproduce bien un aspecto de España; pero que no debe limitarse a este aspecto solo, para no darle al mundo una falsa idea de la totalidad española" [Zuloaga did a good job at reproducing an aspect of Spain; but that he shouldn't limit himself to this aspect alone, to avoid giving the world a false idea of the Spanish totality] (79). Others still believed the Spain of his work to be "falsa de toda falsedad, falsa en el detalle y en el conjunto, falsa absolutamente" [false in every way, false in the details and in the ensemble, absolutely false] (80). In defense of Zuloaga's paintings, Camba reminds his readers that "Zuloaga no reproduce: interpreta" [Zuloaga does not reproduce: he interprets] (80), just as writers of literature such as Azorín, Baroja, and others do. For the remainder of the chronicle Camba goes on to argue that depictions of a place present ideas and interpretations as opposed to images that should be judged to be true or faithful. This is the same predicament as in the evaluation of translations. Discussions of fidelity mask the role of the translator as an interpreter of a literary text. Camba advocates for his own writing as one that interprets rather than observes. Understanding his work in such a way presents possibilities for New York in writing rather than a choice between a favorable or unfavorable city.

Josep Pla

If Julio Camba's death marked the beginning of a decline in his readership, Josep Pla's death marked just the opposite. His worked continued to be read, celebrated, and translated beyond his passing. Pla, like Camba, was an extremely prolific writer. His complete works, which he began to assemble around the age of 70, make up over 40 hefty volumes "averaging more than six hundred pages each" (Bou 568) making a total that exceeds 30,000 pages (Puig ix).[36] As mentioned earlier, "his writing doesn't fit easily into any school or pervading style of the time, yet he is the most important modern stylist in Catalan prose" as well as one of the most important prose writers of the twentieth century (Miles). Perhaps Pla's writing would not have gained such a status had it not been for his interest in and need to travel. The amount of writing that Pla produced is commensurate with the amount of traveling he did. He engaged in international travel throughout a large part of his life as a foreign correspondent for newspapers.[37] The list of cities and countries he visited includes, in no particular order: Paris, Rome, Madrid, Berlin, Cuba, New York, Buenos Aires, Belgium, England, Russia, Holland, Scandinavia, Hungary, Madrid, Valencia, Greece, Israel, Brazil, and Puerto Rico. He was away from his homeland for nearly 20 years, which gave him a unique "bany de cosmopolitisme" [cosmopolitanism bath] (Castellet 73).

---

36 In his introduction to Peter Bush's English translation of Pla's *The Gray Notebook*, Valentí Puig gives a sense of Pla's work as a whole: "Pla's body of work comprises journals, notebooks, novels, stories, aphorisms, reminiscences, a political history of contemporary Spain, and a picture of mid-century Catalonia, including portraits and biographies of its major figures, which has all the minute detail of a modern digital file. Of his few novels, the best is *La calle estrecha* (1952). Better are his many stories—of the sea, the small world of pensions in Barcelona, and Berlin—which emulate the realism of Dutch painting" (x).

37 Of the 47 volumes of Pla's complete works, 21 include articles published in the periodicals *Destino*, *La Publicitat*, and *La Veu de Catalunya*.

Curiously, Pla never considered himself a tourist, nor did he ever travel "pel plaer de fer-lo" [for the pleasure of it]; on the contrary, he thought of himself as a professional traveler (Garolera 126). For Pla, travel, literature, and life are intricately linked to the extent that they are "una mateixa cosa" [the same thing] (Garolera 121).

Unlike the other authors I have studied in this book, Pla did not have a deep affection for or a personal connection to the city. In 1913, he left his home on the Costa Brava to study law at the Universitat de Barcelona, a time that he recounts in "his finest book," *El quadern gris* [The Gray Notebook] (Puig viii). As a young reporter, he was in Barcelona during one of the city's most unsettling periods. He then moved on to Paris as a foreign correspondent. He traveled to and wrote a myriad of European cities during some of their most intense moments. He was in Geneva during the League of Nations, Rome during Mussolini's march on the city in 1922, Moscow in 1925 "when Trotsky and Stalin were caught in a power struggle," and Berlin "during the hyperinflation of the Weimar Republic" (Puig xi). His travel came to a halt when Francisco Franco confiscated his passport (Puig xi). Pla began to travel again when he started writing weekly articles for the Spanish-language newspaper *Destino* in 1940. Valentí Puig notes that Pla's urban-centric texts on the small world of *pensiones* in Barcelona and Berlin are among his best (x).

New York City occupies a special place in his *œuvre* as the only non-European city to which an entire volume is dedicated and one of the few centered around one single city; however, *Week-end (d'estiu) a New-York* has received little critical attention. Pla was a mature writer by the time he first traveled to New York in his late fifties. In fact, in 1951, three years before his trip, he was considered the most prolific and most-read Catalan author due to the growth in books published in Catalan (Bonada 16). Pla enjoyed one of the peaks of his career before crossing the Atlantic. His friend Josep Vergés, owner and editor of *Destino*, proposed the idea of going to New York with the intention that the trip would generate a dozen "reportajes" [features] for the weekly paper (López Gayarre). Pla recounts: "me hizo gracia la propuesta de Vergés y la acepté" [I was amused by Vergés's proposal and accepted it] (López Gayarre). *Week-end* was published in Catalan in 1955, and then later in Spanish in 1959 under the title *Viaje a América* by Vergés's publishing house Áncora y Delfín, with a prologue by the journalist Néstor Luján (1922–95).

In 1946, close to a decade before going to New York, Pla had experienced changes that would greatly impact his career. That year, Franco allowed books to be published in Catalan again. Pla celebrated this with the publication of three books in Catalan: *Cadaqués*, and new editions of *Cartes de lluny*, originally published in 1928, and *Viatge a Catalunya*, first published in 1934.[38] Valerie Miles notes that for Pla "the return to writing in his native language and the ability to travel again—now by tanker, to places like Israel, Cuba, New York, the Middle East, and South America—brought renewed energy to his writing." Revisiting his previous work also granted Pla the opportunity to comment on the significance of publishing in Catalan again. In the prologue to his new and expanded edition of *Viatge a Catalunya*, Lluís Bonada notes that Pla "espera que sigui l'inici de la publicació, en català, de tots els seus llibres i deixa entès que l'edició original dels llibres que fins ara ha hagut de publicar en castellá és la catalana" [hopes that this is the start of the publication of all his books in Catalan, and he makes it clear that the original edition of his books that, until now, he has had to publish in Castilian, is the Catalan version] (Bonada 15). Pla had published seven books in Castilian during the years in which it was prohibited to publish in Catalan: *Guía de la Costa Brava* (1941), *Las ciudades del mar* (1942), *Viaje en autobús* (1942), *Rusiñol y su tiempo* (1942), *El pintor Joaquín Mir* (1944), *Un señor de Barcelona* (1945), and *La huida del tiempo* (1945). Declaring that the Catalan versions of texts first published in Castilian were the originals not only reveals the hindrances of publishing during a dictatorship, but also highlights the fact that a published edition of a book does not always mean that it is the original. To further solidify his status as a Catalan writer, in a 1957 article in *Destino*, Pla refused to be considered a bilingual writer (Bonada 17). Pla's declarations warned against the deformed representations of what his published work says about him as a writer and indirectly speak to the complex and widespread degree to which translation is ingrained in his writing.

Pla as a Translator

Beyond the Castilian-Catalan conflict in publishing, as a frequent and professional traveler and writer, and a speaker of a minority language, Pla was in a sense always translating, insofar as the effects of translation must not have been foreign to him. There is, however, no critical discussion of Pla as a translator. Lluís Bonada claims that Pla's Catalan version of *El lladre de criatures* by the French authors Émile Erckmann (1822–99) and Alexandre Chatrian (1826–90), who jointly wrote nearly all of their works

---

38 Pla received a letter written in Catalan from Josep B. Canudas in New York dated October 7, 1949 (now held by the Fundació Josep Pla, Palafrugell, Spain), in which Canudas thanks him for *Cadaqués* and *Cartes de lluny* because they made him feel closer to Catalonia.

under the name Erckmann-Chatrian, is the only translation *per se* that Pla ever published. Pla was in his late twenties when the translation was released in December of 1924 (8). There are other instances in which Pla translated shorter texts from one language to another. For example, *Week-end (d'estiu) a New-York* includes a Catalan translation of a selection from *Les 48 Amériques* (1953) by the French journalist Raymond Cartier (1904–75), which Pla refers to as *Les 49 Amériques*. In addition, in Pla's description of New York's Washington Square, he shares a Catalan translation of Henry James's 1880 novel by the same name. The text's initial response to the New York locale is bilingual: "a *quiet and gentle retirement* (un lloc tranquil i de qualitat)" (126).[39] In James's short novel the quote is "[t]he ideal of quiet and of genteel retirement, in 1835, was found in Washington Square" (11). Shortly after, Pla quotes more extensively from James, this time solely providing the Catalan version:

> "Washington Square"—escriu James—"exhala una espècie de calma estable que es troba rarament en aquesta ciutat vibrant; el seu aspecte mostra una maduresa, una dignitat, un benestar, que es deuen, sens dubte, al fet que el lloc fou centre, ja historic, d'una societat, cosa que no tenen ni coneixen els barris més sumptuosos." (126)

> ["Washington Square," writes James, "exhales a kind of stable calm that is rarely found in this vibrant city; it exhibits a maturity, a dignity, a well-being, that is undoubtledly due to the fact that it was the center of a now historic society, something that the most splendid neighborhoods neither have nor are familiar with."]

The placement of quotations around James's words suggests that Pla is providing a Catalan translation of a citation from James's text. Given that the first Catalan translation of *Washington Square*, by Jordi Arbonès, was not published until 1984, this translation was most likely produced by Pla specifically for *Week-end*. Whether or not Pla translates from James's *Washington Square* or cites the text from memory, the result appears to be a translation of a selection from the novel which reveals that writing New York literally becomes translating New York as it exists in the literary imagination. Considering the publication year of *Week-end* and the contemporaneous status of the Catalan language in print, Pla's decision to provide Catalan translations of Cartier and James is more than an effort to make his text

---

39 The first Spanish translation by Sergio Pitol was published in 1970. Subsequent Spanish translations include those by Emilio Olcina Aya (1982), Amando Lázaro Ros (1990), and Catalina Martínez Muñoz (2010).

more accessible to his readers. His translations demonstrate a commitment to writing in Catalan and to getting as many words as possible into Catalan, making up for the absence of the language from publications in previous years.

Moreover, the inclusion of Cartier's and James's versions of New York speaks to the fact that writers of the city not only write place but also write in reaction to its former representations, similar to the way in which literary translators, when creating a new translation of a given text, respond to, reject, or borrow from extant versions.[40] Following his quote of James on Washington Square, Pla explicitly refers to other versions of New York by authors who wrote the city before him:

El lector observarà potser que venir a Nova York per parlar d'aquests llocs tocats de vellesa i de decrepitud és romper escandalosament amb una tradició literària europea que exigeix parlar d'aquesta ciutat amb un lèxic crispat, febricitant i dramàtic. Es possible. De tota manera, no crec que sigui cap defecte d'atenir-se a la realitat. En aquesta ciutat hi ha coses molt amables i perfectament humanes, cosa natural, perquè els homes i les dones que viuen aquí són com els altres. En canvi, una gran part de la informació que jo portava m'ha resultat, sino totalment falsa, almenys insuportablement exagerada. He trobat, en aquesta immensa concentració, tantes coses del nord d'Europa, que si s'exceptuen els gratacels, que fan de Nova York una peça única, res de les altres coses no m'ha causa una sensació de desplaçament a un país exotic i estrany. És certament ridícul que jo parli d'aquesta ciutat d'Amèrica en termes generals, però tinc la vaga intuïció—i les intuïcions han d'ésser perdonades—que aquesta és la ciutat d'aquest continent més profundament europea, més acostada als nostres gustos i als nostres habits mentals. (127)

[The reader will perhaps observe that to come to New York to talk about these places that are decrepit and touched by time is to break scandously with a European literary tradition that talks about this city with a tense, feverish, and dramatic lexicon. It's possible. Anyway, I don't think it's a defect to stick close to reality. In this city, there are very nice and perfectly human things, something natural, because the men and women that live here are like others. However, a large part of the information I had, turned out to be, if not totally false, at least unbearably exaggerated. In this immense concentration, I have found

---

40 Besides Henry James, Pla also mentions the work of Ernest Hemingway while discussing the area around Cuba and Key West (Pla, *Week-end* 17).

so many things from northern Europe that—with the exception of
the skyscrapers—make New York unique. None of the other things
has caused me to feel displaced in an exotic and strange country.
It's certainly ridiculous for me to talk about this American city in
general terms, but I have the vague intuition—and intuitions must
be excused—that this is the most profoundly European city on this
continent, more inclined to our tastes and mental habits.]

In making an argument for a New York that is not drastically different from
Europe, Pla detracts from the foreignness of the city for his readers. His
attempt to adhere to reality, to portray the actuality of the city, thus comes
across as novel. In his study of the affinities between translation and travel,
Michael Cronin argues that "Good translations can endure, of course, and
travel accounts can be memorable additions to writing in a language but
most translations, even the very best, have to be reworked and/or reinvented
for a new generation of readers" (*Across* 23). Pla was certainly familiar with
Camba and his work, as is seen in his 1962 essay "Les idees de Julio Camba."
In *Week-end*, without ever mentioning his name, Pla refers to Camba's New
York writing: "Anys enrera Nova York fou anomenada la ciutat automàtica"
[years ago, New York was called the automatic city] (150). Furthermore,
about two months before Pla left for New York, he received a letter from
Antonio Ramón Torres, "el mallorquí, amic [seu] des de 1915, resident a Nova
York des de fa tants anys, magnífic temperament d'artista, d'una companyia
tan agradable i útil" [the Malloriquin, his friend since 1915, resident in
New York for some time, an artist with a wonderful nature, and a nice and
helpful companion] (24). In a letter dated June 4, 1954 (now held by the
Fundació Josep Pla, Frank Keerl Pla Collection, Palafrugell, Spain), Ramón
Torres offers details about Spanish cultural production on and in New York
and references "el gran" [the great] Julio Camba and his assessment of New
York as "el ombligo del mundo" [the navel of the world].[41] Therefore, Pla
was familiar with Camba's representation of New York and at the same
time would have agreed with Cronin's justification for the value of updated
travel accounts. When writing about the city approximately 25 years after
Camba, Pla mentions Camba's "ciutat automática" and finds his account to
have "ridiculitzat" [derided] the city (150). In speaking in general about
Pla's work, Valentí Puig reminds us that he "was not interested in metaphor
but in the language of things. He sought a comprehensive realism, rich in
detail and full of color" (Valentí Puig vii). By sticking to the details, Pla

41 This letter contains details about Iberian artists and culture in New York. This
letter is available at the Fundació Josep Pla.

focuses on the experience of actually being in the city in an effort to move away from a perspective that is exaggerated or overwhelmed by the city and its extant images, and to offer a reworked or reinvented approximation of the city. Pla's text presents a new version of New York for a mid-twentieth-century reader already familiar with a number of representations of the city that contribute to its symbolic meaning.

More than a Weekend, More than New York

Week-end (d'estiu) a New-York is organized into 11 parts with anywhere from four to six individually titled sections in each. The twelfth and final part features an interview with Josep Pla conducted by an unnamed journalist upon Pla's return to Empordà. Although the text includes specific dates and demonstrates awareness of the passage of time, *Week-end* is not a diary but rather a report of Pla's trip to New York City, beginning with the moment the *Guadalupe* leaves the port of Cádiz in the south of Spain at 5:30 pm on August 3, 1954, and ends about a month later, when Pla reaches A Coruña in the early days of September. His arrival in Galicia is facilitated by Fernando Fontana, "el nostre amic i company de viatge" [our friend and travel companion] (170),[42] who accompanies Pla at least on the eastbound trip (see Fig. 3.4).[43] Pla then makes his way across the Iberian Peninsula to the Costa Brava via Santander and Bilbao. According to *Week-end*, on the way to New York, Pla visits Havana and then arrives in the New York harbor on August 19, 1954. He leaves the city from the Hoboken dock on the New Jersey side of the Hudson River on August 22, 1954. The accuracy of these arrival and departure dates is questionable not only because they add up to four days rather than a weekend, but also because they align neither with other dates Pla gives nor with his summation of having been in the city for six days: "I així arribà l'hora de marxar, perquè el *weekend* a Nova York—que fou un final de setmana una mica més llarg del que signifiquen les paraules (sis dies)—s'havia inexorablement acabat" [and then came time to leave, because the weekend in New York—a weekend that was a bit longer than what the word means (six days)—had inexorably come to an end] (168). The length of his stay, however, is less significant than what the miscalculations

---

42 Fontana is the nephew of Rafael Puget i Munt for whom Pla's *Un senyor de Barcelona* is named (Moret 1). Xavier Moret claims that Pla and the Fontanas "van fer tots plegats un viatge a Amèrica" [took a trip to America together] (Moret 2). Fernando reports that there was a time when Pla and Luján spent a lot of time together (Moret 2).

43 I located this photo at the Fundació Josep Pla. It has never been published before.

Fig. 3.4 The Fontanas, Josep Pla, and Néstor Luján aboard the *Guadalupe*. New York, 1954. Fundació Josep Pla, Collection Ed. Destino.

reveal about the disorienting effects of time in the city. During the first quarter of *Week-end*, time and its passage are precisely noted. On his first day in New York, Pla marks the hours: "Vuit hores després de trobar-me a Nova York" [Eight hours after arriving in New York] (4); "Vaig tornar a les idees d'unes hores abans" [I went back to the ideas from a few hours ago] (45). The writing has an immediacy which gives the impression that he is recording the progression and observations of his visit while walking. On that first day alone, while eating lunch, Pla shares that "avui ha estat el dia de la meva vida que he vist més coses" [today I have seen more than on any other day of my life] (46). On the third day, he has still not stopped moving: "[d]esprés de tres dies de córrer per Manhattan sense parar" [after three days of running around Manhattan without stopping" (70). By the fourth day in the city, he has used every form of transportation the city offers (122), allowing him to visit Rockefeller Center, the Upper East Side, the New York Public Library, Washington Square Park, and Harlem, among other places. Similar to José Moreno Villa, Pla is affected by the accelerated speed, the "ritme frenètic" [frenetic rhythm] (38), at which the city operates, a pace that gives no respite. As the text develops, attention to time becomes less and less frequent. Nearing the final pages of *Week-end*, Pla says that he has been in the city for six days "sense parar un moment, dormint poc, anant de la Seca a la Meca sense reposar" [without stopping for a moment, sleeping little, going from here to there without resting] (157). The effects of his fatigue penetrate the writing as the sense of time is lost. His sense of movement around the city becomes scarcer the longer he is there. Pla recognizes that a "defecte fenomenal" [phenomenal defect] of the city is that "és massa gran, donades les mides humanes" [it is too big, given human sizes] (129). Observations of this nature recall Federico García Lorca's remarks on New York: "the two elements the traveler first captures in the big city are extrahuman architecture and furious rhythm" ("Lecture" 187).[44] Pla's text attests to these two characteristics that Lorca highlights as fundamental for understanding New York. In a way, the title *Week-end (d'estiu) a New-York* is a statement about the treatment of time in the city not being what it seems. As *Week-end* progresses, the abundance of details eclipses references to time, and Pla realizes that his report on the city cannot keep up with the abundance that surrounds him. In his description of the Metropolitan Museum of Art, Pla notes on two occasions that "No tinc pas lloc per a detallar" [I have no space for the details] (74) and "No tinc espai suficient per a ocupar-me dels altres aspectes de la institució" [I don't have enough space to get into the other aspects of the institution] (75). Abundance is another word that has traditionally characterized the city. Now abundance describes the amount of detail that Pla offers his readers with the possibility of tiring them out as they read his city.

The book's title is also notable for its language choice. In the prologue to volume 34 of Pla's *Obra completa*, *Les Amériques*, he comments on the title of *Week-end (d'estiu) a New-York* and says that it could seem that it responds to "un esnobismo de extranjerización acentuada" [a snobbishness of accentuated foreignization] (López Gayarre). Writing this prologue in 1977, about 20 years after the publication of *Week-end*, Pla contests that this is not the case and that he is from a generation in which the reasonable use of foreignization was not considered snobbish (López Gayarre). Pla's perspective on the title further supports the idea that he does not subscribe to larger trends, generalizations, or "the service of the symbolic" (Puig vii), but this short title encapsulates much more that can be said about the work. In spring 1955, a little less than a year after Pla's return home from his trip to the United States, *Week-end (d'estiu) a New-York* was published by Selecta in Barcelona (see Fig. 3.5). While Pla's title uses English words, subsequent printings of the book and references to it have chosen to substitute the English *New York* with the Catalan *Nova York* and have eliminated the hyphen

44 Pla talks about Columbia University without making any mention to Lorca's stay (86–87).

in "weekend."[45] Spanish-language versions of the book have introduced other alterations. *Fin de semana en Nueva York* is the title of the 2016 edition of the 1959 Spanish version *Viaje a América* with translations of previously unedited parts by Concha Cardeñoso Sáenz de Miera. These versions are not faithful to Pla's original title, which highlights one of the fundamental aspects of writing New York: the encounter with the English language. Throughout the book, Pla switches between "New York" and "Nova York," mostly favoring the Catalan version, thus making his choice of New York for the title even more notable. The use of the word *week-end* is noteworthy not only because his stay in New York exceeded a weekend but also because throughout the text the use of English is scarce. The title in part presents a distortion of some of the key aspects of the book. In doing so the title is faithful to Pla's approach to New York, in which he strives to supersede the existing image of the city.

Descriptions of *Week-end*—such as that of Carles Capdevila's "un llibre on relata la seva experiència i desciu la ciutat dels gratacels" [a book in which he tells of his experience and describes the city of skyscrapers] (Capdevila 240)—limit the book's scope in terms of content and the overall complexity of a travel account. On the one hand, New York is not the only place described in the book. The text commences the moment Pla leaves the port of Cádiz and incorporates descriptions of sea life, sunsets, the changing sea, and other landscapes. The *Guadalupe* travels to New York via Havana, where Pla sees his first skyscraper, another gesture to subvert the strong association of New York and skyscrapers:

> Embadalits davant del moderns gratacels, no ens adonàrem gairebé que el «Guadalupe», navegant lentament, entrava a la boca de trabuc del port, deixant a l'esquerra la mediocre ruïna colonial del Castell del Morro i les decrepituds casernàries de La Cabaña. (16)

> [Spellbound before the modern skyscrapers, we almost didn't realize that the *Guadalupe*, sailing slowly, was entering the gun-barrel mouth of the port, leaving to the left the mediocre colonial ruin of the Morro Castle and the decrepit quarters of La Cabaña.]

The inclusion of the journey to New York underlines Pla's attention to travel, to the experience of travel, and not just the destination. Travel, as Joan Ramon Resina points out, was a major component of Pla's life, to the extent that "travel is a metaphor or, better, a modality of life, and like life, it cannot

---

45 The 1985 edition reprints the work as *Weekend (d'estiu) a Nova York*, which comes from the edition in Pla's *Obra completa*.

JOSEP PLA

WEEK-END
(D'ESTIU)
A NEW-YORK

TERCERA SÈRIE DE «CARTES DE LLUNY»

Fig. 3.5 Cover of first edition
Week-end (d'estiu) a New-York
by Josep Pla, 1955.

be grasped as a still image or place but unfolds in time" (Resina 227). Thus, the opportunity to provide an account of a journey reduces the anxiety about reach New York. What is more, while in New York for a few days, Pla asks his cicerone, Mr. Ellers,[46] to take him to the countryside. On Sunday, August 22, the two travel 20 miles outside the city to "visitar un poblet situat al camp" [visit a small town in the country] (99): "Eaglenwood" (103), presumably Englewood, and Leonia in New Jersey. Pla's description of the New Jersey houses likens them to those of northern Europe, alluding to his vast travels. Pla's descriptions of the journey to New York and the areas beyond the city serve as a reminder that "[l]andscape for Pla was his homeland" (Puig ix). They also allow Pla's writing to expand literary representations of New York

---

46 According to *Week-end*, Ellers worked for Crown Cork International in New Jersey (*Week-end* 24). See Pla's "Agraïment" in *Week-end* for a list of the the other individuals who facilitated this trip.

to the outlying areas, thereby demonstrating how the city fits into the U.S. landscape. In *Week-end*, Pla notes that

> La literatura sensacionalista sobre Nova York és molt abundant. La literatura dedicada a descriure extravagancies més o menys fantasistes—més aviat més que menys—sobre aquesta ciutat és també important. En canvi, són raríssims els autors que ens parlen de la geografia de Nova York. (143)

> [The sensationalist literature about New York is very abundant. The literature that describes the more or less fantastic extravagances—or rather more than less—of this city is also considerable. On the contrary, authors who speak to us about the geography of New York are very rare.]

Throughout *Week-end* Pla demonstrates his familiarity with a literary New York and seeks to respond to it, making this text much more significant than a descriptive travel account.

The Language of *Week-end (d'estiu) a New-York*

Pla's treatment of New York's skyscrapers, reflects his endeavor to rework or reinvent New York at a time when the city's images are accessible to a large audience. After Havana, the next skyscrapers appear in New York. A touch of humor accompanies the text's initial description of the city's primary architectural feature: the skyscrapers of Lower Manhattan. Pla likens them to "un manat fantàstic d'espàrrecs" [a fantastic handful of asparagus] (22), reducing their awesome presence to a common garden vegetable. What is more, throughout *Week-end*, but most frequent in the early pages, Pla's use of the word skyscraper, "gratacel" in Catalan, is notably replaced by a descriptive combination of words such as "estructures verticals" [vertical structures] (22), "les superbes estructures" [the superb structures] (22), "les estructures estretes, primes" [the narrow, slim structures] (23), "les verticals de Nova York" [the New York verticals] (23), "grans edificis verticals" [grand vertical buildings] (30), "una superestructura" [a superstructure] (34), "les fantàstiques estructures verticals" [the fantastic vertical structures] (117). Referring to skyscrapers in these terms allows Pla's readers enduring the "anys encara durs i difícils" [still difficult and trying years] under Franco's dictatorship, who have never physically seen a skyscraper, to comprehend the spatial implications of such a structure (Iborra 68). This example not only speaks to Pla's care for language but also to his "predilection for the concrete and the minute" as "a defense against the voiding of life through false expectations or utopia" (Resina 238). Discussing the skyscrapers as such "familiarize[s] the foreign element and render[s] it in terms immediately intelligible to the target (home) reader, thus operating what has become known as a 'domesticating' strategy'" (Polezzi 83). Speaking of New York architecture in these terms increases its significance to a Catalan-speaking audience.

Week-end (d'estiu) a New-York continues to use a variety of strategies that could be classified as domesticating. First, Pla's conversations with his cicerone, Mr. Ellers of Crown Cork International in New Jersey, of whom the reader knows very little, are fluid and pose no communication obstacle. The text masks any trace of the language of their conversation as they appear in Catalan. *Week-end* is also made comfortable for the non-English-speaking Catalan reader as it translates proper nouns, such as Saint Patrick's Cathedral to "Sant Patrici" and Fifth Avenue to "Cinquena Avinguda," Battery Park to "Parc de la Bateria" (163), and Morgan Bank to "Banque Morgan" (164). On the one hand, this strategy seems to be an unproductive over-translation of New York City, while on the other, it enhances the description of the place, underlining the significance of its name as the author makes sure that his readers will understand its meaning. Furthermore, this gesture can be understood as an effort to work these grand places of New York into the sounds of Catalan, thereby internationalizing the language. However, there are some instances in which the decision to translate place names into Catalan falls short. In a discussion of Harlem, Pla avoids using "Spanish Harlem" and instead refers to it as "el barri porto-riqueny, erròniament anomenat espanyol" [the Puerto Rican neighborhood, erroneously called Spanish] (30). Pla comprehends that this neighborhood "és un barri d'immigrants de l'Amèrica Llatina dins del qual tenen una absoluta preponderància els porto-riquenys" [is a neighborhood of immigrants from Latin America in which Puerto Ricans are the dominant group] (76–77), but he fails to see that "Spanish" in this case refers to the presence of the language instead of the national group.

Although domestication appears to be the strategy of choice overall, *Week-end* does allow space for English and, with less frequency, Italian words. These words visually mark the text as they are almost always presented in italics. A sampling of the English words included in Pla's travel account attests to the text's variety of subject matter: "*borough*" (19), "*cottages*" (20), "*hall*" (36, 67), "*flash*" (39), "*melting pot*" (43, 64, 77), "*building*" (44), "*subway*" (49), "*trading floor*" (54), "*lunch*" (54), "*barman*" (59), "*slums*" (65, 148), "*campus*" (86), "*saloons*" (90), "*mayor*" (96), "*poor fellows*" (98), "*bungalow*" (102), "*hot music,*" "*night clubs*" (127), "*frozen*" (130), "*cowboy*" (131), "*highlanders*" (131), "*income tax*" (147), and "*skyviews*" (161). The text neither defines nor provides a Catalan translation for these words, asking the reader to deduce the meaning from context. On a few occasions, the text facilitates the readers' experience by incorporating an explanation of an English term. For example, when walking around the city, Pla notes that the word "shelter" is frequently seen: "*Shelter*, que vol dir refugi, si no estic equivocat" [*Shelter*, which means "refugi," if I'm not mistaken] (139). In a discussion of Wall Street, "*brokers*" is followed by "que peremptòriament traduirem per borsistes" [which we will peremptorily translate as "borsistes"] (54). "*Check, please ...!*" (59) appears twice in *Week-end*, first without a translation, and later followed by "D'una factura, en diuen un xec. *Check please ...* Aquestes paraules, les sentiu constantment" [They call the bill a *xec. Check please ...* You hear these words constantly] (136). Both examples suggest that Pla is aware of the complexities of travel and translation, in that his translations call attention to themselves by giving the reader something more than a translation of just the English words. They prove that Pla does not just translate words, but rather context. Another example of the inclusion of words in languages other than Catalan is the use of "*negritos*" [blacks] (80, 81, 82) in Spanish three times in the description of Harlem. Pla's use of words in English and Spanish, and the choice to give prices in dollars and cents, and distances in miles—"De l'Havana a Nova York hi ha mil dues-centes milles" [Havana and New York are 1,200 miles apart] (19)—could be perceived as moving toward foreignization as a translation strategy. Instead, considering Pla's attention to detail and his faithfulness to the concrete, these moments in which foreignization seems to be the strategy of choice, or translation is absent, can be understood as an effort to capture the concrete or proof of his visit to the city.

As a result, if travel accounts are to be read as a type of translation, the traditional binary of foreignization and domestication to classify translations and comprehend translation strategies masks the complicated linguistic, cultural, and historical circumstances surrounding the creation of Pla's New York writing. In 2000, Michael Cronin argued for the recognition of travelers as translators, speaking of "fractal differentialism" to "express the notion of a cultural complexity which remains constant from the micro to the macro scale" ("Across" 16–21). A few years later, in 2006, Cronin marked a new turn in translation studies by coining the term "micro-cosmopolitanism," which "provides a conceptual framework for better articulating and understanding the relationship between the local and the global, the particular and the universal, the self and the other at the core of contemporary thinking in translation" (Lane-Mercier 241). In her review of Cronin's *Translation and Identity* (2006), where this term first appeared, and quoting from the book, Gillian Lane-Mercier states that:

the most powerful defining feature of micro-cosmopolitanism is its ability to at once reconnect the opposing poles that binary systems are so anxious to uphold, undermine the hierarchies that enable them to do so, and reserve dominant ideological and theoretical trends by arguing that "the same degree of diversity is to be found at the levels of entities judged to be small or insignificant as at the level of large entities" (15). (242)

The diversity of translation strategies in Pla's *Week-end (d'estiu) a New-York* does not indicate empty inconsistencies in his work or a range of unresolved ideas about the city. Rather, the range of approaches to representing New York further testifies to his commitment to the Catalan language and its development, and to his predilection to display the concrete details of life. Pla's connection to travel and the many ways in which he traveled to and within New York also provided him with a large spectrum of experiences and perspectives from which to write the city.

Critical reception of Pla's *Week-end (d'estiu) a New-York*—such as the aforementioned review by Carles Capdevila and the 1957 review by Josephine de Boer referring to the book as "[a] complete, detailed description of the physical setting and the daily life of the city conveyed in a sound, unbiased manner" (430)—does not do justice to the intracacies of the work, or to the significance of the visit to the city. But if travel is read as translation, there is bias in the text because there are choices which the writer must make. Polezzi argues that "the travel writer has no way of being faithful since multiple layers of interpretation and representation are always present in his/her accounts—in fact, they are also always already there in the reality s/he describes" (Polezzi 102). Pla's first trip to New York was not just an opportunity to gather fascinating material for a home readership with limited prospects to travel across the Atlantic, it also was an excuse to think about his own continent and *país* [country], Catalonia, seen throughout the text in references to the way Europe was before the Second World War. New York represents a welcome hiatus from the oppression of Franco's dictatorship and postwar Europe. Experiencing New York with this context in mind contributes to the degree of interpretation of the text. In a discussion about New York commerce, Pla wonders why there are not more Catalans in the city since "Nova York hauria pogut ésser la terra de promissió de l'emigració catalana" [New York could have been the promised land of Catalan emigration] (28). While the statement might suggest humor on some level, on another it speaks to the contemporaneous precarious economic situation of Pla's home. (117). Despite the trip's short duration or "l'absurdidat d'haver vingut ací per tan pocs dies" [the absurdity of having come here for so few days,' he concludes that "Sento que tot m'incita a tornar en aquest país, encara que el retorn sigui una pura illusió de l'esperit" [I feel that everything urges me to come back to this country, even if the return is purely all in my head] (*Week-end* 117), suggesting that the impression New York made on him would not easily be left behind.

The Writing Continues

Pla's writing on New York was not limited to *Week-end d'estiu a New-York*. He continued to feature the city in articles published in *El Correo Catalan* and *Destino* as the result of subsequent trips to New York. Some of these contain the same features as his New York book. For instance, in the two-part article "José Pla cuenta las impresiones de su nuevo viaje de Barcelona a Nueva York, con escala en Londres" [José Pla Gives His Impressions of His New Trip from Barcelona to New York, with a Layover in London] published in *El Correo Catalan* on September 26, 1963, Pla continues to avoid the word "skyscraper," opting instead for "fantásticos edificios verticals" [fantastic vertical buildings] (14). Pla's attention to words and his quest to describe his experiences concretely, force him to provide an explanation for the inclusion of the vague word "impresionante" [impressive]:

> El lector creerá quizás que la utilización de estos adjetivos tan voluminosos es un poco provincial. El caso es que no tengo otros para dar una idea del espectáculo. A mí me disgustan esta clase de adjetivos, pero, ¿cómo hacerse entender de otro modo? ("Cuenta" 14)

> [The reader will perhaps think that the use of these really bulky adjectives is a bit provincial. The thing is, I don't have any others to give an idea of the spectacle. I don't like this type of adjective, but how can I make myself understood in another way?]

This example illustrates the challenge of putting New York into written language, let alone for an audience who has not witnessed the city. Pla's determination to capture the details was challenged by New York.

Just over a month later, in another article for *El Correo Catalan*, "El Punto Preciso para ver New York" [The Precise Point to See New York], from the "Trybourough" [Triborough] Bridge, Pla ponders:

> ¿Cómo describir el espectáculo que se ofrece a la vista? Es la ciudad en su mayor totalidad posible y adjetivar un fenómeno semejante exigiría la pluma de un poeta—como lo exigen las montañas, el cielo o el mar. La prosa es para los detalles habituales, para lo de cada día. No creo

que estas consideraciones contengan la menor exageración, porque si en alguna cosa esta todo el mundo está de acuerdo es en creer que la ciudad es el mayor esfuerzo constructivo (urbanístico) que en el curso de la historia ha hecho el hombre sobre la tierra. Esta construcción no tiene un aspecto cósmico, ciertamente, pero un aspecto aberrante, único, sorprendente si lo tiene. Y en el curso de uno de mis viajes al referido puente, se me ocurrió pensar lo que esta ciudad sería si en lugar de utilizar las formas geométricas regulares que sus arquitectos han empleado, el constructor hubiera sido don Antonio Gaudí. Es una hipótesis naturalmente muy alejada, desde luego, porque en definitiva estos edificios elevados han sido construidos para acumular en el menor espacio, la mayor cantidad de despachos y oficinas. Sin embargo, la imaginación es libre ...

How to describe the spectacle the view offers? It is the city in its greatest possible totality and to give adjectives to a similar phenomenon would demand a poet's pen—as do the mountains, sky, and sea. Prose is for habitual details, for the everyday. I don't think these considerations contain the least bit of exaggeration, because if there's something everyone agrees on, it's that the city is the greatest constructive (urbanistic) effort in the course of history that man has made on earth. This construction certainly doesn't have a cosmic aspect, but it does have an abnormal, unique, and surprising aspect. And in the course of one of my trips to the aforementioned bridge, it occurred to me to think about what this city would be if instead of using the regular geometric forms that its architects have employed, the builder had been Don Antoni Gaudí. Of course, it's a very far-fetched hypothesis, because these elevated buildings have definitely been built to provide in the least amount of space the largest number of workplaces and offices. Nevertheless, imagination is free ... (Pla, "Punto")

This later New York text is notable for two reasons. First, having written many pages on it, Pla is more concerned with the macro discussion of how to represent the city in writing, comparing it to that of a poet before the natural world. New York poses a challenge to writing, shifting the focus from an abundantly detailed description to a search for a language with which to describe the city. Second, in the face of such a dilemma, Pla reaches to familiarize New York by imagining the city in the architectural language of Gaudí, while at the same time expanding the dimensions of Gaudí by imagining his work in the language of New York.

Early in his career, Pla was a foreign correspondent in Paris for the Spanish-language newspaper *La Publicidad*. During that time, he published a chronicle titled "Los libros de junio." It turns out that Pla's chronicle was a translation of an article from the Parisian newspaper *Le Temps* (Lluís Bonada 5). When the director of *La Publicidad* found out, he fired Pla (Bonada 5), although Pla would again write for the newspaper in the future. This was not the only time that Pla would take a text written by another author, translate it, and then publish it in a newspaper with his name attached.[47] In 1975, Pla published "Una carta de New York" [A Letter from New York] (26) in *Destino*, which includes a letter he claims to have "transcrito" [transcribed] from a New York-based friend (26). In his introduction, Pla describes the letter as "sencilla, clara, objetiva, sin ninguna hinchazón literaria" [simple, clear, objective, without any literary puffiness] (26). He identifies its author, Ramon Boixareu, as "un amigo de este país que por razones de su actividad industrial se ha marchado a New York, con su familia, a pasar una temporada un poco larga" [a friend from this country who because of reasons having to do with his business has gone off to New York, with his family, for a fairly long time] (26). Pla did not *transcribe* the letter from Boixareu, which is part of the archives at the Fundació Josep Pla (Frank Keerl Pla Collection, Palafrugell, Spain), he *translated* it. Boixareu originally wrote the letter to Pla in Catalan on December 7, 1974, on stationary from the Spanish Embassy in New York, where he had been living for three months. Some readers might have been aware of the letter's Catalan-language origins as Pla introduces Boixareu as "un amigo de este país" (26): throughout *Week-end (d'estiu) a New-York* Pla uses "país" to talk about Catalonia. For other readers, the article hides the fact that the letter is a translation. Pla's interest in New York continued 20 years after his initial visit to the city, but this time he turned his writing of New York to the act of translating New York. Pla left *Destino* that same year, in 1975, after 35 years with the paper.

Conclusions

Pla and Camba have contributed a significant amount of writing to the history of the twentieth century. Their writings on New York serve as key texts for understanding the city's vibrancy. Comparing the initial publications of the two men's work, the impact of Pla's New York was not as widespread as Camba's. Pla's initial audience was patient and savored the details, while Camba's was large and on the move. The amount of travel

---

47 These Spanish-language articles are not signed by a translator. Cotoner Cerdó lists the Spanish-language translators of Pla's work, many of them poets and writers: Juan Chabás, Joan Vinyoli, Dionisio Ridruejo and Gloria de Ros, Josep M. Espinàs, and Néstor Luján (160).

each did and the amount of writing each produced indicates that travel, like translation, renews writing. Travel gave them other worlds to put into words for the home audience. It brought new scenes, objects, and ideas into the Catalan and Spanish languages. But their texts suffer, because they are read as objects of pure curiousity. Reading their New York writing together is like comparing multiple translations of a single text: the process reveals much more about what the city meant to their own writing. Moreover, the examples of Camba's and Pla's works, texts that together span the course of about 40 years, indicate that writing about the city is not only a response to the city itself as a place but also to the existing images and literature of that place. As a result, the challenge for the writer presents itself not as a quest to write new areas of the city, but rather to write the city in a new way.

Coda:
Re-Creating a Classic

Translating New York: The City's Languages in Iberian Literatures was motivated by the need to go beyond discussions of New York that look at the city as a constant binary battle between love and hate, between attraction and disgust. Such readings contribute to the creation and persistence of stereotypes of the city. After all, Josep Pla indicates that, by definition, "Nova York—és necessari repetir-ho—és la ciutat dels contrastos continuats" [New York—it's necessary to say it again—is a city of continuous contrasts] (*Week-end* 117). As fascinating as it may be to address these tensions, critical conversations of the sort do not touch on how the actual city is more than a theme. This book has pursued the goal of examining how New York influences the language, and appears as a shaper, of literary writing.

The authors I have studied throughout this book traveled to New York for different reasons, circumstantial, personal, and professional; and they produced writing in several forms—novels, poetry, travel-centered sketches for a limited audience, and travel writing for a general audience. In every case, the actual city—or physical contact with it, experiencing its sights and sounds—figures significantly, either as a place from which to write or a place to write about. Many writers have written the city at some point, and in their New York texts, they are in dialogue with one another through their own New York. I postulate, therefore, that New York emerges as a classic text for Iberian writers. The writing New York corpus grows simultaneously with the city's expansion in the imagination. As a result, attention to travel, or to the physical encounter with New York, becomes distorted, neglected, or erased in more contemporary literary examples. British travel writer and novelist Colin Thubron has noted that halfway through the twentieth century, "'the old sense of wonder has been deeply and forever diminished', and therefore the traveler 'must be conscious that almost always he has been preceded in his path by a host of others', and his account 'has been robbed of its old, empirical usefulness, and must look to other ways of excellence'" (qtd. in Polezzi 173).

In addition to the ways of writing and translating New York outlined in this book, another tendency has emerged within Iberian literatures. Alfau, Moreno Villa, Camba, and Pla all left the Iberian Peninsula to travel to New York. For most of them, the two locations inform their New York texts to varying degrees. But for a number of other Iberian writers, whose literary activity took off in the latter part of the twentieth century or in the beginning of the twenty-first, travel is a certainty, and so is access to diverse and multiple images of faraway places. As such, writing New York requires a different way of portraying the city in the Iberian literary imagination. Carmen Martín Gaite, Quim Monzó, Antonio Muñoz Molina, and Ernest Farrés seek alternate ways to recreate a version of the city. This diverse collection of writers has dialogued with the life and paintings of Edward Hopper as a way to write New York. Martín Gaite's collage travel notebook from the 1980s *Vision of New York* (2005), Monzó's early novel *Benzina* (1983), and Muñoz Molina's hybrid *Ventanas de Manhattan* (2004) are examples of overlooked works by widely recognized authors that engage New York thus in a meaningful way. The contemporary author Ernest Farrés dedicates an entire collection of poetry to the late painter in *Edward Hopper Poems* (2009), available in a bilingual edition with a translation from the Catalan by the prominent translation theorist Lawrence Venuti. These texts could be considered examples of intersemiotic translations of New York, as they shift from the source of the city itself to an image of it born from a tangible medium with universal appeal. These works are "not so much dictated by place as by how much and what has been said about the place" (Cronin, *Across* 36), thereby pushing the writer to experiment with new strategies by which to re-create New York. In a context in which New York is vastly familiar, the novel is found in a way that surpasses actuality and speaks to a moveable city only possible in literature.

Bibliography

Ackers, Kathy. *Don Quixote: A Novel.* New York: Grove, 1986. Print.

Alarcón Sierra, Rafael. *Una rana viajera: las crónicas y los libros de viaje de Julio Camba.* Sevilla: Renacimiento, 2010. Print.

Alberti, Rafael. *La arboleda perdida/2, Tercero y cuarto libros (1931–1987).* Madrid: Alianza Editorial, 1998. Print.

Alborg, Concha. *Beyond Jet-Lag: Other Stories.* New Jersey: Ediciones Nuevo Espacio, 2000. Print.

Alfau, Felipe. *Chromos.* Elmwood Park, IL: Dalkey, 1990. Print.

——. *Cromos.* Trans. María Teresa Fernández de Castro. Barcelona: Seix Barral, 1991. Print.

——. *Cuentos españoles de antaño.* Prólogo y trad. Carmen Martín Gaite. Il. Rhea Wells. Barcelona: Siruela, 1991. Print.

——. *Locos: A Comedy of Gestures.* Prologue Felipe Alfau. Afterword Mary McCarthy. Elmwood Park, IL: Dalkey, 1988. Print.

——. *Old Tales from Spain.* Illust. Rhea Wells. Garden City, NY: Doubleday, Doran & Company, 1929. Print.

——. *Sentimental Songs (La poesía cursi).* Trans. and intro. Ilan Stavans. Elmwood Park, IL: Dalkey, 1992. Print.

Alfau de Solalinde, Jesusa. *Los débiles.* New York: Prentice-Hall, 1930. Print.

Allen, Esther. "The Perils of Polyglossia." University of Massachusetts Amherst. Herter Hall, Amherst, MA. 4 Apr. 2014. Invited Lecture.

——. "What Does Nueva York mean in Spanish? Episodes in a History of Linguistic Invisibility." *Translation Review* 81.1. Special issue ed. Carmen Boullosa and Regina Galasso (2011): 1–11. Print.

Allones, Carlos. "Las crónicas norteamericanas de Julio Camba. Una nueva lectura." *Foro interno* 12 (Jan. 2012): 159–80. Web. 4 Aug. 2015.

Anderson, Andrew A., ed. *Poeta en Nueva York.* Barcelona: Galaxia Gutenberg, Círculo de Lectores, 2013. Print.

Andrian, Gustave W., ed. *Modern Spanish Prose: An Introductory Reader with a Selection of Poetry.* 2nd ed. London: MacMillan, 1969. Print.

Apter, Emily. *The Translation Zone: A New Comparative Literature.* Princeton, NJ: Princeton University Press, 2006. Print.

Arranz, Fermín Galindo. *Julio Camba: una lección de xornalismo.* Santiago de Compostela: Ediciones Lea, 2013. Print.

Azancot, Nuria. "Eduardo Lago: En *Llámame Brooklyn* conviven Cervantes y Don DeLillo." *El Cultural* 8 Jan. 2007. Web. 15 Mar. 2008.

Balder, Artur, dir. *Little Spain*. Bluechromatic Productions; Chinstrap Films; Meatpacking Productions, 2011. Film.

Ballesteros, Rafael, and Julio Neira. "Introducción y biográfia crítica." In Rafael Ballesteros and Julio Neira (eds), *Jacinta la pelirroja*. Madrid, Castalia, 2000. 7–65. Print.

Basile, Giambattista. *El archipámpano de las pulgas*. Trans. Rafael Sánchez Mazas. Illust. José Moreno Villa. Sevilla: Renacimiento, 1989. Print.

——. *Las siete palomas*. Trans. Rafael Sánchez Mazas. Illust. José Moreno Villa. Sevilla, Renacimiento, 1989. Print.

Bassnett, Susan. *Translation*. London: Routledge, 2014. Print.

——. *Translation Studies*. 3rd ed. London: Routledge, 2002. 1–10. Print.

——. *Translation Studies*. 4th ed. London: Routledge, 2014. 1–13. Print.

——. "When Is a Translation Not a Translation?" In Susan Bassnett and André Lefevere (eds), *Constructing Cultures: Essays on Literary Translation*. Clevedon: Multilingual Matters, 1998. 25–40. Print.

Beerbohm, Max. *Seven Men and Two Others*. Harmondsworth: Penguin, 1954. Print.

Begnal, Michael H. "Review of *Chromos*, by Felipe Alfau." *Choice: Current Literary Reviews for College Libraries* 27.10 (1990): 1674. Print.

Belda, Joaquín. *En el país del bluff: veinte días en Nueva York*. Madrid: Biblioteca Hispania, 1926. Print.

Benítez, Enrique. "Lorca y Camba en Nueva York." *Faro de Vigo* 27 May 2015. Web. 1 Sept. 2015.

Benjamin, Walter. "The Task of the Translator." In Hannah Arendt (ed.), *Illuminations*. Trans. Harry Zohn. New York: Harcourt Brace Jovanovich, 1968. 69–82. Print.

Bercovici, Konrad. *Around the World in New York*. Illust. Norman Borchardt. Ann Arbor, IL: University of Michigan Press, 2004. Print.

Bonada, Lluís. *L'obra de Josep Pla*. Barcelona: Editorial Tede, S.A., 1991. Print.

Bou, Enric. *Invention of Space: City, Travel and Literature*. Madrid: Iberoamericana Vervuert, 2012. Print.

Brenkman, John. "Review of *Chromos*, by Felipe Alfau." *New York Times Book Review* 13 May 1990: 25. Print.

Brossard, Chandler. "Two or Three Things I Know about Him." *The Review of Contemporary Fiction* 13.1. Special issue ed. David Bellos and Ilan Stavans (1993): 194–97. Print.

Boullosa, Carmen, et al. "Manifesto Neoyorkino." Unpublished manifesto, 2006.

Buffery, Helena. "Iberian Identity in the Translation Zone." In S. Pérez Isasi and A. Fernandes (eds), *Looking at Iberia: A Comparative European Perspective*. Bern: Peter Lang, 2013. 249–64. Print.

Butor, Michel. "Le Voyage et l'écriture." *Romantisme* 2.4 (1972): 4–19. Print.

Cabrera de Tablada, Eulalia. *José Juan Tablada en la intimidad: con cartas y poemas inéditos*. Mexico: Imprenta universitaria, 1954. Print.

Calvo Serraller, Francisco. "José Moreno Villa: Historiador y crítico de arte." In Juan Pérez de Ayala (ed.), *José Moreno Villa [1887–1955]*. Madrid: Ministerio de Cultura; Dirección general de libro y biblioteca, 1987. 17–30. Print.

Camba, Julio. *Alemania: Impresiones de un español*. Sevilla: Renacimiento, 2012. Print.

——. *Alemania: Londres; Un año en el otro mundo; La casa de Lúculo*. Barcelona: Editorial Vergara, 1962. Print.

——. *Aventuras de una peseta*. Barcelona: Alhena Media, 2007. Print.

——. *Caricaturas y retratos*. Madrid: Forcola, 2013. Print.

——. *La casa de Lúculo o el arte de comer*. Prólogo Eduardo Riestra. Illust. Miguel Ángel Martín. Madrid: Reina de Cordelia, 2010. Print.

——. *La ciudad automática*. Madrid: Espasa-Calpe, 1932. Print.

——. *La ciudad automática*. Madrid: Espasa-Calpe, 1934. Print.

——. *La ciudad automática*. Buenos Aires: Austral, 1942. Print.

——. *La ciudad automática*. Barcelona: Alhena Media, 2008. Print.

——. *La ciudad automática*. Ed. José Luis García Martín. Sevilla: Renacimiento, 2015. Print.

——. *Come un giramondo prende il mondo in giro*. Trans. Carlo Boselli. Milan: Sperling & Kupfer, 1941. Print.

——. *Crónicas de viaje: Impresiones de un corresponsal español*. Ed. Francisco Fuster. Prologue Antonio Muñoz Molina. Madrid: Fórcola, 2014. Print.

——. *Dos novelas bastante cortas*. La Coruña: Ediciones del Viento, 2007. Print.

——. *Esto, lo otro y lo de más allá*. Madrid: Cátedra, 1995. Print.

——. *Etc... Etc...* Madrid: Editorial Plus-Ultra, 1945. Print.

——. *Haciendo de República*. Madrid: Luca de Tena Ediciones, 2006. Print.

——. "Iberian Sketches." Trans. Oscar Handlin. In Oscar Handlin (ed.), *This Was America: True Accounts of People and Places, Manners and Customs as Recorded by European Travelers to the Western Shore in the Eighteenth, Nineteenth, and Twentieth Centuries*. Cambridge, MA: Harvard University Press, 1949. 453–64. Print.

——. *Londres: Impresiones de un español*. Madrid: Renacimiento, 1916. Print.

——. *Maneras de ser periodista*. Ed. and prologue Francisco Fuster García. Madrid: Libros del K.O., 2014. Print.

——. *Millones al horno*. Buenos Aires: Espasa-Calpe, 1980. Print.

——. *Playas, ciudades y montañas*. Madrid: Reino de Cordelia, 2012. Print.

——. *La rana viajera*. Barcelona: Alhena Media, 2008. Print.

——. *Sobre casi nada*. Sevilla: Renacimiento, 2013. Print.

——. *Sobre casi todo*. Sevilla: Renacimiento, 2013. Print.

——. *Un año en el otro mundo*. Madrid: Biblioteca Nueva, 1917. Print.

——. *Un año en el otro mundo*. Prólogo Ignacio Carrión. Madrid: Rey Lear, 2009. Print.

Cano Ballesta, Juan. *Literatura y tecnologia: Las letras españolas ante la revolución industrial (1900–1933)*. Valencia: Pre-Textos, 1999. Print.

Cañas, Dionisio. *El poeta y la ciudad: Nueva York y los escritores hispanos*. Madrid: Cátedra, 1994. Print.

——. "New York City: Center and Transit Point for Hispanic Cultural Nomadism." In Mario J. Valdés and Djelal Kadir (eds), *Literary Cultures of Latin America: A Comparative History*. New York: Oxford University Press, 2004. 679–702. Print.

Capedevila, Carles. *Nova York a la catalana: Les històries viscudes a Nova York pels catalans famosos: de Dalí a Pau Casals, cantants, arquitectes, metges, polítics ... i gàngsters. I una guia turística del rastres catalans més significatius a Manhattan*. Barcelona: Edicions La Campana, 1996. Print.

Caponegro, Mary. *The Star Café*. New York: W.W. Norton, 1990. Print.

Carmona Mato, Eugenio. *José Moreno Villa y los orígenes de las vanguardias artísticas en España (1909-1936)*. Málaga: Universidad de Málaga y Colegio de Arquitectos en Málaga, 1985. Print.

Carnero, Guillermo. "Recuperación de Moreno Villa." *Ínsula* (1977): 368-69. Print.

Carrión, Ignacio. "La mirada escribe." In Julio Camba, *Un año en el otro mundo*. Prólogo Ignacio Carrión. Madrid: Rey Lear, 2009. 13-17. Print.

Cartier, Raymond. *Les 48 Amériques*. Paris: Plon, 1953. Print.

Castedo, Elena. *Paradise*. New York: Grove Press, 1990. Print.

Castellet, J.M. *Josep Pla o la raó narrativa*. Barcelona: Destino, 1978. Print.

Castillo, Debra A. "Latina or Americaniard?" *Revista Canadians de Estudios Hispánicos* 30.1 (2005): 47-59. Print.

Cela, Camilo José. *Viaje a U.S.A. o el que la sigue la mata*. Illust. Lorenzo Goñi. Madrid: Alfaguara, 1967. Print.

"Chiquita Villet." Obituary. *Los Angeles Times* 2-3 Jun. 2015. Web. 20 May 2015.

Ciplijauskaité, Biruté. "Los 'cuadros cubistas' de José Moreno Villa." In Charles B. Faulhaber, Richard P. Kinkade, and T.A. Perry (eds), *Studies in Honor of Gustavo Correa*. Preface Manuel Durán. Potomac, MD: Scropta Humanistica, 1986. 47-57. Print.

Cirre, José Francisco. *La poesía de José Moreno Villa*. Madrid: Ínsula, 1962. Print.

Cocco De Filippis, Daisy. "Alfau Galván de Solalinde, Jesusa (1890-1943)." In Vicki L. Ruiz and Virginia Sánchez Korral (eds), *Latinas in the United States: A Historical Encyclopedia*. Bloomington, IN: Indiana University Press, 2006. 37-38. Print.

Collins, Glenn. "Postmodern, in a Manner of Speaking; a Shape out of 1908 is Offered Downtown." *New York Times* 21 Jan. 2003. Web. 16 Jan. 2008.

Collins, George R. "The American Hotel." In Robert Descharnes and Clovis Prèvost (eds), *Gaudí: The Visionary*. Preface Salvador Dalí. New York: The Viking Press, 1982. 193-201. Print.

Colón, Jesús. *A Puerto Rican in New York and Other Sketches*. New York: Mainstream Publishers, 1961. Print.

Compitello, Malcolm Alan, and Susan Larson. "Cities, Culture … Capital? Recent Cultural Studies Approaches to Spain's Cities." *Journal of Spanish Cultural Studies* 2.2 (2001): 231-38. Print.

Cortázar, Julio. *Hopscotch: A Novel*. Trans. Gregory Rabassa. New York: Random House, 1966. Print.

Cortés Ibáñez, Emilia. "José Camprubí y *La Prensa*, pilar del Hispanismo en Nueva York." *Oceánide* 5 (2013). Web. 26 Jun. 2015.

Costa, Lluís. "The Catalan Migration to New York: A View from *La Llumanera de Nova York (1874-1881)*." *New York History Review* (2012): 1-12.

Costa, María Dolores. "The Travel Writing of Julio Camba." *Monographic Review/ Revista Monográfica* 12 (1996): 154-65. Print.

Cotoner Cerdó, Luisa. "Ética y estética de la autotraducción: una cala en las versiones al castellano de Josep Pla, Joan Perucho y Carme Riera." In Emilio Ortega Arjonilla (ed.), *Panorama actual de la investigación en traducción e interpretación. Vol. 3*. 2nd ed. Granada: Atrio, 2004. 159-67. Print.

Couceiro Freijomil, Antonio. *Diccionario bio-bibliográfico de escritores. Vol. 1*. Santiago de Compostela: Editorial de los Bibliófilos Gallegos, 1951-53. Print.

Crandall, Marjorie L. "Review. *La ciudad automática*." *Books Abroad: An International Literary Quarterly* 7.3 (1933): 350. Print.

Crispin, John. *Oxford y Cambridge en Madrid: La Residencia de Estudiantes (1910–1936) y su entorno cultural.* Santander: La Isla de los Ratones, 1981. Print.

——. "Review of *Chromos,* by Felipe Alfau and *Cromos* translated by Javier Fernández de Castro." *World Literature Today* 65.4 (1991): 673. Print.

Cronin, Michael. *Across the Lines: Travel, Language, Translation.* Cork. Cork University Press, 2000. Print.

——. *Translation and Identity.* New York: Routledge, 2006. Print.

Cronin, Michael, and Sherry Simon. "Introduction: The City as Translation Zone." *Translation Studies* 7.2 (2014): 119–32. Print.

Crow, John A, ed. *Cuentos hispánicos.* New York: Holt, Rinehart and Winston, 1939. Print.

Dalí, Salvador. "Photography, Pure Creation of the Spirit." In Christopher Phillips (ed.), *Photography in the Modern Era: European Documents and Critical Writings, 1913–1940.* New York: The Metropolitan Museum of Art/Aperture, 1989. 198–99. Print.

Darío, Rubén. "La gran cosmópolis (Meditaciones de la madrugada)." *rubendario.org* 11 Jan. 2016. Web. 7 Jun. 2016.

Davidson, Robert A. "Periphery with a View: Hotel Space and the Catalan Modern Experience." *Romance Quarterly* 53.3 (2006): 169–83. Print.

De Boer, Josephine. "Review: *Week-end (d'estiu) a New-York* by Josep Pla." *Books Abroad* 31.4 (Autumn 1957): 430. Print.

De Onís, Federico. "El Humorismo de Julio Camba." *Hispania* 10.3 (May 1927): 167–75. Print.

——. "Julio Camba." In Julio Camba, *La rana viajera.* Ed. Federico de Onís. Boston, MA: Heath and Co., 1928. vii–xviii. Print.

——. "Dos libros de Camba (*Sobre casi todo* y *Sobre casi nada*)." *Revista de Estudios Hispánicos* I (1928): 421–22.

de Pereda, Prudencio. *All the Girls We Loved.* New York: Farrar, Straus, 1948. Print.

——. *Fiesta: A Novel of Modern Spain.* New York: A.A. Wyn, 1953. Print.

——. *Windmills in Brooklyn.* New York: Atheneum, 1960. Print.

de Unamuno, Miguel. *Niebla.* Madrid: Cátedra, 1982. Print.

DeGuzmán, María. *Spain's Long Shadow: The Black Legend, Off-Whiteness, and Anglo-American Empire.* Minneapolis, MN: University of Minnesota Press, 2005. Print.

Del Arco, Miguel Ángel. "Sólo he escrito para burlarme de las novelas." *Tiempo* 20 May 1991, 138–41. Print.

Del Villar, Arturo. "De cómo el poeta malagueño José Moreno Villa conoción y se enamoró de una joven neoyorquina, pelirroja por más señas." *La estafeta literaria* 617 (1977): 4–7. Print.

Derrida, Jacques. "Des Tours de Babel." Trans. Joseph F. Graham. In Joseph F. Graham (ed.), *Difference and Translation.* Ithaca, NY: Cornell University Press, 1985. 218–27. Print.

Díaz, Roberto Ignacio. *Unhomely Rooms: Foreign Tongues in Spanish-American Literature.* Lewisburg, PA: Bucknell University Press, 2002. Print.

Díaz de Castro, Francisco Javier. "La poesía vanguardista de José Moreno Villa." In Cristóbal Cuevas García (ed.), *José Moreno Villa en el contexto del 27.* Barcelona: Anthropos, 1989. 30–67. Print.

Eisenberg, Daniel. *Poeta en Nueva York: Historia y problemas de un texto.* Barcelona: Ariel, 1976. Print.

Fabrés, Xavier. *Les dones de Josep Pla.* Barcelona: Edicions 62, 1999. Print.

Fajardo, Salvador J. "José Moreno Villa: Exile and Community." In Cecile West-Settle and Sylvia Sherno (ed.), *Contemporary Spanish Poetry: The Word and the World.* Madison, NJ: Fairleigh Dickinson University Press, 2005. 39–58. Print.

Farrés, Ernest. *Edward Hopper Poems.* Trans. Lawrence Venuti. Minneapolis, MN: Graywolf Press, 2009. Print.

"Felipe Alfau 1902–1999." Obituary. *New York Times* 23 Feb. 1999. Web. 2 Apr. 2015.

Fernández, Carlos. "La voz ofrece mañana el libro 'La ciudad automática', de Julio Camba." *La voz de Galicia.* 22 May 2005. Web. 14 Sept. 2015.

Fernández, James D. "'Longfellow's Law': The Place of Latin America and Spain in U.S. Hispanism, circa 1915." In Richard L. Kagan (ed.), *Spain in America: The Origins of Hispanism in the United States.* Urbana, IL: University of Illinois Press, 2002. 122–41. Print.

——. "Poets, Peasants, Painters, Professors and Performers in New York." In Richard Kagan and Ignacio Suárez Zuloaga (eds), *When Spain Fascinated America.* Madrid: Fundación Zuloaga; Gobierno de España, Ministerio de Cultura, 2010. 47–59. Print.

Fernández, James D., and Luis Argeo, eds. *Invisible Immigrants: Spaniards in the U.S. (1868–1945).* New York: White Stone Ridge, 2014. Print.

Fernández, Pelayo H. "Norteamérica vista por Ramón Pérez de Ayala y Julio Camba." *Cuadernos Hispanoamericanos* 367–68 (1981): 71–80. Print.

Figueira, Gastón. "Review. *La ciudad automática.*" *Books Abroad: An International Literary Quarterly* 17.1 (1943): 63–64. Print.

Fonollosa, José María. *Ciudad del hombre: New York.* Barcelona: Edhasa, 1990. Print.

Fontcuberta, Joan. "The New Objectivity." In Christopher Phillips (ed.), *Photography in the Modern Era: European Documents and Critical Writings, 1913–1940.* New York: The Metropolitan Museum of Art/Aperture, 1989. 39–40. Print.

——. "Spanish Photography: Memory of its Avant-garde." In Christopher Phillips (ed.), *Photography in the Modern Era: European Documents and Critical Writings, 1913–1940.* Ed. and intro. Christopher Phillips. New York: The Metropolitan Museum of Art/Aperture, 1989. 25–37. Print.

Fraser, Benjamin. *Henri Lefebvre and the Spanish Urban Experience: Reading the Mobile City.* Lewisburg, PA: Bucknell University Press, 2011. Print.

Fussell, Paul. *Abroad: British Literary Traveling between the Wars.* Oxford: Oxford University Press, 1979. Print.

Fuster García, Francisco. "Imagen periodística de Julio Camba." *Cuadernos hispanoamericanos* 754 (2013). 67–80. Print.

——. "Introducción: Un español por el mundo." *Crónicas de viaje: Impresiones de un corresponsal español.* Prólogo Antonio Muñoz Molina. Ed. Francisco Fuster. Madrid: Fórcola, 2014. 9–35. Print.

——. "Yo, Periodista." *Maneras de ser periodista.* Ed. and prologue Francisco Fuster García. Madrid: Libros del K.O., 2014. 5–13. Print.

Galasso, Regina. "An Interview with Mark Statman." *Translation Review* 90.1 (2014): 1–14. Print.

García Lorca, Federico. "Lecture: A Poet in New York." Trans. Christopher Maurer. In Christopher Maurer (ed.), *Poet in New York.* Trans. Greg Simon and Steven F. White. Introduction and notes Christopher Maurer. New York: The Noonday Press, 1998. 184–201. Print.

——. *Poet in New York*. Trans. Ben Belitt. Intro. Ángel del Río. New York: Grove Press, 1955. 1985. Print.

——. *Poet in New York*. Trans. Pablo Medina and Mark Statman. Intro. Edward Hirsch. New York: Grove Press, 2007. Print.

——. *The Poet in New York and Other Poems of Federico García Lorca*. Trans. Rolfe Humphries. Intro. José Bergamin. New York: W.W. Norton, 1940. Print.

——. "The Poet Writes to His Family from New York and Havana." Trans. Christopher Maurer. In Christopher Maurer (ed.), *Poet in New York*. Trans. Greg Simon and Steven F. White. New York: The Noonday Press, 2000. 203–86. Print.

——. *Poeta en Nueva York*. Ed. Andrew A. Anderson. Barcelona: Galaxia Gutenberg, 2013. Print.

——. *Poeta en Nueva York. Cita en Manhattan*. Prologue Mario Hernández. Photographs José Antonio Robés. Trans. Greg Simon and Steven F. White. Barcelona: Fundación Federico García Lorca; Lunwerg, 2011. Print.

——. *Poeta en Nueva York y otros poemas de Federico García Lorca*. Trans. Rolfe Humphries. Preface Antonio Muñoz Molina. Granada: Diputación de Granada; Patronato Cultural Federico García Lorca; Román y Bueno, 2010. Print.

——. *Obras, VI Prosa, 2 Epistolario*. Ed. Miguel García-Posada. Madrid: Akal, 1994. Print.

——. "Theory and Play of the Duende." In Christopher Maurer (ed. and trans.), *In Search of Duende*. Christopher Maurer. New York: New Directions, 1998. 48–62. Print.

——. *Un poeta en Nueva York*. Red Ediciones, S.L., 2011. Print.

García Márquez, Gabriel. *The Autumn of the Patriarch*. Trans. Gregory Rabassa. London: Cape, 1976. Print.

Garolera, Narcís. *L'escriptura itinerant: Verdaguer, Pla i la literatura de viatges*. Prologue Antoni Marí. Lleida: Pagès editors, 1998. Print.

Gerchunoff, Alberto. *Jewish Gauchos of the Pampas*. Trans. Prudencio de Pereda. Foreword Ilan Stavans. Albuquerque, NM: University of New Mexico Press, 1998. Print.

Gibson, Ian. *Federico García Lorca: A Life*. New York: Pantheon, 1989. Print.

——. *The Shameful Life of Salvador Dalí*. New York: W.W. Norton, 1998. Print.

Gili, Marta. "Pictorialism and Amateur Photography." In Christopher Phillips (ed.), *Photography in the Modern Era: European Documents and Critical Writings, 1913–1940*. New York: The Metropolitan Museum of Art/Aperture, 1989. 133–34. Print.

Grossman, Edith. *Why Translation Matters*. New Haven, CT: Yale University Press, 2010. Print.

Gutiérrez, Margo. "Latina and Latino Literature: Anthologies of the 1990s, A Selected Bibliography." Ed. Ann Hartness. *BiblioNoticias* 95 (1998). Web. 3 Jan. 2008.

Guzmán, María Constanza. *Gregory Rabassa's Latin American Literature: A Translator's Visible Legacy*. Lewisburg, PA: Bucknell University Press, 2010. Print.

Hagedorn, Jessica. *Dogeaters*. New York: Penguin, 1990. Print.

Handal, Nathalie. *Poet in Andalucía*. Pittsburgh, PA: University of Pittsburgh Press, 2012. Print.

Handlin, Oscar. "Introduction." In Oscar Handlin (ed.), *This Was America: True Accounts of People and Places, Manners and Customs as Recorded by European Travelers to the Western Shore in the Eighteenth, Nineteenth, and Twentieth Centuries*. Cambridge, MA: Harvard University Press, 1949. 1–4. Print.

Herrero-Senés, Juan. "El Arte Nuevo y el jazz: El cifrado del siglo XX." In Mechthild Albert (ed.), *Vanguardia española e intermedialidad: artes escénicas, cine y radio*. Madrid: Iberoamericana/Vervuert, 2005. 317–30. Print.

Hijuelos, Oscar. *The Mambo Kings Play Songs of Love*. New York: Farrar, Straus and Giroux, 1989. Print.

Huergo, Humberto. "La poética del retrato en *Jacinta la Pelirroja*." *Torre de papel* 5.2 (1995): 17–33. Print.

Hutchinson, George. *In Search of Nella Larsen: A Biography of the Color Line*. Cambridge, MA: Belknap Press, 2006. Print.

Iannone, Carol. "Literature by Quota." *Commentary* 91.3 (1991): 50–53. Print.

Iborra, Josep. "La Ciutat de Nova York a la vista." *El Temps* 11–17 Jan. 2000, p. 68. Print.

Infante, Ignacio. *After Translation: The Transfer and Circulation of Modern Poetics Across the Atlantic*. New York: Fordham University Press, 2013. Print.

James, Henry. *Washington Square*. Raleigh, NC: Alex Catalogue, n.d.

——. *Washington Square*. Trans. Sergio Pitol. Barcelona: Seix Barral, 1970. Print.

——. *Washington Square*. Trans. Emilio Olcina Aya. Barcelona: Fontamara, 1982. Print.

——. *Washington Square*. Trans. Amando Lázaro Ros. Barcelona: Orbis-Fabri, 1990. Print.

——. *Washington Square*. Trans. Catalina Martínez Muñoz. Barcelona: Alba, 2010. Print.

Jakobson, Roman. "On Linguistic Aspects of Translation." In Rainer Schulte and John Biguenet (eds), *Theories of Translation: An Anthology of Essays from Dryden to Derrida*. Chicago, IL: University of Chicago Press, 1992. 144–51. Print.

Jiménez, Francisco. *Taking Hold: From Migrant Childhood to Columbia University*. New York: Houghton Mifflin Harcourt, 2015. Print.

Jiménez, Juan Ramón. *Diario de un poeta recien casado*. Madrid: Calleja, 1917. Print.

——. *Diary of a Newlywed Poet/Diario de un poeta recien casado*. Trans. Hugh A. Harter. Intro. Michael P. Predmore. Selinsgrove, PA: Susquehanna University Press, 2004. Print.

Johnson, Charles. *Middle Passage*. New York: Scribner, 1990. Print.

Kagan, Richard L. "Prescott's Paradigm: American Historical Scholarship and the Decline of Spain." In Richard L. Kagan (ed.), *Spain in America: The Origins of Hispanism in the United States*. Urbana, IL: University of Illinois Press, 2002. 247–76. Print.

——. "*The Spanish Craze*: The Discovery of Spanish Art and Culture in the United States." In Richard L. Kagan and Ignacio Suárez Zuloaga (eds), *When Spain Fascinated America*. Madrid: Fundación Zuloaga, 2010. Print.

Kanellos, Nicolás, and Helvetia Martell. *Hispanic Periodicals in the United States, Origins to 1960: A Brief History and Comprehensive Bibliography*. Houston: Arte Público Press, 2000. Print.

Kutzinski, Vera M. *The Worlds of Langston Hughes: Modernism and Translation in the Americas*. Ithaca, NY: Cornell University Press, 2012. Print.

Laffoley, Paul. "A Grand Hotel on the Hudson." *Paranoia: The Conspiracy & Paranormal Reader*. 2002. Web. 29 Jan. 2008.

Lago, Eduardo. *Call Me Brooklyn*. Trans. Ernesto Mestre-Reed. Elmwood Park, IL: Dalkey, 2013. Print.

——. *Ladrón de mapas*. Barcelona: Destino, 2008. Print.

——. *Llámame Brooklyn*. Barcelona: Destino, 2006. Print.

——. *Siempre supe que volvería a verte, Aurora Lee*. Barcelona: Malpaso, 2013. Print.

Lago, Eduardo, et al. "Manifiesto Neoyorkino." *Carmenboullosa.net*. Web. 18 Aug. 2015.

Lahuerta, José Juan. *Universo Gaudí*. Barcelona: Diputació de Barcelona; Centre de Cultura Contemporània de Barcelona; Museo Nacional Centro de Arte Reina Sofía, 2002. Print.

Lane-Mercier, Gillian. "Michael Cronin. *Translation and Identity*. Oxford/New York, Routledge, 2006, 166 p." *TTR: traduction, terminologie, rédaction* 21.1 (2008): 241–47. Print.

Lang, Fritz, dir. *Metropolis*. Universum, 1927. Film.

Lefevere, André. *Translation, Rewriting and the Manipulation of the Literary Frame*. Shanghai: Shanghai Foreign Language Press, 2004. Print.

Lewis, Hunter. *A Question of Values: Six Ways We Make Personal Choices that Shape Our Lives*. Mount Jackson, VA: Axios Press, 2003. Print.

Levine, Philip. "On the Meeting of García Lorca and Hart Crane." In Philip Levine, *The Simple Truth: Poems*. New York: Knopf, 1994. Print.

Lindner, Christopher. *Imagining New York City: Literature, Urbanism, and the Visual Arts, 1890–1940*. Oxford: Oxford University Press, 2015. Print.

Little Ashes. Dir. Paul Morrison. Factotum, 2008. Film.

Little Spain. Dir. Artur Balder. Bluechromatic Productions, Chinstrap Films, Meatpacking Productions, 2011. DVD.

Llera, José Antonio. *El humor en la obra de Julio Camba: Lengua, estilo e intertextualidad*. Madrid: Editorial Biblioteca Nueva, 2004. Print.

López García, Pedro Ignacio. *Julio Camba: el solitario del Palace*. Madrid: Espasa Calpe, 2003. Print.

López Gayarre, Pedro A. "Fin de semana en Nueva York. Josep Pla." *El digital CLM* 18 Jun. 2016. Web. 26 Oct. 2016.

McDowell, Edwin. "Nominees for the National Book Awards." *New York Times* 19 Oct. 1990. Web. 20 May 2015.

——. "Small-Press Celebrity." *New York Times* 24 Oct. 1990. Web. 20 May 2015.

Mañas, José Ángel. "La literatura española explicada a los asnos: Julio Camba." *PliegoSuelto: Revista de Literatura y Alrededores* 23 May 2014. Web. 14 Sept. 2015.

Manrique, Jaime. *Eminent Maricones: Arenas, Lorca, Puig, and Me*. Madison, WI: University of Wisconsin Press, 1999. Print.

——. *My Night with Federico García Lorca*. Bilingual ed. Trans. Edith Grossman. Hudson, NY: The Groundwater Press, 1995. Print.

Marbán, Jorge. "Martí, Camba y Uslar Pietri: Tres originales enfoques ensayísticos sobre la ciudad de Nueva York." *Círculo: Revista de Cultura* 39 (2010): 60–68. Print.

Martí, José. "Impressions of America (By a Very Fresh Spaniard)." In Esther Allen (ed. and trans.), *José Martí: Selected Writings*. Intro. Roberto González Echevarría. New York: Penguin, 2002. 32–40. Print.

Martín Gaite, Carmen. *Caperucita en Manhattan*. Madrid: Siruela, 2014. Print.

——. "Introducción: El triunfo de la excepción." In Felipe Alfau, *Cuentos españoles de antaño*. Trans. and prologue by Carmen Martín Gaite. Madrid: Siruela, 1991. xi–xxvii. Print.

——. "The Triumph of the Exception." Trans. Ilan Stavans. *The Review of Contemporary Fiction* 13.1. Special issue ed. David Bellos and Ilan Stavans (1993): 174–82. Print.

——. *Visión de New York*. Madrid: Siruela, 2005. Print.

Mata, Rodolfo. "José Juan Tablada: Translator." Trans. Nicholas Goodbody. *Translation Review* 81.1. Special issue ed. Carmen Boullosa and Regina Galasso (2011): 34–43. Print.

Maurer, Christopher. "Introduction." In Federico García Lorca, *Poet in New York*. Trans. Greg Simon and Steven F. White. Ed. Christopher Maurer. New York: Farrar, Straus and Giroux, 2013. ix–xxix. Print.

——. *Sebastian's Arrows: Letters and Mementos of Salvador Dalí and Federico García Lorca*. Chicago, IL: Swan Isle Press, 2004. Print.

Mauthner, Fritz. *Contribuciones a una crítica de lenguage*. Trans. José Moreno Villa. Madrid: Daniel Jorro, 1911. Print.

Mayhew, Jonathan. *Apocryphal Lorca: Translation, Parody, Kitsch*. Chicago, IL: University of Chicago Press, 2009. Print.

——. "Reading Poetry: A Conversation with Jonathan Mayhew." *Creative Writing Now*. Web. 4 Aug. 2014.

Miles, Valerie. "The Weather Man." *The Paris Review* 25 Mar. 2014. Web. 14 Jun. 2016.

Millhauser, Steven. *The Barnum Museum*. Champaign, IL: Dalkey, 1990. Print.

Miranda-Barreiro, David. "Primitivist Modernism and Imperialist Colonialism: The View of African Americans in José Moreno Villa's *Pruebas de Nueva York* and Julio Camba's *La ciudad automática*." *Journal of Spanish Cultural Studies* 14 (2013): 52–69. Print.

——. *Spanish New York Narratives 1898–1936: Modernization, Otherness and Nation*. London: LEGENDA, 2014. Print.

Mobilio, Albert. "Loco Heroes: Felipe Alfau's Alien Nation." *Village Voice Literary Supplement* Jun. 1990: 18. Print.

Monzó, Quim. *Benzina*. Barcelona: Quaderns Crema, 1983. Print.

——. *Gasoline*. Trans. Mary Ann Newman. Rochester, NY: Open Letter, 2010. Print.

Moore, Steven. "Recalled to Life." *The Review of Contemporary Fiction* 13.1. Special issue ed. David Bellos and Ilan Stavans (1993): 245–47. Print.

Morand, Paul. *New-York*. Paris: Flammarion, 1930. Print.

Moreno Villa, José. *Jacinta la pelirroja*. Ed., introduction, and notes Rafael Ballesteros and Julio Neira. Madrid: Castalia, 2000. Print.

——. *Pruebas de Nueva York*. Valencia: Pre-textos, 1989. Print.

——. *Vida en claro: autobiografía*. México: El Colegio de México, 1944. Print.

Moret, Xavier. "Aquells senyors de Barcelona: Els germans Puget, retratats per Josep Pla, són recordats pels seus nebots." *El país Quadern* 913 (11 Jan. 2001): 1–3. Print.

Muñoz Molina, Antonio. "Epílogo." *El País Semanal* 24 Feb. 2002: 112. Print.

——. *In the Night of Time*. Trans. Edith Grossman. Boston, MA: Houghton Mifflin Harcourt, 2013. Print.

——. *La noche de los tiempos*. Barcelona, Seix Barral, 2009. Print.

——. "Paisajes del idioma." *El País* 24 Mar. 2007. Web. 19 Aug. 2015.

——. "El secreto de Julio Camba." In Julio Camba, *Crónicas de viaje: Impresiones de un corresponsal español*. Prólogo Antonio Muñoz Molina. Ed. Francisco Fuster. Madrid: Fórcola, 2014. 5–8. Print.

——. "Spanish in New York: A Moving Landscape." Trans. Dan Newland. In Claudio Iván Remeseira (ed.), *Hispanic New York: A Sourcebook*. New York: Columbia University Press, 2010. 355–58. Print.

——. *Ventanas de Manhattan*. Barcelona: Seix Barral, 2004. Print.

Neira, Julio. "Ciudad y poesía: Imagen dual." *Geometría y angustia: Poetas españoles en Nueva York*. Sevilla: Vandalia, 2012. 9–63. Print.

——, ed. *Geometría y angustia: Poetas españoles en Nueva York*. Intro. Julio Neira. Sevilla: Fundación José Manuel Lara; Vandalia, 2012. Print.

——. *Historia poética de Nueva York en la España contemporánea*. Madrid: Cátedra, 2012. Print.

Noel, Urayoán. *Buzzing Hemisphere/Rumor Hemisférico*. Tucson, AZ: The University of Arizona Press, 2015. Print.

"Now This Is How Translation Reviews Should Be Done." *Two Lines Press*. 21 Jan. 2014. Web. 4 Jun. 2016.

Novo Blankenship, Silvia. "Julio Camba: Spain and the World." University of Virginia. MA thesis, 1962. Print.

Oates, Joyce Carol. *Because it Is Bitter, Because it Is My Heart*. New York: Plume, 1991. Print.

Obiols, Isabel. "Reedición de 'Weekend (d'estiu) a Nova York' de Josep Pla." *El país* 5 Jul. 1999. Print.

Ordaz, Jorge. "Prudencia de Pereda." *Obiter Dicta: Una bítacora con notas, comentarios y reflexiones sobre libros y literatura* 9 May 2015. Web. 15 Jun. 2015.

——. "Prudencio de Pereda, español de Brooklyn." *Clarín: Revista de nueva literatura* 20.116 (2015): 41–43. Print.

O'Sullivan, Carol. "Psuedotranslation." In Yves Gambier and Luc van Doorslaer (eds), *The Handbook of Translation Studies Vol. 2*. Amsterdam: John Benjamins, 2011. 123–25. Print.

Pane, Remigio Ugo. *English Translations from the Spanish, 1484–1943: A Bibliography*. New Brunswick, NJ: Rutgers University Press, 1944. Print.

Paredes, Julio. "El escritor y la ciudad." *El Diario La Prensa* 27 Jul. 2008. Web. 4 Aug. 2015.

Perec, Georges. *Life, A User's Manual*. Trans. David Bellos. Boston, MA: David R. Godine, 1987. Print.

Pérez Firmat, Gustavo. *Life on the Hyphen: The Cuban-American Way*. Austin, TX: University of Texas Press, 1994.

Pérez de Ayala, Juan, ed. *José Moreno Villa [1887–1955]*. Madrid: Ministerio de Cultura; Dirección general de libro y biblioteca, 1987. Print.

——. "Las otras pruebas neoyorkinas de José Moreno Villa." In José Moreno Villa, *Pruebas de Nueva York*. Valencia: Pre-textos, 1989. iii–v. Print.

Pirandello, Luigi. *The Late Mattia Pascal*. Trans. William Weaver. Intro. Charles Simic. New York: New York Review of Books, 2004. Print.

Pla, Josep. "Antoni Gaudí (1852–1926)." In Josep Miquel Sobrer (ed. and trans.), *Catalonia, a Self-Portrait*. Bloomington, IN: Indiana University Press, 1992. 160–90. Print.

——. *El carrer Estret*. Barcelona: Destino, 2004. Print.

——. *Fin de semana en Nueva York*. Barcelona: Destino, 2016. Print.

——. *The Gray Notebook*. Trans. Peter Bush. New York: New York Review of Books, 2014. Print.

——. "Les idees de Julio Camba." In Josep Pla, *El passat imperfecte*. Barcelona: Destino, 1962. Print.

——. "José Pla cuenta las impresiones de su nuevo viaje de Barcelona a Nueva York, con escala en Londres." *El Correo Catalan* 26 Sept. 1963: 14. Print.

——. *Life Embitters*. Trans. Peter Bush. Brooklyn: Archipelago, 2015. Print.

——. "El Punto Preciso para ver New York." *El Correo Catalan* 9 Nov. 1963. Print.

——. "Una carta de New York." *Destino* 1975: 26. Print.

——. *Week-end (d'estiu) a New-York: tercera sèrie de "Cartes de lluny."* Barcelona: Selecta, 1955. Print.

——. *Weekend (d'estiu) a Nova York*. Barcelona: Ediciones Orbis, 1985. Print.

Polezzi, Loredana. *Translating Travel: Contemporary Italian Travel Writing in English Translation*. Aldershot: Ashgate, 2001. Print.

Predmore, Michael P. "Introduction." In Juan Ramón Jiménez, *Diary of a Newlywed Poet*. Trans. Hugh A. Harter. Selinsgrove, PA: Susquehanna University Press, 2004. 21–78. Print.

Prados, Emilio. *Diario íntimo*. Málaga: Centro Cultural de la Generación del 27; Centro de Ediciones de la Diputación de Málaga, 1998. Print.

Pratt, Mary Louise. *Imperial Eyes: Travel Writing and Transculturation*. London: Routledge, 1992. Print.

Puig, Valentí. "Introduction." In Josep Pla, *The Gray Notebook*. Trans. Peter Bush. New York: The New York Review of Books, 2013. vii–xii. Print.

Rabassa, Gregory. *If This Be Treason: Translation and its Discontents, A Memoir*. New York: New Directions, 2005. Print.

——. "The Power of *Chromos*." *The Review of Contemporary Fiction* 13.1. Special issue ed. David Bellos and Ilan Stavans (1993): 223–24. Print.

Ramos, Carlos. "Modernidades desplazadas: *Locos* (1928) de Felipe Alfau y *Locura y muerte de nadie* (1929) de Benjamín Jarnés." *Revista Hispánica Moderna* 56.1 (2003): 105–15. Print.

Rath, Bridgitte. "Pseudotranslation." *The 2014–2015 Report on the State of the Discipline of Comparative Literature* 1 Apr. 2014. Web. 27 Jul. 2015.

Remeseira, Claudio Iván. *Hispanic New York: A Sourcebook*. New York: Columbia University Press, 2010. Print.

Resina, Joan Ramon. "Lisbon as Destination: Josep Pla's Iberianism through his Travels to Portugal." In Joan Ramon Resina (ed.), *Iberian Modalities: A Relational Approach to the Study of Culture in the Iberian Peninsula*. Liverpool: Liverpool University Press, 2013. 225–42. Print.

Revilla Guijarro, Almudena. *Periodismo y literatura en la obra de Julio Camba*. Vigo: Diputación Provincial de Pontevedra—Servicio de Publicaciones, 2002. Print.

Rodríguez Martorell, Carlos. "Eduardo Lago—An Ode to Brooklyn." *Críticas Magazine* 15 Apr. 2006. Web. 19 Aug. 2015.

——. "Eduardo Lago: Call Me Brooklyn." *She Pushes a Mad Whip* 27 Jan. 2007. Web. 11 Jul. 2015.

——. "Hispanic Authors Celebrate Literary Works in the Big Apple." *Críticas Magazine* 15 Feb. 2007. Web. 19 Aug. 2015.

Rogers, Gayle. *Modernism and the New Spain: Britain, Cosmopolitan Europe, and Literary History*. New York: Oxford University Press, 2012. Print.

Roser i Puig, Montserrat. "Review of Xavier Pla, *Josep Pla: Ficció autobiogràfica i veritat literària*." *The Modern Language Review* 93.2 (1998): 554–55. Print.

Rothenberg, Jerome. *The Lorca Variations: I–XXXIII*. New York: New Directions, 1990. Print.

Saenz de la Calzada, Margarita. *La Residencia de Estudiantes 1910–1936*. Madrid: Consejo Superior de Investigaciones Científicas, 1986. Print.

Sahagun, Felipe. *El mundo fue político: Corresponsales españoles en el extranjero: La información internacional en España.* Madrid: Fundación Banco Exterior, 1986. Print.

Scaramella, Evelyn. "Literary Liaisons: Translating the Avant-Garde from Spain to Harlem." *Nueva York. Translation Review* 81.1. Special issue ed. Carmen Boullosa and Regina Galasso (2011): 61–72. Print.

——. "Translating the Spanish Civil War: Langston Hughes's Transnational Poetics." *The Massachusetts Review* (Summer 2014): 177–88. Print.

Schanke, Robert A. *"That Furious Lesbian": The Story of Mercedes de Acosta.* Carbondale, IL: Southern Illinois University Press, 2003. Print.

Schnapp, Jeffery T. "Crash: Speed as Engine of Individuation." *Modernism/modernity* 6.1 (1999): 1–49. Print.

Schnitzler, Arthur. *La señorita Elisa.* Trans. José Moreno Villa. México: Leyenda, 1945. Print.

Schor, Sandra. *The Great Letter E.* San Francisco, CA: North Point Press, 1990. Print.

Scott, Joanna. *Arrogance: A Novel.* New York: Picador, 1990. Print.

Scott, Joseph. "Thundering out of the Shadow: Modernism and Identity in the Novels of Felipe Alfau." MA thesis. University of Missouri-Columbia, 2005. Print.

Senabre, Ricardo. *"Llámame Brooklyn."* El Cultural 9 Feb 2006. Web. 11 Jul. 2015.

Shapiro, Anna. "Sixty-one Years of Solitude." *The Review of Contemporary Fiction* 13.1. Special issue ed. David Bellos and Ilan Stavans (1993): 203–06. Print.

Shapiro, Doris. "Hidalgo Remembered." *The Review of Contemporary Fiction* 13.1. Special issue ed. David Bellos and Ilan Stavans (1993): 198–202. Print.

Shearer, James. "Introducción a Julio Camba." In Julio Camba, *Países, gentes y cosas.* New York: Holt, Rinerhart and Winston, 1962. Print.

Shearer, James F. "Periódicos españoles en los Estados Unidos." *Revista Hispánica Moderna* 1–2 (1954): 45–57. Print.

Simmons, Charles. "From *Powered Eggs.*" *The Review of Contemporary Fiction* 13.1. Special issue ed. David Bellos and Ilan Stavans (1993): 186–93. Print.

Simon, Sherry. "Across Troubled Divides: Translation, Gender, Memory." Nida School of Translation Studies, Misano Adriatico, Italy. 31 May 2013. Lecture.

——. *Cities in Translation: Intersections of Language and Memory.* New York: Routledge, 2012. Print.

——. *Translating Montreal: Episodes in the Life of a Divided City.* Montreal: McGill-Queen's University Press, 2006. Print.

Sommer, Doris. "Introduction." In Doris Sommer (ed.), *Bilingual Games: Some Literary Investigations.* New York: Palgrave Macmillan, 2003. 1–19. Print.

——. "Invitation." In Doris Sommer, *Bilingual Aesthetics: A New Sentimental Education.* Durham, NC: Duke University Press, 2004. xi–xxv. Print.

Spain in Flames. Dir. Helen van Dongen. 1937. Film.

The Spanish Earth. Dir. Joris Ivens. Commentary and narration Ernest Hemingway. Spanish adaptation Prudencio de Pereda. Dokumentarfilm, 1937. Film.

Stainton, Leslie. "Oh Babilonia! Oh Cartago! Oh Nueva York! El europeo ante Manhattan, Manhattan ante el europeo, 1917–1932." *FGL: Boletín de la Fundación Federico García Lorca* 4.10–11 (1992): 191–212. Print.

Stavans, Ilan. "Anonymity: An Interview with Felipe Alfau." *The Review of Contemporary Fiction* 13.1. Special issue ed. David Bellos and Ilan Stavans (1993): 146–57. Print.

——. "Felipe Alfau: Curriculum Vitae." *The Review of Contemporary Fiction* 13.1. Special issue ed. David Bellos and Ilan Stavans (1993): 143–45. Print.

——. "Felipe Alfau y La Prensa." *El Diario La Prensa* 26 Jun. 2007: 21. Print.

——. *The Hispanic Condition: Reflections on Culture & Identity in America*. New York: HarperPerennial, 1995. Print.

——, ed. *The Norton Anthology of Latino Literature*. New York: Norton, 2011. Print.

Sullivan, Edward J., ed. *Nueva York, 1613-1945*. New York: New York Historical Society/ London: Scala, 2010. Print.

Sweeney, Susan Elizabeth. "Aliens, Aliases, and Alibis: Alfau's *Locos* as a Metaphysical Detective Story." *The Review of Contemporary Fiction* 13.1. Special issue ed. David Bellos and Ilan Stavans (1993): 207–14. Print.

——. "'Subject Cases' and 'Book-Cases': Impostures and Forgeries from Poe to Auster." In Patricia Merivale and Susan Elizabeth Sweeney (eds), *Detecting Texts: The Metaphysical Detective Story from Poe to Postmodernism*. Philadelphia, PA: University of Pennsylvania Press, 1999. 247–70. Print.

Talbot, Toby. "The Return of the Native." *The Review of Contemporary Fiction* 13.1. Special issue ed. David Bellos and Ilan Stavans (1993): 183–85. Print.

Thompson, B. Bussell, and J.K. Walsh. "Un encuentro de Lorca y Hart Crane en Nueva York." *Ínsula* 41.479 (Oct. 1986): 1. Print.

Torres, Lourdes. "In the Contact Zone: Code-switching Strategies by Latino/a Writers." *Melus* 32 (2007): 77–97. Print.

Torres-García, Joaquín. *Historia de mi vida*. Barcelona: Paidós, 1990. Print.

Toury, Gideon. *Descriptive Translations Studies and Beyond*. Amsterdam: John Benjamins, 1995. Print.

——. "Translation, Literary Translation, and Pseudotranslation." In E.S. Schaffer (ed.), *Comparative Criticism* 6. Cambridge: Cambridge University Press, 1984. 73–85. Print.

Trachtenberg, Alan, ed. *Classic Essays on Photography*. Notes Amy Weinstein Meyers. New Haven, CT: Leete's Island Books, 1980. Print.

Trivedi, Harish. "Translating Culture vs. Cultural Translation." In Paul St-Pierre and Prafulla C. Kar (eds), *In Translation: Reflections, Refractions, Transformations*. Amsterdam: John Benjamins, 2007. 277–87. Print.

Umbral, Francisco. "Julio Camba." *El Cultural* 13 Mar. 2003. Web. 14 Sept. 2015.

Usary, Carolyn S. "Rhea Wells (1891–1962), Jonesboro, Tennessee: Author and Illustrator of Children's Books." MA thesis. East Tennessee State University, 1973. Print.

Valdés, Mario, and Linda Hutcheon. *Rethinking Literary History—Comparatively*. New York: American Council of Learned Societies, 1994. Print.

Valendar, James. "A propósito de las 'Poesías completas' de José Moreno Villa." *NRFH* 47.2 (1999): 385–98. Print.

Valls, Fernando. "Luces y sombras de Brooklyn." *Revista de Occidente* 307 (2006): 139–45. Print.

Varela-Lago, Ana María. "Conquerors, Immigrants, Exiles: The Spanish Diaspora in the United States (1848–1948)." PhD dissertation. University of California, San Diego, 2008. Print.

Venuti, Lawrence. *The Translator's Invisibility: A History of Translation*. New York: Routledge, 1995. Print.

Vila-Matas, Enrique. *Bartleby y compañía*. Barcelona: Anagrama, 2002. Print.

Villeneuve, Philippe. "Confabulation, Collaboration, and Chromolithography: Memory as a Construct in the Works of Felipe Alfau." PhD dissertation. University of Ottawa, 2013. Print.

von Schlegel, Friedrich. *Lucinda: una novela.* Trans. José Moreno Villa. Madrid: Ediciones de la pluma, 1921. Print.

Weinberger, Eliot. "Anonymous Sources (On Translators and Translation)." In Esther Allen and Susan Bernofsky (ed.), *In Translation: Translators on their Work and What it Means.* New York: Columbia University Press, 2013. 17–30. Print.

West, Paul. "Felipe Alfau and the NBA." *The Review of Contemporary Fiction* 13.1. Special issue ed. David Bellos and Ilan Stavans (1993): 241–44. Print.

Weston, Edward. "Seeing Photographically." In Alan Trachtenberg (ed.), *Classic Essays on Photography.* New Haven, CT: Leete's Island Books, 1980. 169–75. Print.

Wölfflin, Heinrich. *Conceptos fundamentales de la historia del arte.* Trans. José Moreno Villa. Madrid: Calpe, 1924. Print.

Young, Howard. "Federico de Onís (1888–1966)." *Hispania* 80.2 (May 1997): 268–70. Print.

Zangrilli, Franco. "Pirandello and Alfau." *The Review of Contemporary Fiction* 13.1 Special issue ed. David Bellos and Ilan Stavans (1993): 215–22. Print.

Zelich, Cristina. "Portraiture, Social Documentation, and Photojournalism." In Christopher Phillips (ed.), *Photography in the Modern Era: European Documents and Critical Writings, 1913–1940.* New York: The Metropolitan Museum of Art/Aperture, 1989. 161–62. Print.

Index

Note: Page numbers in italics indicate photographs.

www.ingramcontent.com/pod-product-compliance
Lightning Source LLC
Chambersburg PA
CBHW071108100726
47908CB00008B/2312